JOHN HEDGECOE CREATIVE PHOTOGRAPHY WORK BOOK

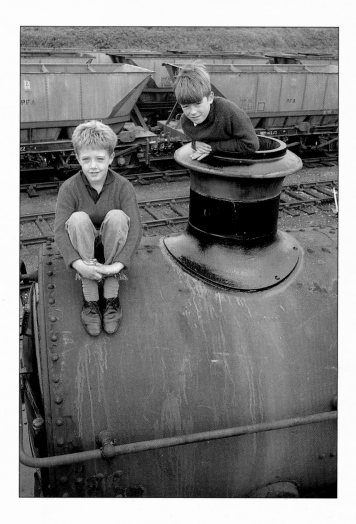

JOHN HEDGECOE'S
CREATIVE
PHOTOGRAPHY
WORK BOOK

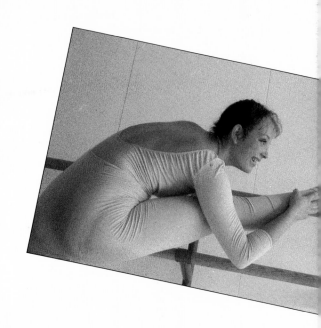

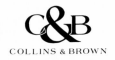

C&B
COLLINS & BROWN

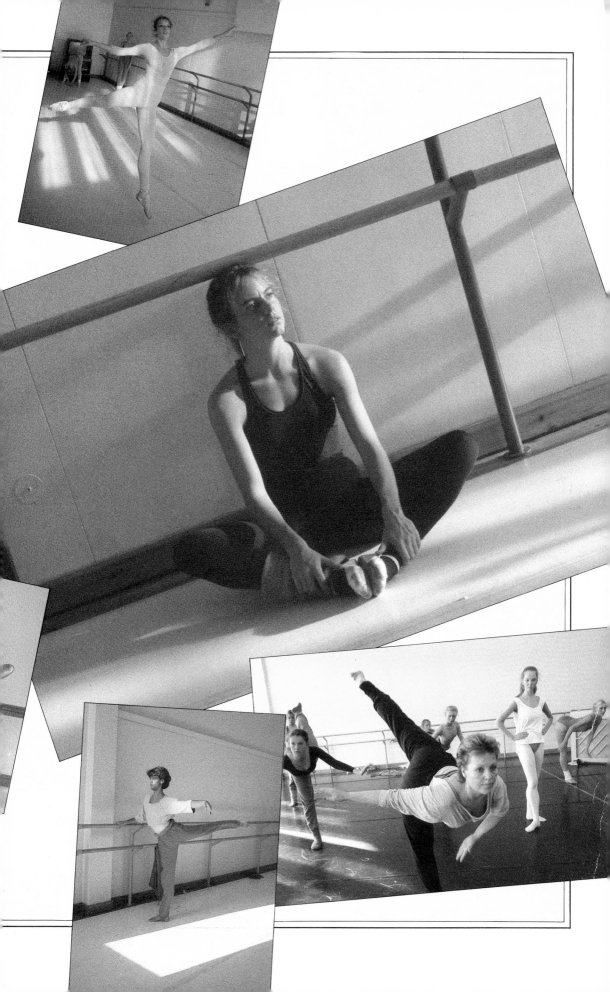

First published in 1986, as

John Hedgecoe's New

Manual of Photography

This revised paperback edition

published by Collins & Brown

London House

Great Eastern Wharf

Parkgate Road

London SW11 4NQ

Distributed in the United States and Canada

by Sterling Publishing Co, 387 Park Avenue

South, New York, NY 10016, USA

Copyright © Collins & Brown 1999

Photographs copyright © John Hedgecoe 1999

1 3 5 7 9 8 6 4 2

ISBN 1-85585-608-5

Reproduction by Grafiscan, Italy

Printed by Midas Printing,

Hong Kong

CONTENTS

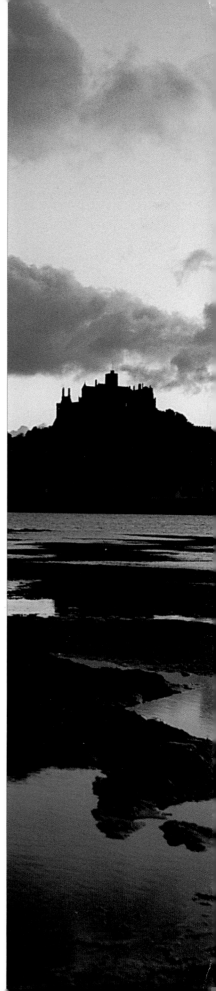

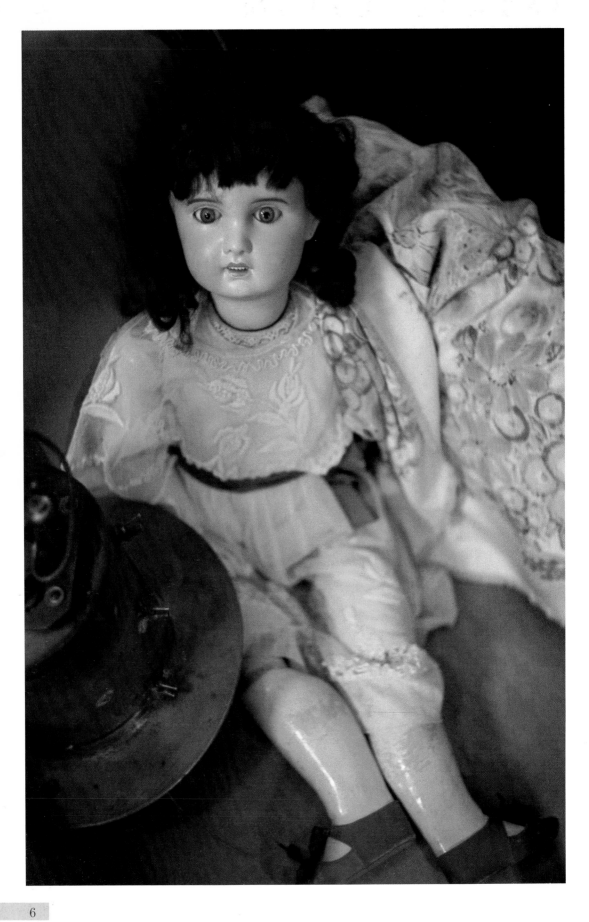

INTRODUCTION

The aim of this book is to help the photographer to exploit his or her own ideas. I have tried to show how to do this – with full technical information and practical advice – and, at the same time, to demonstrate how even familiar subjects, approached with imagination and enthusiasm, can offer the chance to come up with new images.

The first section of the book explains the techniques and skills used in making pictures. None of them is complex and all are explained in terms that are easy to understand.

Important though technical skill is, the camera is just the means by which a photographer expresses his creative vision. In the second part of this book, there are numerous examples that I hope will stimulate your imagination and trigger new ideas for pictures. Arranged thematically, this section explores the potential of many of the most popular photographic subjects, such as landscapes, the nude, portraits, sport, wildlife, and fashion. Making successful pictures means understanding what lies behind a subject's appeal, rather than just reacting intuitively. Analyse your reactions to a scene, deciding what is visually attractive and emotionally stimulating; which elements need emphasis and which should be ignored. It is the ideas behind the pictures that stimulate the senses and, after the initial impact, engage the imagination.

John Hedgecoe

The tools that are available to the photographer today have changed substantially from those used a decade or so ago. Labour-saving camera systems, such as autofocus, and multi-pattern meters, have removed much of the mystique from the picture-taker's art. Advances in digital photography, meanwhile, mean that effects that once took hours to perform in the darkroom can now be achieved with a click of a computer's mouse. Although it is important for photographers to understand, and exploit, such new technologies, we must not forget that such devices are only tools. Without the skills and artistry to see the picture in the first place, such electronic marvels are worthless.

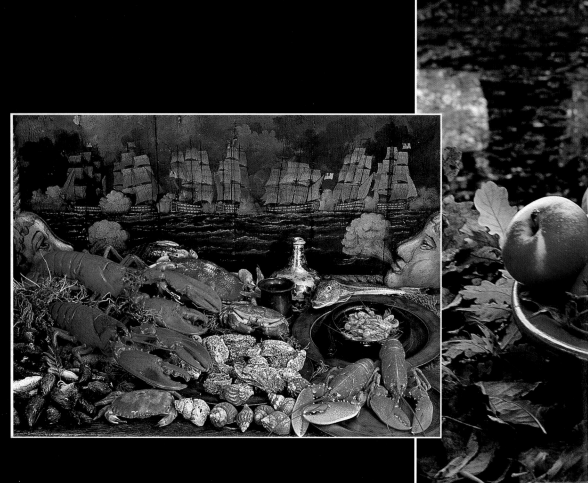

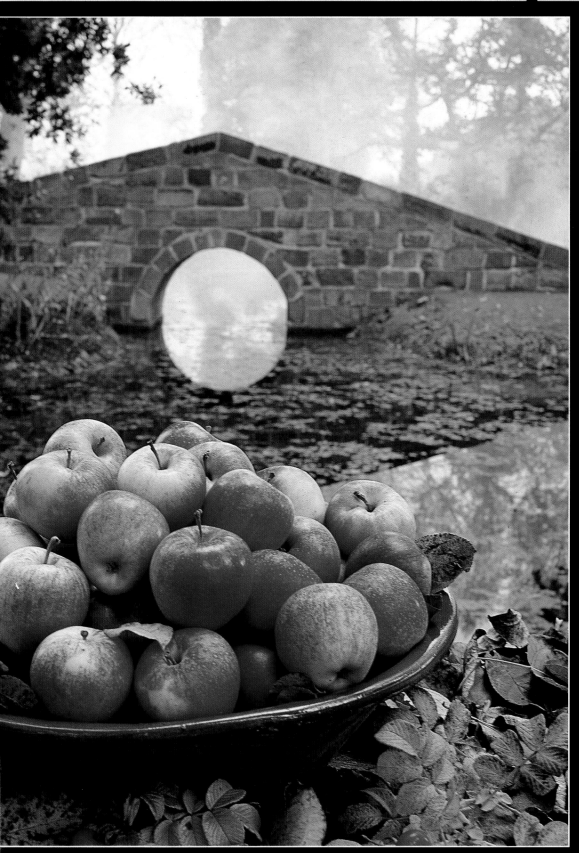

EXPLOITING WIDE-ANGLES

Zooms have done much to lighten the load for the modern photographer. Not so long ago, enthusiasts would carry around half a dozen lenses – to ensure that they always had the right tool for the job. Today, just one or two zooms can provide photographers with practically every focal length they need – and a lot more in between. With the popularisation of 'all-in-one' lenses, such as the 28–200mm for the 35mm SLR, the term wide-angle no longer refers, necessarily, to a particular lens, but to a range of focal lengths. Special wide-angle zooms, such as the 21–35mm for the 35mm SLR, are available.

For the 35mm format, a wide–angle lens setting is one that has a focal length that is around 40mm or shorter. In essence, it is one that gives an angle of view that is appreciably wider than that given by a standard lens setting – a focal length that most closely approximates the field of vision of the human eyes (excluding periphery vision).

Whilst a 35mm lens is counted as a wide-angle lens for the 35mm camera, this is not necessarily the case for users of other formats. Focal length is directly proportional to the size of the image; thus a 35mm lens setting for a digital stills camera would be a telephoto, as this has a much smaller imaging area (in this case, a CCD chip rather than an area of film).

Wide-angles become a necessity in confined spaces, as they allow you to fit more into the frame where it is impossible to move further away from the subject. For interior photography, and for architecture, therefore, they are often *de rigueur*.

Wide-angles have their creative uses, too, in other forms of photography. By allowing the photographer to work close to a subject, yet to include as much of a scene as a longer lens would from further away, wide-angle lenses make foreground objects loom large while distant objects recede and appear miniaturised. Emphasis, therefore, can be deliberately placed on the foreground. If used for close-up portraits, the wide-angle will exaggerate the size of the features of the face nearest the camera, for instance, making the nose look unnaturally large.

Depth of field is far greater with wide-angles than telephotos. With a suitable aperture, objects just a few feet away to the distant horizon can appear sharp in the same frame.

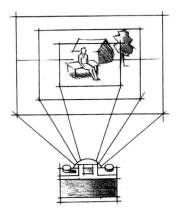

△ The picture areas illustrated here show the coverage of 35mm, 28mm, and 18mm wide-angle lenses for the 35mm format. The angles of view for these lenses is 62°, 74°, and 100° respectively.

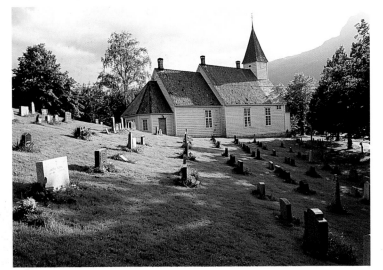

◁ A 28mm wide-angle setting was deliberately chosen for this shot to accentuate the lines of gravestones. They then lead the viewer's eyes through the picture to main subject of the shot – the Norwegian church itself. Note how the gravestones that are closest to the camera appear larger than those further away.

▷ This shot of Ayers Rock in Australia shows the immense depth of field that is possible when using a wide-angle lens. Here, I used a 24mm lens setting with an aperture of f16 and focussed so that everything in the picture was sharp – from the grass just in front of me to the horizon.

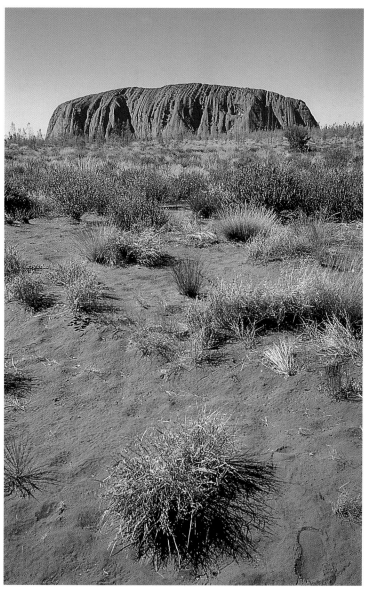

▽ Wide-angle lenses are more likely to be affected by flare than longer focal lengths and need careful shading from light sources. Flare patterns, created by light reflecting off the iris diaphragm, are distinctive and form 'images' of the opening repeated across the picture – as in this shot taken with a 24mm wide-angle.

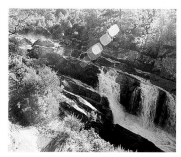

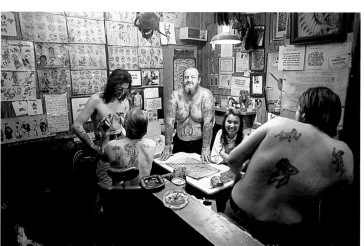

◁ To include the full extent of this tatooist's salon, I used a super-wide 21mm lens setting with my 35mm SLR. In such confined spaces, it is not possible to move further back to include more of the subject.

See also:
EXPLOITING TELEPHOTOS pp12–13
SPECIAL LENSES pp14–15
UNUSUAL VIEWPOINTS pp46–47
LINEAR PERSPECTIVE pp146–147

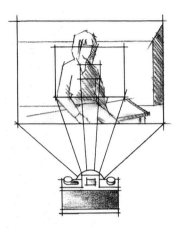

△ The angles of view for the 85mm, 200mm and 1000mm focal lengths for a 35mm SLR are illustrated here. Their respective angles of view are approximately 28°, 12°, and 3.5°, and they represent the extremes of most manufacturers' ranges of telephoto lenses.

The telephoto lens lessens the gap between the photographer and a distant subject. It acts like a telescope, drawing the subject in and filling the frame. In the 35mm format, zooms offering telephoto settings from 70mm to 300mm are available for most system cameras. Longer lenses (up to 1000mm) are usually found as fixed focal length (or 'prime') lenses.

Long telephoto lens settings are ideal for sports, action and wildlife photography, where it impractical, or even unsafe, to approach any closer to the subject. They are also invaluable for candid shots in which photographers want to avoid influencing behaviour through their own presence. The exact focal length for these types of uses will depend on the size of the subject, and the distance to the subject. A 300mm lens, for instance, is ideal for close-up soccer action, but a 600mm is a better starting point for full-length shots of a cricketer at the wicket.

Shorter telephoto lens settings (70–150mm for 35mm SLR users) are well suited to portrait photography. Using longer focal lengths means that you are generally too far away to communicate with your sitter, whilst shorter focal lengths can cause unflattering facial distortions.

These settings are harder to use than wide-angle ones – even if on the same lens – as the extra magnification in the image exaggerates any movement of the camera during exposure. For this reason, either faster shutter speeds must be used to keep the image from blurring – or the camera supported.

Telephoto lenses afford less depth of field than wide-angle settings. To ensure picture sharpness from 10 metres to infinity with a 135mm lens, for instance, a 35mm SLR would have to be set to an aperture of f32. Accurate focusing therefore is crucial.

As telephotos are used at greater distances from their subjects than other lenses, they appear to affect perspective. Subjects which in reality are some distance away from each other can appear that they are standing back-to-back. This can create dramatic impact in a picture – presenting views that you would not think possible. However, the apparent compression can also have its disadvantages. Spectators on the other side of the sports field, for instance, can appear as prominent in your action pictures as the athletes you are photographing.

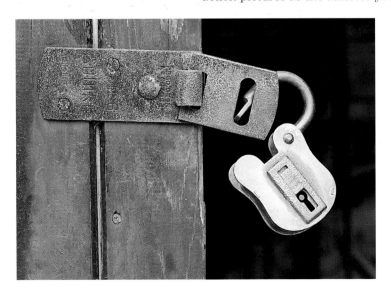

◁ Many zoom lenses have a so-called 'macro' mode. The facility does not usually allow true macro photography, but it does reconfigure the optics to allow you to get much closer to small subjects. This shot was taken with the macro mode of a 70–210mm telephoto zoom for a 35mm SLR, and produced an image on the film that was about a quarter life-size.

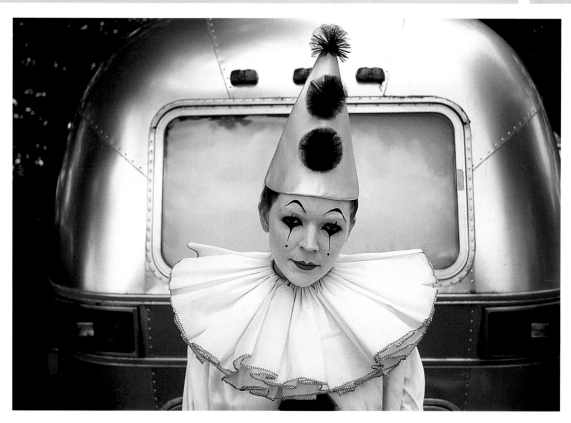

△ Zoom lenses are ideal for in-camera cropping, so that the image fills the frame precisely.

▷ The perspective in this portrait has been flattened by using a 350mm lens. The hurdles seem to be positioned very close together; in reality they were several feet apart.

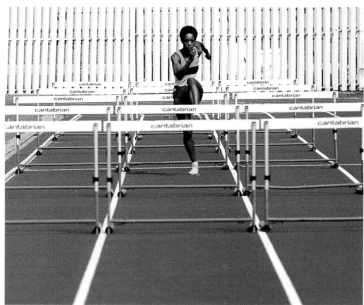

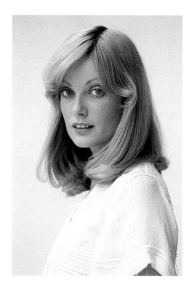

◁ For portraits that fill a large part of the picture it is best to use a short telephoto. Perspective is flattened, making a more attractive picture, and a wide aperture used to throw the background out of focus.

See also:
EXPLOITING WIDE-ANGLES pp10–11
SPECIAL LENSES pp14–15
BEHIND THE SCENES pp50–51
THE HIGHPOINT pp124–125

SPECIAL LENSES

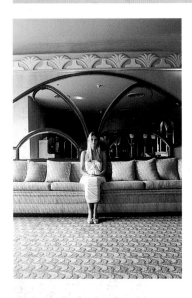

△ A standard prime lens is a sensible investment for those who enjoy lowlight photography. I used a 50mm lens for this portrait taken in a Brazilian hotel.

Zoom lenses are designed to be as versatile as possible, but unusual picture requirements, such as extreme close-ups or extreme angles of view, require specially designed lenses.

Whilst a zoom lens eliminates the need for several prime lenses, it does have one major disadvantage – that of speed. Whilst many 35mm SLRs are now sold with standard zooms with focal length ranges of, say, 35–80mm, a decade or so ago the SLR body came with a standard 50mm lens. The zoom lens will have a maximum aperture of f3.5-4.5, whilst the 50mm lens had a typical maximum aperture of f1.8. In lowlight the 50mm lens can let in four times as much light as the modern equivalent – allowing you to use a shutter speed two stops faster. 50mm lenses are still cheaply available (secondhand and new) and are a good addition to any camera bag.

Of the true specialist lenses, the macro lens is probably the most useful. They are designed for working at close focusing distances, offering images that are life-size or half life-size. The magnification afforded is adjustable – as if you want to fit more of your subject in you just move back slightly. The most popular macro lens for the 35mm format is the 90 or 100mm. As these lenses focus from a few centimetres away up to infinity, they can also be used for everyday photography.

Shift lenses have been designed to overcome the architectural photographer's commonest problem – that of keeping vertical lines parallel when taking shots from ground level. With a normal lens, and the camera facing upwards, the structure's sides seem to converge. With a shift lens, the camera back can be kept parallel to the side of the building, and the lens itself is shifted up to include the top of the structure in the picture.

Mirror lenses are really no more than telephoto lenses – but they are built using a special 'catadioptric' design where the light path is folded using mirrors. This makes them much lighter and shorter than traditional long telephotos.

Fisheye lenses are extreme wide-angles where image distortion is not corrected for in order to provide angles of view of 180° and greater. Image magnification varies across the frame, creating an image as though viewed through a fishbowl.

▷ Macro lenses are probably the most versatile lenses available to the SLR photographer. Not only can they be used for normal, distant, subjects, but they can focus down to a few centimetres to produce images that are, usually, one-half life-sized. The 90/100mm versions are the most popular, although 50mm and 200mm versions are available for those who need to work that bit closer (or further away) from their subjects.

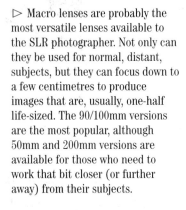

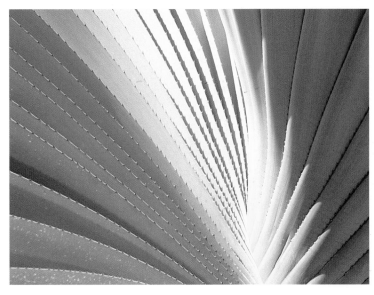

▷Perspective control (PC) or shift lenses give the SLR camera some ability to imitate the extensive rising front of large-format technical cameras. Rather than tilting the camera back upwards to include the top of the building, it is kept level, and the lens itself is raised. This avoids converging verticals. Other effects are possible by tilting the lens sideways or downwards.

▽A mirror lens is lighter than conventional long telephotos, but is more fragile. A useful side-effect of its construction are the attractive doughnut-shaped highlights, as seen in this shot taken with a 500mm mirror lens.

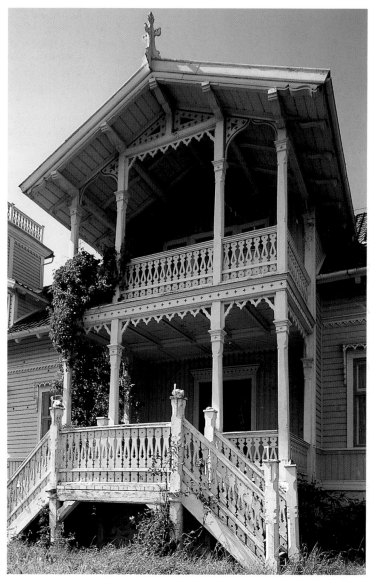

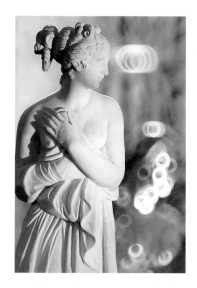

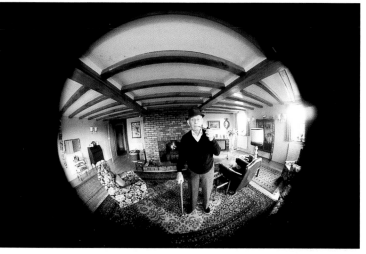

◁ The curved distortion in this image is typical of that produced by a fisheye lens. These lenses have an extremely wide coverage and practically infinite depth of field, making focusing unnecessary. This shot was taken with a 16mm circular fisheye.

See also:
EXPLOITING WIDE-ANGLES pp10–11
EXPLOITING TELEPHOTOS pp12–13
THE VERSATILE LENS pp116–117

CREATIVE EXPOSURE

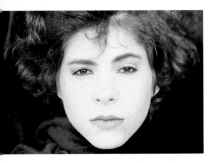

△ Overexposure must be executed carefully, or too much tone and detail will be lost and the image will have an unattractive, washed-out appearance. In the portrait above, slight overexposure draws attention to the girl's features and lifts the face from the dark background.

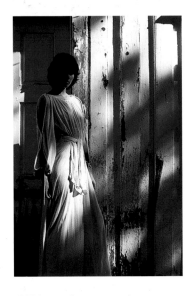

△ Using underexposure is more straightforward than overexposure, as the eye more readily accepts the darker, enriched tones. In this portrait, the dark shadow areas contrast well with the highlights and help to strengthen the atmosphere.

Determining the correct exposure for a particular shot is a skill that can depend as much upon instinct as upon science. In general, a photographer tries to select a shutter speed and aperture combination in which records full detail in all areas of the subject, whether brightly lit or cast in shadow. If too much exposure is given (the aperture is too wide, or shutter speed too slow), the image will be washed out, with detail lost in the brighter areas of the picture. With an underexposed image (where the aperture is too small, or the shutter speed too fast), the picture is too dark and shadow areas become indistinct.

Fortunately, much of the difficulty is taken away from the photographer by the increasingly sophisticated metering systems built into today's SLRs. Matrix metering, for instance, will take dozens of readings from across the image, and then compare the relative values to data stored in its databank. By doing this it can predict the type of picture you are taking, and the most likely effect needed (the down side is this type of metering is harder to predict). Older centre-weighted metering systems concentrate on the light intensity in the middle of the frame – where they assume the subject will be.

Whatever the metering system, however, there are times when the film itself cannot record detail across the whole image – regardless of the exposure settings used. Film is nowhere near as sensitive to extreme variations in light intensity as the human eye. If there is too much contrast between the brightest and darkest areas of the scene, then detail has to be sacrificed.

Photographers must train themselves to recognise situations where the film that they are using will struggle, and to make a suitable compromise on exposure. For example, nightscapes are characterised by the harsh contrast between dark shadows and bright street lights and neons. In this case, however, it is best to expose for the light sources themselves, rather than trying, unsuccessfully, to penetrate the night shadows.

Even in less contrasty scenes, the metering system built into your camera will not pick the right exposure 100% of the time. With a scene that is predominantly white, for example, such as a snowy landscape, the metering system will try and average the exposure – turning the whites a shade of grey or blue. Manual exposure compensation, or handheld meter readings, are therefore needed to show the snow at its correct brightness. Again, these situations must be recognised by the photographer, through practice.

As a fail-safe in difficult lighting conditions, it is best to shoot a scene at a range of different exposures. If using slide film, which is far less tolerant to exposure inaccuracies than print film, the exposures should be taken at $\frac{1}{2}$–1 stop apart. This technique is known as 'bracketing' – a procedure which some SLRs can undertake automatically. Colour print film is far more tolerant to overexposure than underexposure – so if in any doubt use a longer shutter speed or larger aperture.

The choice of overall exposure can also be part of the creative process. By varying exposure you highlight different things within the frame. An overexposed picture can take on a dreamy appearance; an underexposed picture can appear moody and sombre. Slight underexposure can increase colour saturation, whilst slight overexposure can create more pastel hues.

▷ Evenly lit scenes such as this cause few exposure problems for the photographer, as the metering systems built into any SLR can produce a well-exposed result. Generally, when the sun is behind the photographer, the frontal lighting will mean that the brightness range will be well within the limits of all film types.

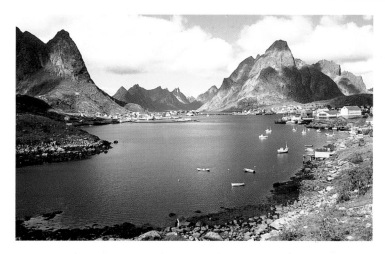

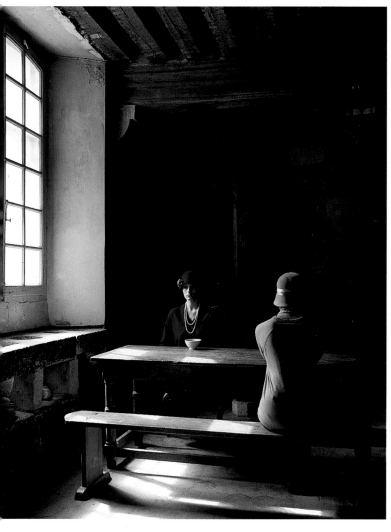

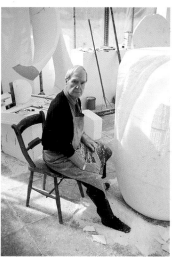

△ Meter readings will often be misleading if the image contains large light or dark areas, as the meter assumes that the average brightness value for the scene should be a mid-tone grey. In the scene above, the sculptor Henry Moore is surrounded by huge slabs of white stone – which the camera's built-in meter would tend to expose as a grey. Here I compensated by overriding the meter and giving an extra two-thirds of a stop exposure.

See also:
SOFT AND HARD LIGHT pp18–19
COLOUR INTENSITY pp24–25
EVENING LIGHT pp78–79
FLARE FOR EFFECT pp84–85

△ All films have a limited contrast range over which they can record detail. In a contrasty scene like this, detail has either to be lost in the shadows or in the highlights. Here, the shot has been exposed for the skin tones of the woman facing the camera.

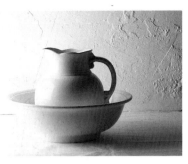

△ ▽ The still-life above has been shot under semi-diffused light, while the same subject below has been illuminated with more diffused lighting. The harder lighting above has a directional quality, throwing a distinct shadow. The jug's curved form and depth have been emphasized by the tonal gradation. The diffused-light picture below has indistinct shadows, and looks more two-dimensional, but more detail is revealed.

Light is fundamental to all photography — and all photographers need to understand the qualities, moods, and uses that can be made of light. It is important to appreciate how light can change and what effects different lighting has on its surroundings. Most people are aware of light intensity, whether it is dim or bright, and can quickly learn to estimate its direction. These are qualities are essential to the photographer — but of equal importance is the light's hardness or softness.

Hard light typically gives strong shadows with hard edges. In soft light, subject outlines are less well defined or disappear entirely. Overall shape and form better revealed with soft light, and the contrast between dark and light is subdued; colours are muted. In daylight, direct sunlight gives hard lighting, while soft lighting is produced when the sun is hidden by cloud.

The hardness of the lighting can be defined by the relative size of the light source to the subject. The larger the light source is comparatively the softer its illumination. The sun, in a clear sky, is a small source, giving hard, directional light. When obscured by cloud, the cloud acts as a large diffuser and effectively becomes the light source. Light can also be softened by the surroundings: in built-up areas light reflects off buildings partly filling in the shadows caused by direct sunlight.

A common mistake is to confuse a softening in light quality with a drop in intensity. This is not true — direct sunlight is no harder than light from the much dimmer moon, as pictures shot by moonlight will show; shadows are just as strong.

In general, hard light is best for subject that have strong simple shapes and brilliant colour. Texture is revealed by hard directional light that skims the surface to create a myriad of contrasting highlights and shadows.

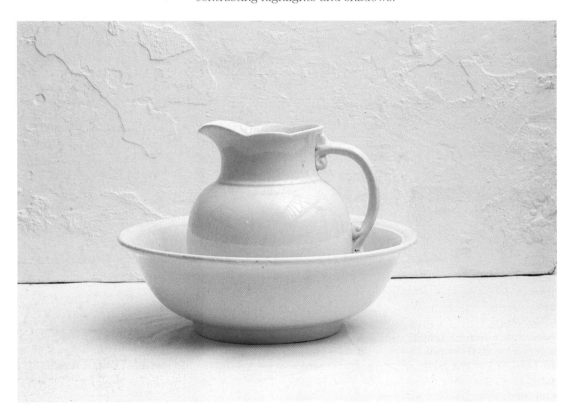

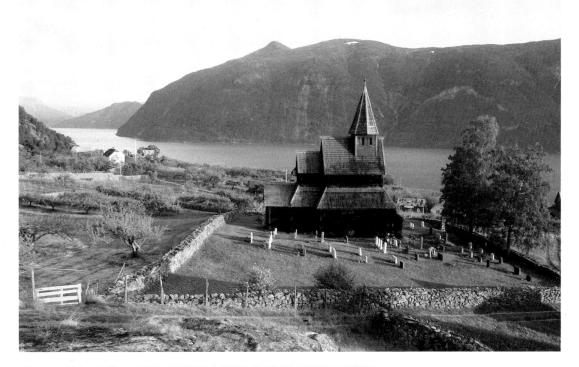

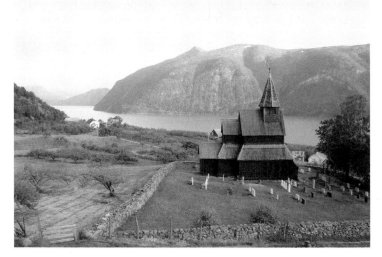

◁ △ In the shot above the early evening sun throws long, distinct shadows, characteristic of a hard light source. Each tree, wall and building is given extra depth and is lifted from the background by contrasting shadows against highlights. In the second picture, on the left, a cloud has passed over the sun, bathing the landscape in diffuse light. Without the shadows and bright highlights, the picture has less depth and little textural quality, making the scene appear flat.

Diffuse lighting with its soft shadows can often be easier to work with, as hard shadows can often interfere with composition and obscure detail. Soft light creates a soft mood, and can be used to reveal overall form as the light wraps itself around objects to give delicate modelling. Texture and colour are subdued, but more detail is revealed.

Remember that there are many degrees of softness and hardness. Often hard light can be softened slightly by the use of a reflector. In the studio, overall diffuse lighting can sometimes be bettered by the addition of a smaller, hard spotlight on a particular detail. Outdoors, a small change in the cloud cover can have a significant impact on the way a scene looks.

See also:
COLOUR INTENSITY pp24–25
LANDSCAPE MOODS pp62–63
A TOUCH OF LIGHT pp82–83
THE STILL LIFE pp162–163

FRAMING THE SUBJECT

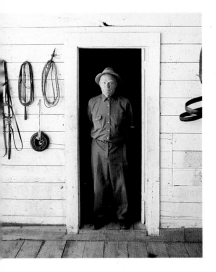

△ The combination of several framing devices in this portrait of an American horse owner serves to echo his solid stance. The squarish format suggests stability and placing him in a centrally framed doorway concentrates the attention on his figure. On a smaller scale, his face is framed by the hat and his light skin stands out against the darkness of the interior.

Framing is one of the photographer's principal compositional aids, concentrating the viewer's attention on the picture. The camera's viewfinder is a window on the world, hiding from view all that lies outside its boundaries.

The film format is obviously key to the relative dimensions of this window. Most film formats are rectangular as this is generally thought to be more interesting than a square frame, as it evokes more tension and energy. However, whatever the format, you should occasionally be prepared to crop pictures when they are printed, for the simple reason as this will add variety to your portfolio. Turning the camera through 90°, between 'landscape' and 'portrait' orientations, is also important if you don't want your pictures to look too similar.

The placing of the subject within the frame has a profound effect on compositional balance. Many artists instinctively put the centre of interest approximately one-third of the way into the frame from any side. 'The rule of thirds' is a useful device that pays premiums with many forms of photography. Horizons respond well to this treatment — placing them a third, or two thirds, of the way down when taking landscapes. Like any photographic rule, the rule of thirds is not inflexible. The key to success is to experiment — many successful images have been placed dead centre in the frame.

Colour is one of the strongest aids to composition; we are very aware of it and our response to different hues is almost instinctive. Reds, oranges, and yellows are warm, assertive colours that 'come forward' in a picture. Reds, in particular, grab the viewer's attention. Blues, violets, and greens are cool and restful, and seem to 'recede' into the background. Pictures that make use of colour contrast between the centre of interest and the surroundings are given dramatic emphasis.

Shape and line are two further powerful tools in composition. A common fault in pictures is that there is no centre of interest, or that there are too many. Shapes within the picture can be used to frame the subject, but it is best if they have an obvious connection — such as a doorway into a room.

Lines leading to an important element within the scene are useful aids — particularly if they lead from the corner of the frame, rather than from the side. Rivers, roads, and paths can all be pressed into service in this way, particularly when shooting landscapes, as they guide the eye through the picture.

▷ When there are strong diagonal lines in a picture, their impact is strengthened if they are framed so that they enter from a corner. In this picture, the bridge and horizon line meet where two imaginary lines drawn one-third in from the bottom and right sides would intersect.

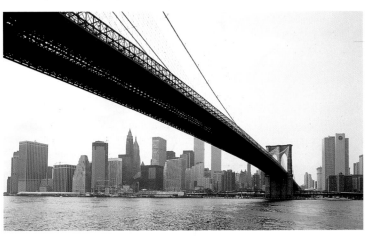

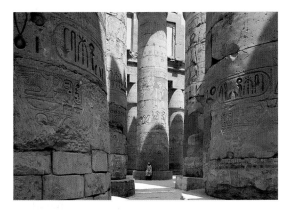

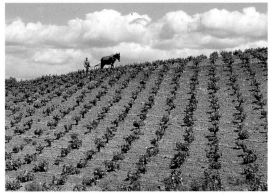

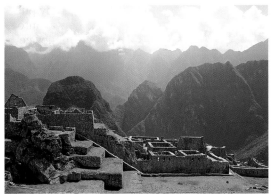

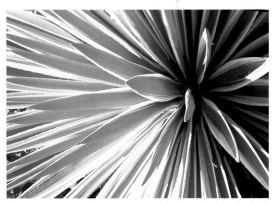

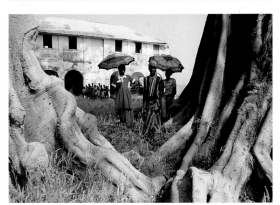

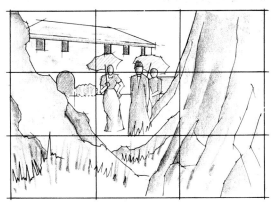

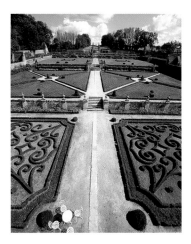

△ The pictures on this page illustrate several of the basic guidelines to composition, but remember that these aren't hard-and-fast laws that impose a straitjacket on your creativity, but should be thought of as a basis from which to start. Placing horizon lines near the top or bottom of the frame is more dynamic than placing them centrally. Using strong shapes as frames concentrates attention on the subject, while dividing the frame into thirds, then arranging elements of the composition to coincide with the lines and their intersections, helps pictorial balance. Try tracing the grid lines on the diagram and then overlay it on each of these pictures to see the 'rule of thirds' at work.

See also:
DESIGN WITH FIGURES pp58–59
THE CLOUDSCAPE pp64–67
DIAGONAL DESIGNS pp134–135
FRAMING THE SHOT pp148–149

BLACK AND WHITE

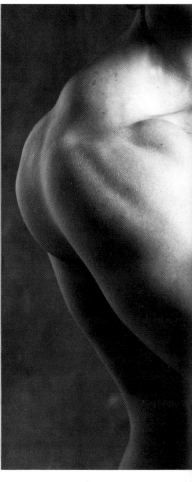

Many experienced photographers prefer working in black and white. This is probably because the medium has a graphic quality that is more interpretative and less rooted in the real world than is colour photography. Black and white also lends itself to image manipulation, allowing the photographer great creative freedom. But in order to gain this freedom, the photographer needs to invest in a darkroom in addition to his camera equipment. Treating black and white film like colour negative film, and sending it to a commercial laboratory rarely produces results that do justice to the process.

Composition in black and white follows the same guidelines as for colour. Light is the most vital element; its character and mood will have a profound effect on the atmosphere as well as image contrast. Subject qualities such as shape, form, line, pattern, texture, and tone all play crucial roles in image structure, but perhaps surprisingly, colours have to be taken into account, as they affect the tonal balance of the picture. Tonal balance can suggest different moods – predominantly pale tones suggest a light sunlit atmosphere, and tend to give the image an ethereal quality, whereas large areas of dark tones or black can lead to a sombre atmosphere and a sense of drama. Contrast also affects mood. Pictures containing bright and dark tones next to each other heighten the sense of drama, adding energy, but pictures containing similar, more subtle tones create a quiet, harmonious impression.

The choice of film will have an important influence on the final image. There are many different types on the market from ultra-fine grained graphic films which produce only blacks and whites, to highly sensitive, grainy films with panchromatic response, which produce a full range of tones. There are some special black and white films, designed for specific uses, such as medical photography.

▷ This picture was shot on high-speed film and shows the obvious granular pattern typical of this film type. It breaks up fine detail, especially in the mid-grey tones, but can introduce a pleasing textural effect with the right subject and create a moody atmosphere.

Hasselblad, 500 mm, Kodak Tri-X, ¹/₂₅₀ sec, f16

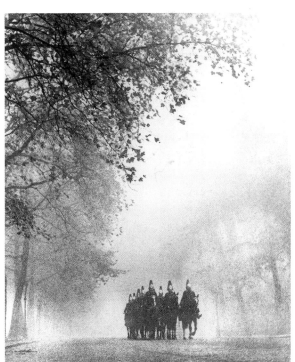

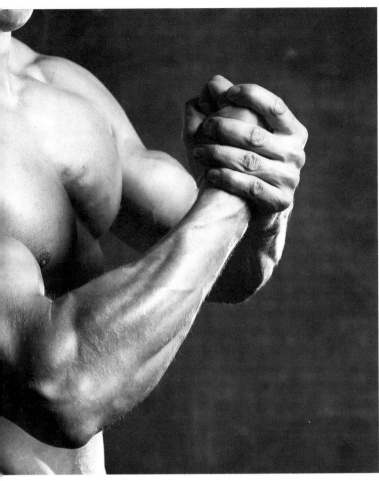

◁ In a black and white image tone plays an important compositional role. In this picture the three-dimensional form of the man's torso is largely expressed in terms of tonal variation. Soft, directional light has revealed skin texture without losing detail in highlight and shadow areas.

Hasselblad, 120 mm, Kodak Tri-X, flash, f16

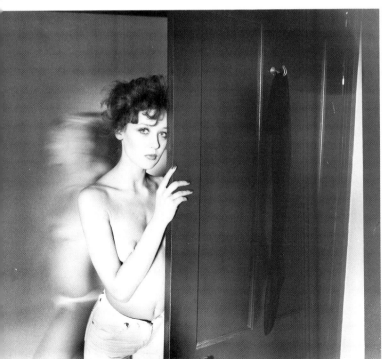

◁ Fine-grained films of slow speed are ideal for subjects that have delicate textural qualities and large areas of even tone where grain is most noticeable. They are also sharper than fast films and can be enlarged to a greater extent without a severe loss in image quality.

Pentax LX, 50 mm, Ilford FP4, ISO 100, 1/30 sec, f8

See also:
SOFT AND HARD LIGHT pp18–19
MONOCHROME VIEWS pp74–75
DOWN ON THE FARM pp100–101

COLOUR INTENSITY

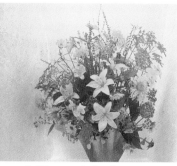

△ Warm muted colours predominate in this simple still life study of flowers. The tonal range is limited to lighter colours from mid-grey to white – making this a high-key image – but the shot still contains colour. The misty effect is produced by using a soft, overhead light and fitting a diffuser and fog filter to the lens.

Pentax LX, 85 mm, Scotch (3M) 100, ¹⁄₂₅₀ sec, f8

▽ The warm reds and yellows in this image seem to evoke a sense of intimacy and well-being.

Pentax LX, 50 mm, Kodak Kodachrome 64, ¹⁄₅₀₀ sec, f8

Colour has a profound effect on a picture's mood. Bold, striking colours are eye-catching and energetic; pastel tones suggest harmony and invite the eye to explore the photograph at leisure. Understanding and controlling colour so that it can be enriched or muted to achieve the desired mood is an essential part of the photographer's skill.

Vibrant colours can form the dominant element in a photograph's composition. Strong colour contrasts intensify the impact of different tones, especially if there are just one or two pairs set against each other. Colour pairs that have the most contrast are complementaries – blue-yellow, green-magenta, and red-cyan – but any warm colour placed next to a cool one will add impact. A similar effect is achieved when a photograph is largely composed of one bold colour with small areas of black, grey, or white as a neutral counterpoint.

Colours can be manipulated and strengthened by appropriate choice of exposure, film, lighting, and filters. Exposure plays an important role in manipulating colour. If you are using colour transparency film, you must avoid underexposure, as this will desaturate colour. However, many photographers increase colour contrast by underexposing slightly – usually by ⅓ to 1 stop. But remember, if you are using colour negative film, the reverse is true: colour contrast can be increased by overexposing, but subjects with a wide brightness range may lose colour in the highlights if overexposure is extreme. Precise exposure control is crucial, so a separate light meter with an incident-light attachment is recommended.

Lighting quality can also be exploited to enhance colour. Notice how the colour quality of, for example, a familiar building, changes in the sunlight at different times of the day. With landscapes, the clear air produced after heavy rain allows distant

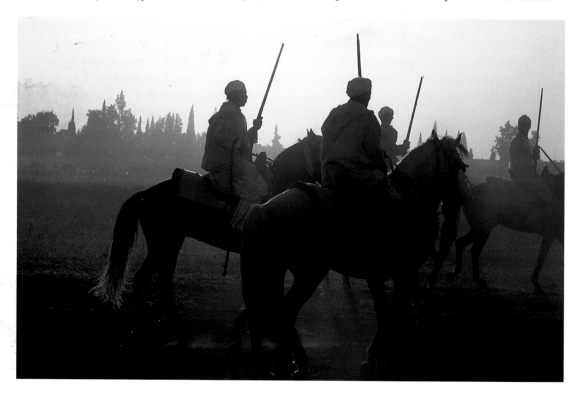

colour to record with extra clarity, and the wet surfaces also deepen the colour balance. Hard, strong light – typical of noonday summer sun – is ideal for giving emphasis to bold colour, and any desaturation caused by glare from reflections or heat haze can be reduced by using a polarizing filter.

If, on the other hand, you wish to evoke a poignant or romantic atmosphere, you should aim to use soft, muted colours. Harmony is suggested by pastel colours of similar tones and hues. Soft, diffuse light is ideal for recording subdued colour, and slight overexposure – about ⅓ to 1 stop – of the transparency will dilute it further to enhance the effect even more. It is also possible to mimic the softening effect of mist by using a fog or diffusing filter over the lens, or by using as the prime lens a cheap plastic magnifying glass fitted to extension rings or bellows.

▽ It can be argued that monochromatic subjects are just as effective in black and white as in colour but, as this portrait shows, large areas of neutral tone bring out any slight colour tints that are present – here, in the girl's skin and hair – making them much more effective.

Pentax LX, 85 mm, Kodak Ektachrome 64, ¹/₂₅₀ sec, f8

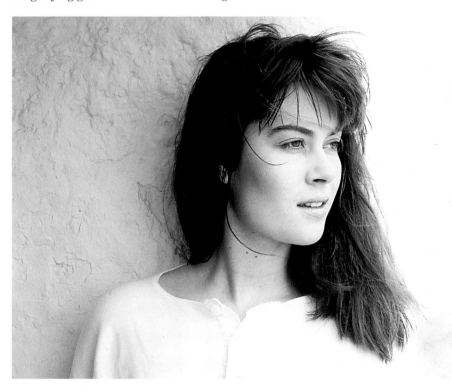

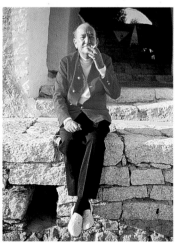

◁ Colour photographers have to take into account not only tone but the characteristics of colours when composing photographs. If shot in black and white, this portrait of Noel Coward would show a good range of tones, with mid-tone values applying to the jacket and face. In colour, the scarlet has a striking effect on composition, immediatley seizing the attention and ensuring that the figure is dominant.

Lecaflex, 35 mm, Kodak Ektachrome 200, ¹/₂₅₀ sec, f8

COMPUTER MANIPULATION

Digital imaging is fast changing the face of photography. Although traditional cameras and film will still be used by photographers for many years to come, there is no escaping the many advantages that digital cameras, and, in particular, computer manipulation, can bring to the photographer.

Although digital cameras are now widely available, they can not compete with 35 mm film in terms of picture quality. However, the fact that their pictures do not need to be processed saves time and money. Professional news and sports photographers can send pictures to their editors, over the phone lines of mobile networks, within moments of shooting pictures. That shots can be sent over telephone lines, and over the internet, within seconds of being taken mean that they are increasingly used by professionals on a tight deadline.

Digital cameras are also used by amateurs – for sending pictures to friends via e-mail, for incorporating into home-compiled newsletters, or for jazzing up world wide web sites.

Those using traditional film do not need to miss out on the digital revolution. Low-cost scanners for home computers allow you to turn prints, negatives and slides into a digital form. Once translated into this series of ones and noughts, the computer can then be used to store, print, transmit and manipulate these electronic copies of your original images.

It is the ability to alter pictures with such ease that excites photographers. Tricks that used to demand years of experience to master, and hours locked away in the darkroom to undertake, can now be carried out, in minutes, with simple image manipulation software and a computer.

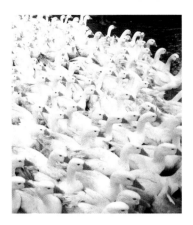

△ ▽ The original picture of this flock of geese (above), shot from a high viewpoint to emphasize pattern, was taken on slide film with a 35 mm SLR. Once digitized using a scanner, changing just some of the birds (below) is surprisingly straightforward.

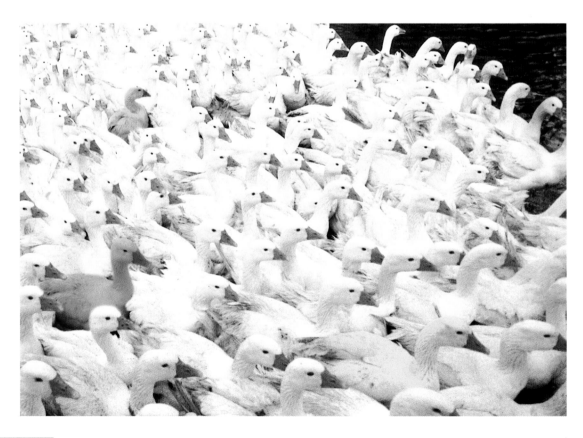

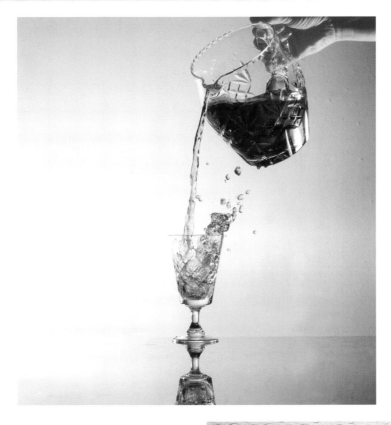

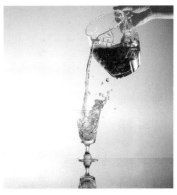

◁ △ A 'magic wand' tool means that you can automatically select areas of the same colour when manipulating an image on computer – these can then all be changed simultaneously. Originally I shot this picture using green liquid (above), but the shot looks better with claret!

▽ ▷ Once upon a time, when you took a picture you could only wonder what a portrait would look like if you'd found the right coloured backdrop – or if your subject had worn different clothes. Now such changes can be made with a few clicks of the computer mouse. Here the original colours of the photograph have been subtlely enhanced.

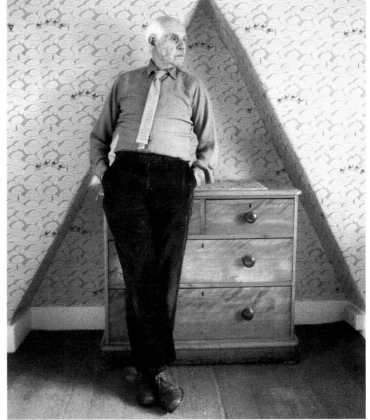

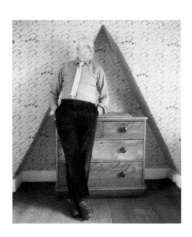

DIGITAL TRICKS

Digital manipulation software allows you to carry out, without the need for chemicals, many of the effects that have been available to the darkroom worker for decades. Retouching scratches, removing dust marks, colour toning, increasing/decreasing contrast – all can be done with ease. Photomontages can be created on screen, and traditional darkroom effects, such as solarization, can be reproduced.

But the computer allows you to go much further. Most image software comes with a selection of 'filters' – digital effects that will add blur lines to your pictures, create ripples over the background, or distort a face as if it were made out of latex.

Often it is the subtler tools that such software provides that prove the most useful. You can soften and sharpen images, for instance – and do so selectively within the picture area. Backgrounds that are too distracting can be made unrecognizable – limiting the depth of the field after the picture has been taken. Crucial areas in the picture, such as a person's eyes, can be sharpened so that the shot looks crisper. Subtle changes in colour balance, can get around problems of pictures taken in mixed lighting. Sunsets, that prove disappointing when processed, can be made to look more dramatic.

When working on images on the computer, it is easy enough to try an effect or alteration – and then revert to where you were if you don't like the result. There are two important tips however. First, crop your picture before you start manipulating, so that the digital image takes up less of your computer's memory, and valuable processing power. Secondly, save different versions of the shot as you go – giving the part-finished picture a new file name. This way, you can always go back several stages without having to start all over again.

▽ For the digital montage of the 'flower girl' on the opposite page, I started with two slides. the shot of the girl had been taken from above, with the model lying on the ground so that her red hair could be arranged like tongues of flame. The picture of the single yellow bloom was shot using diffused flash, which threw the background into darkness, and let me use a much smaller aperture than available light would have allowed.

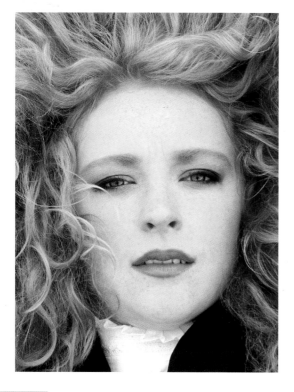

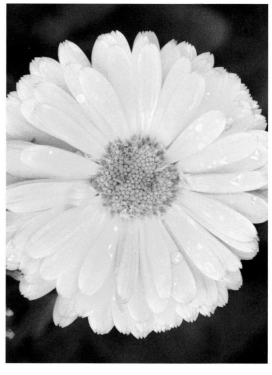

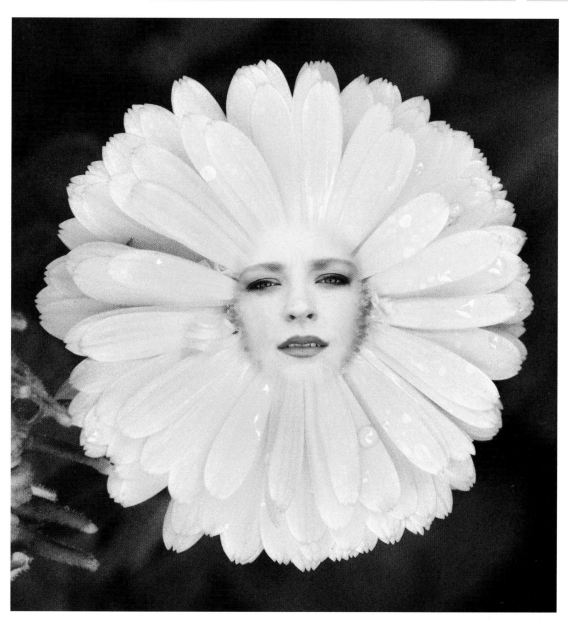

△ To combine the images of the flower and the girl on the computer, both slides were first scanned in. The digital image of the girl was then adjusted in size so that the face would fit neatly into the centre of the petals. This part of the face was then digitally cut from the portrait , and pasted onto the flower. With professional image manipulation software, these two components of the montage can be left separate – as 'layers' – allowing you to adjust relative positions, sharpness and so on at a later stage. It was then necessary to remove some of the hair which was obscuring the model's face. This was done by 'cloning' small areas of the similarly-toned flesh, and copying so they hid the hair. Finally the joins between the two pictures were softened usng a 'smear' tool which allows you to blend colours together, as if you were using pastels.

See also:
COMPUTER MANIPULATION pp26–27
DIGITAL REMODELLING pp30–31
SPLITTING IMAGES pp136–139
FRAMING THE SHOT pp148–149

DIGITAL REMODELLING

Who said the camera never lies?! Back in the days of the old Soviet Union, Communist leaders had a habit of rewriting history by doctoring photographs. Stalin had Trotsky painted out of official photographs, when his former comrade fell out of favour. Russian pictures of Gorbachev never showed the prominent birthmark on his forehead.

Today, computers allow anyone to improve photographs to their liking in a similar way. In the United States there has been a fad for divorcees to have ex-husbands removed from a cherished snap and replacing the image with a current companion. Company reports use computer techniques to give their sites a 'facelift' – considerably cheaper than redecorating.

The techniques used are straightforward, and can be used by any photographer with access to a computer to improve pictures. An annoyingly-modern sign in a shot of a picturesque village can be surgically removed – as can unwanted passers-by.

Removing miniature picture elements (or pixels), or whole objects, from a shot is very easy. It is what you put in the space that is left that is the problem. Although parts of other digital images can be used, in many cases it is possible to make do with copying small sections that are already in the shot. Areas of missing wallpaper can be copied from the wallpaper that is in the shot. When removing a pimple from a model's face, similar-coloured pixels of flesh can be painted in electronically.

The real art to digital doctoring is learning how to hide all traces of your meddling – so that no one knows that the shot has been altered. Particular attention must be paid to shadows. If an object is taken away, so must its shadow. Similarly if something else in the shot casts a shadow over what is removed, it must be carefully painted in.

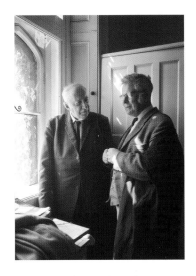

△ I wanted to remove the person on the right in this portrait, to leave the man standing by the window. As ever, the first step in the process was to scan the picture into the computer, turning it into a digital form.

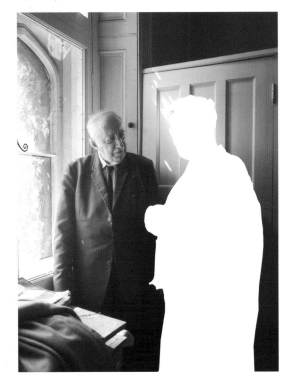

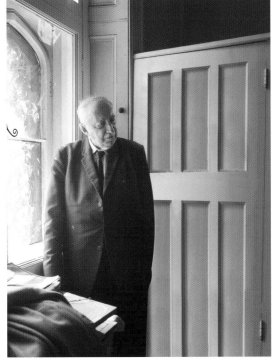

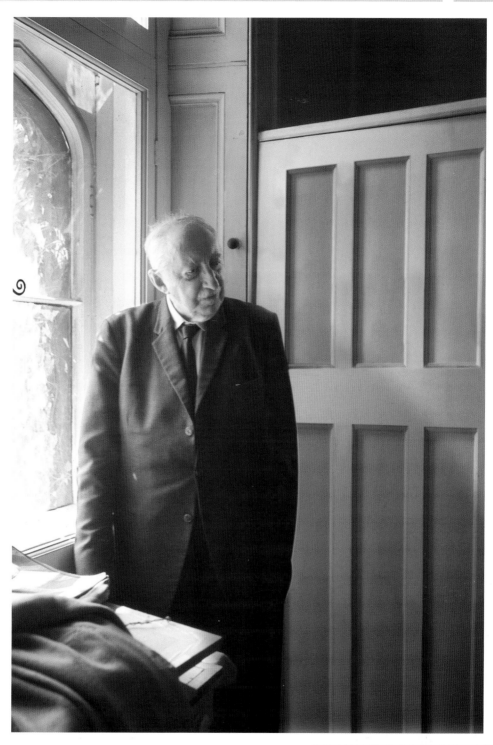

◁ The unwanted subject was cut by magnifying this area, then the outline was marked using the 'lasso' tool and the area deleted (far left). Next, the door and the missing parts of the subject's sleeve were rebuilt by 'cloning'.

△ The final step was to add a shadow to the door. This is simply done by 'painting' the required area. Image software normally includes various painting tools – including sprays, brushes and pencils of different sizes.

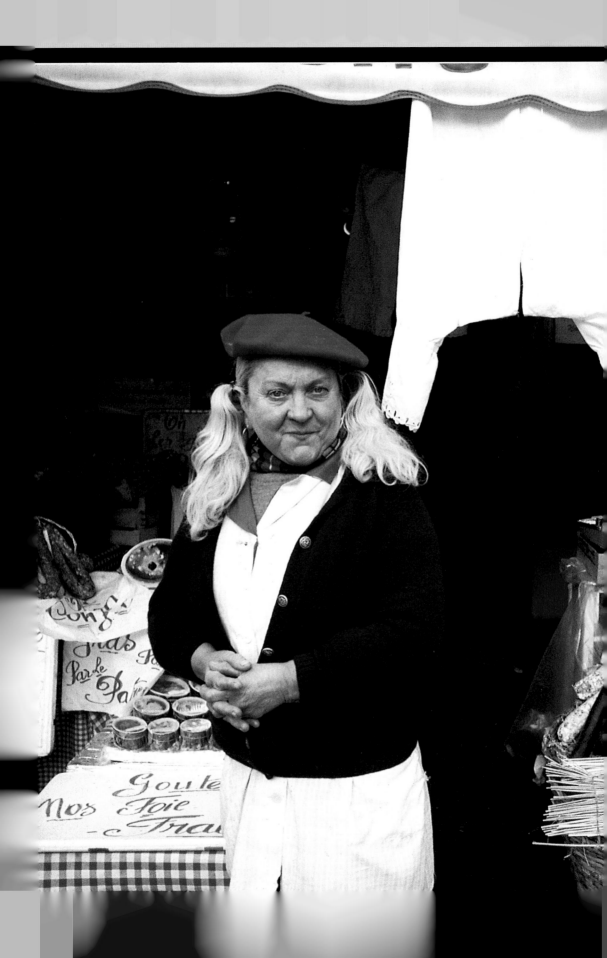

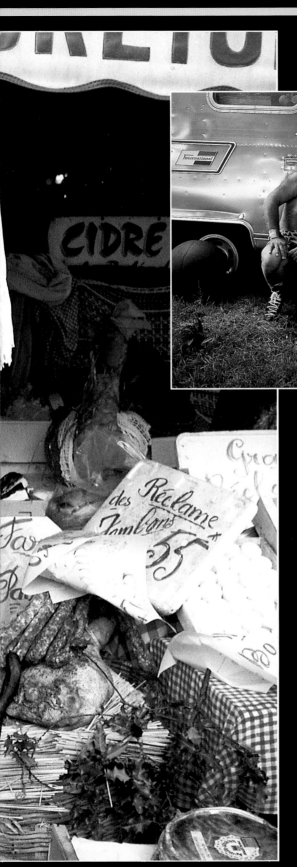

People have been the most popular subject since the earliest days of photography and it is often someone's desire to record his closest friends and relatives that is the catalyst for his future development of photographic expertise. Frequently, it is the relationship that people have with their environment that becomes the main subject of the photograph, although it is a sad fact that many photographers only exploit the situation if it is unusual – for example, when they are travelling away from home. In fact, those whom we know well offer the best opportunities to make truly good portraits that capture the essence of a personality, as it is essential for photographer and subject to have a close rapport.

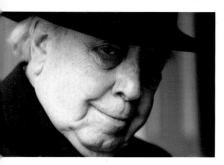

△ A tilted hat and sloping collar frame novelist J B Priestley's wry expression. The angles emphasize the modelling in the face and add interest themselves.

Pentax LX, 100 mm macro, Kodak Ektachrome 200, ¹/₃₀ sec, f16

▷ The subject's direct gaze, hidden by dark glasses, gives this portrait of artist Graham Sutherland a sinister air.

Leicaflex, 90 mm macro, Kodak Ektachrome 64, ¹/₂₅₀ sec, f8

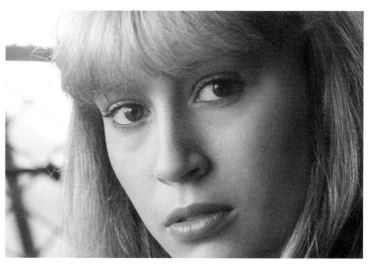

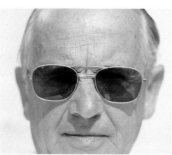

△ Soft colouring and gentle winter sunlight help to create the delicate harmony of this portrait. A romantic impression is conveyed by the gently inclined head and thoughtful expression.

Pentax LX, 135 mm, Scotch (3M) 1000, ¹/₆₀ sec, f16

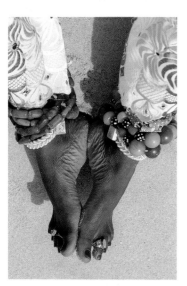

△ This woman used her feet to display her jewellery for sale. Although her wares were striking in themselves, it was the method of display that gave the picture its eloquence.

Pentax LX, 85 mm, Kodak Ektachrome 64, ¹/₂₅₀ sec, f8

The face is the most expressive part of the body and pictures which concentrate on it usually contain both intimacy and impact. The viewer is given a rare chance of seeing in detail the nuance of expression and gaze, so it is not surprising that close-ups can reveal a person in a frank way. Isolating the face can make people appear younger, by excluding tell-tale signs of age, such as grey hair or a wrinkled neck, but any blemishes on the skin will be exaggerated. This factor is naturally of considerable importance when the aim is to make a flattering portrait. Softer lighting and even the use of a soft-focus technique may be required to produce the right effect.

Making successful close-ups demands careful technique. Normally, they should be very sharp, and to achieve this critical focusing and an adequate depth of field are required. With portraits it is particularly important to have the eyes sharply focused. A portrait with blurred eyes will not work, because people depend on the eyes to read a person's expression. But portraits in which the eyes are hidden, or those in which the eyes are averted, may have an added sense of mystery.

After the face, the other most important close-up features in portrait studies are the hands and feet. Like the face, the hands reflect the age and suggest the experience of the person. They can be tiny and perfectly formed, like those of a baby, or they can be clear and soft-skinned like those of a young woman, or they can be gnarled and tanned by a lifetime's toil. As with any portrait, background and setting can add a great deal to the image, and making close-ups of hands, feet and other details can often help to relax a person before a full-figure picture is taken.

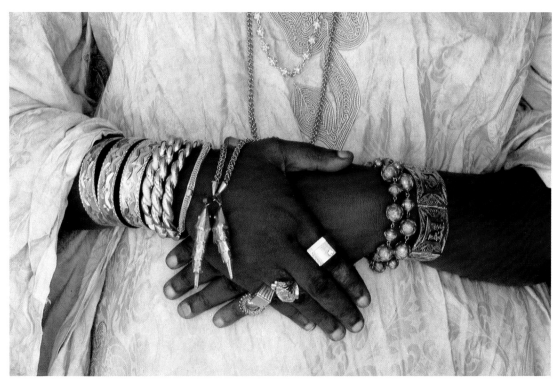

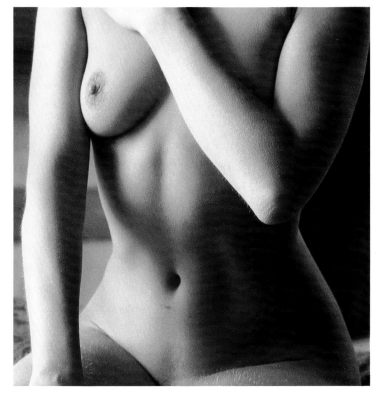

△ The native women of Gambia
display their wealth in gold
bracelets and bangles of which
they are rightly proud. This
woman welcomed the chance to
exhibit her most prized
possessions for the benefit of the
photographer.

*Pentax LX, 135 mm, Kodak
Ektachrome 64, ¹/₂₅₀ sec, f8*

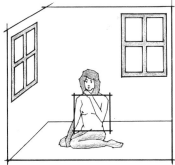

△ Bright side-light from a
window gives good modelling,
while a second small window
behind provides a slight rim-light

(see diagram, above right).

*Pentax LX, 135 mm, Kodak,
Ektachrome 200, ¹/₆₀ sec, f16*

See also:
SOFT AND HARD LIGHT pp18–19
THE VERSATILE LENS pp116–117

P O R T R A I T G R O U P S

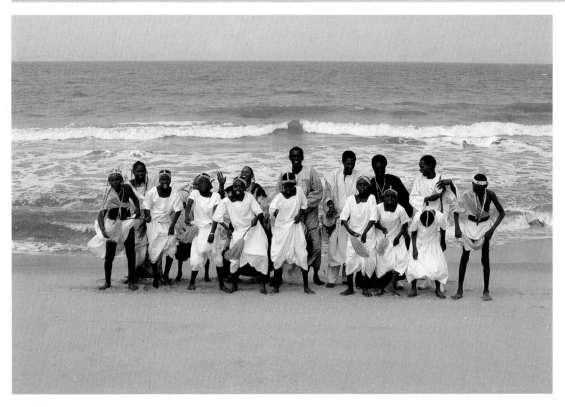

△ This group of native Gambian dancers on a West African beach was rehearsing under the guidance of their director. A chance encounter produced an animated picture that captured the mood of the moment.

Pentax LX, 85 mm, Kodak Ektachrome 64, $^1/_{250}$ sec, f8

Many people buy cameras to enable them to record family events and occasions. Even for professionals, the essential problems of photographing groups of people remain the same. The aim is to produce a result that is not only pleasing to the photographer (and, perhaps, the picture editor), but to the people involved too. To achieve this, care must be taken with every detail – lighting, the setting, positioning and direction – so that the session can proceed with the minimum of fuss and the maximum of enjoyment.

With formally posed groups, it is important to have a clear view of every individual; it is always a disappointment afterwards if anyone finds himself wholly or partially obscured. Although it is seldom attractive, the rank-upon-rank arrangement is often the easiest, especially for large numbers of, say, 20 or more, and so is often fitting for groups such as sports teams, clubs, and societies. To avoid totally predictable results, vary the usual procedure of standing the tallest individuals at the back and the shortest at the front, by, for example, having some people standing on chairs at the back. You can also pose the gathering in a curve, with the ends towards the camera, to break the monotony of the line. A few well chosen props can add interest too. To avoid confusion, arrange each person's position beforehand, have ready any props, and use a tripod to fix the camera position so that you are free to move around.

Although informally posed groups give the photographer a chance to make more interesting pictures, they still need the same care taken over arrangements. There is often a group hierarchy and, though it does not necessarily mean putting the most important person at the front, he or she usually wants to be prominent in some way.

▷ Another chance encounter in Africa – this time with a solitary girl on her hammock – evolved into a group shot. As news of the event spread, children were collected to form a background. The girl's relationship to the group and dominance of the picture is retained by the choice of lens and viewpoint and by controlling the focus.

Pentax LX, 28 mm, Kodak Ektachrome 200, 1/60 sec, f8

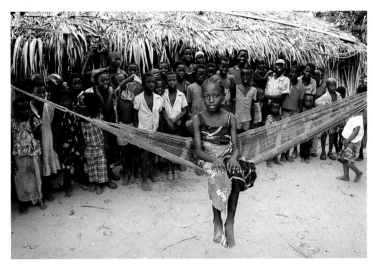

▷ A common sight at London events is the Pearly Kings and Queens and their children. These Pearly Princesses were posed against a simple but brightly coloured background, as a counterpoint to their ornate black and white costumes. The self-conscious poses of the older girls contrast with the shy, retiring pose of their little sister.

Pentax LX, 50 mm, Kodak Ektachrome 64, 1/250 sec, f8

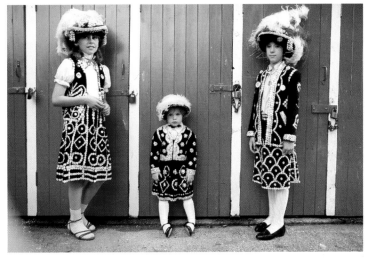

◁ For family portraits in the studio, a soft, even light is ideal. Keeping the attention of young children is not always necessary, and insisting on a particular pose can cause upsets and tension that ruin the results.

Hasselblad, 80 mm, Kodak Ektachrome 64, 1/250 sec, f8

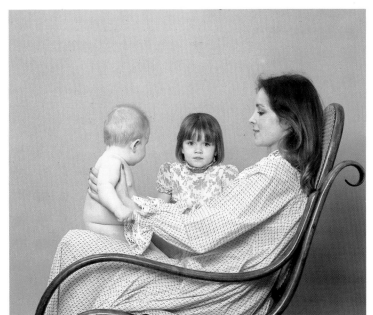

See also:
POSED PORTRAITS pp42–43
DESIGN WITH FIGURES pp58–59
THE WEDDING ALBUM pp92–95

BENDING REALITY

A reflection in a mirror is always a source of interest when included in a photograph. Mirrors have a strange and almost mystical fascination and add an extra dimension and lend an element of mystery and ambiguity when the subject of the reflection is not included in the composition.

Plastic mirrors have opened up new possibilities for the photographer. Not only are they light and portable, but they are unbreakable and therefore quite safe. There are no handling problems when it comes to using large mirrors and a great deal of fun can be had by distorting reflections to create bizarre and surreal images. Large mirrors also make ideal reflectors and, because of their high reflectivity, can be used as a second light source. Placing mirrors within the picture calls for careful positioning of all elements and of the camera. It is also important to focus on the reflected image and not on the mirror's surface. If the subject is in view you will need to use a very small aperture to give sufficient depth of field.

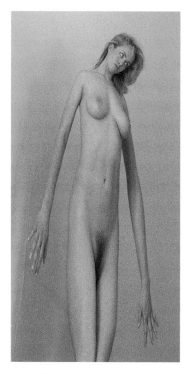

△ Most people are familiar with the distorted reflections seen in a fairground 'Hall of Mirrors' and the same effects can be achieved by bending plastic mirrors. Nudes make interesting distorted images which can be extreme or as subtle as you like, depending on the flexibility of the mirror, and it is possible to create shapes reminiscent of modern figure sculpture where emphasis and form are used to create impact.

Pentax LX, 85 mm, Scotch (3M) 640 Tungsten, ¹/₃₀ sec, f8

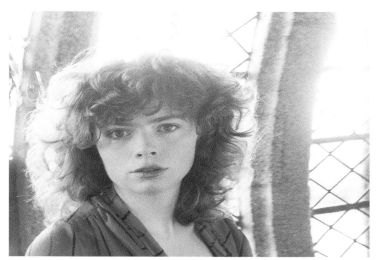

△ ▷ Plastic mirrors can be used in ways that do not shock or surprise the viewer with bizarre distortions. Slightly bending a mirror can subtly alter the shape of a face or figure in ways that are both flattering and intriguing. In this picture, the camera and model were positioned in front of and facing away from a window. The model looked into a plastic mirror that was curved into a concave shape. The camera was then focused on the reflected scene, as shown in the diagram.

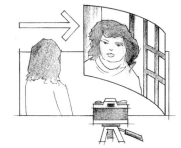

Pentax LX, 85 mm, Kodak Ektachrome 200, ¹/₂₅₀ sec, f11

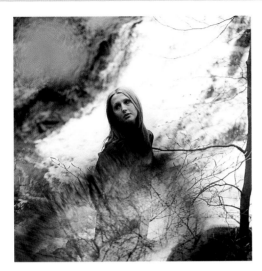

◁ The original intention was to portray this girl in the romantic setting of a secluded waterfall, but the image seemed too cluttered and needed extra impact. A small plastic mirror provided the solution. Placed very close to the lens, which was set to a wide aperture to ensure that the mirror surface was out of focus, the reflection surrounded the girl in an ethereal flow of water.

Hasselblad, 60 mm, Kodak Ektachrome 64, ¹/₁₂₅ sec, f4

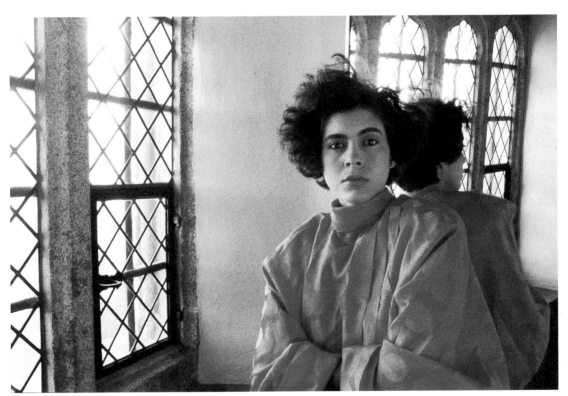

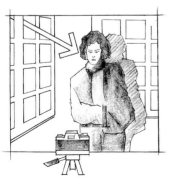

◁ △ This portrait was composed so that the only window provided a rich side light against a background of a blank white wall. To relieve the monotony, a mirror was used to cover part of the wall and introduce a second area of interest.

Pentax LX, 85 mm, Kodak Ektachrome 200, ¹/₃₀ sec, f16

See also:
COMPUTER MANIPULATION pp26–31
FRAMING THE SHOT pp148–149
MIRRORED IMAGES pp188–189

PATTERN AND PORTRAIT

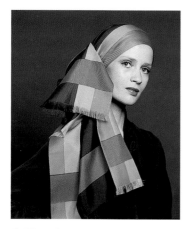

Patterns are a good way of strengthening a portrait, either as a background or as a complementary feature. Background patterns are viewed as a setting and therefore need careful handling, otherwise they will overwhelm the subject. It is like selecting wallpaper for a room: one has to live with the choice. Portraites of people dressed in pastel colours, or where a contemplative atmosphere is required, need a harmonizing pattern of complementary colours and rhythm. To inject drama and energy into portraits of, say, children or creative people, bright colours and a vibrant pattern can be used effectively, as long as a sense of balance and proportion is maintained. Balance depends largely on matching the background to the subject. As the background to a portrait, pattern can be used in a variety of ways. It can lead the eye to the person, either by isolating him or her, or by echoing a colour, shape, or design featured in his or her figure. Pattern can also provide a counterpoint, where its colour, design, and scale contrast with the subject and strengthen the overall impact. Patterns lends an element of design to a portrait and experimentation can lead to fresh and exciting results.

△ The colour and pattern of the scarf are what first attracts the eye, which is then drawn to the face. Dressing the model in dark clothes and using a dark background have isolated the scarf and the face, their colours striking a bold contrast. Flash with a reflective umbrella provided the soft light.

Hasselblad, 80 mm, Kodak Ektachrome 64, f16

▷ This shot was one of a series experimenting with a nude against a powerful geometric setting. Although there was a contrast both in form and colour, the model was lost until the dark sofa provided a local background.

Hasselblad, 80 mm, Kodak Ektachrome 200, 1/30 sec, f16

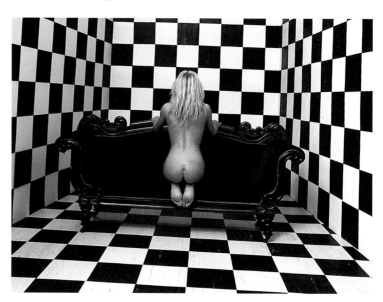

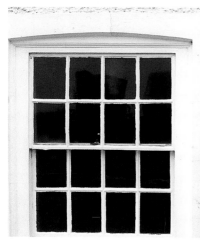

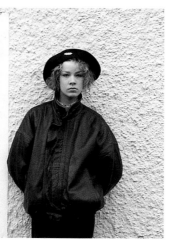

◁ Another image where pattern is a crucial part of the composition. The regular squares of the dark window provide a strong counterpoint to the less symmetrical shape of the girl.

Pentax LX, 50 mm, Kodak Ektachrome 200, 1/30 sec, f8

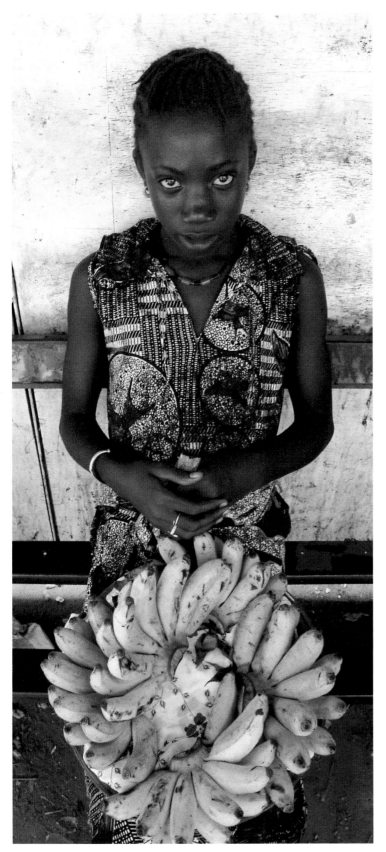

◁ In an African marketplace there were dozens of children selling fruit, but this girl's arrangement of her wares caught the eye at once. The circle of bananas provided a pattern rich in colour, shape, and texture.

Pentax LX, 35 mm, Kodak Ektachrome 200,¹/₃₀ sec, f11

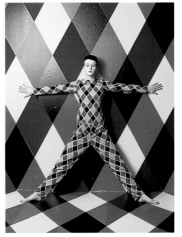

△ The design of the harlequin suit inspired the background for this picture. Different degrees of balance could be achieved by moving the girl away from the pattern, but here the intention was to emphasize the backdrop.

Hasselblad, 80 mm, Kodak Ektachrome 64, f16

POSED PORTRAITS

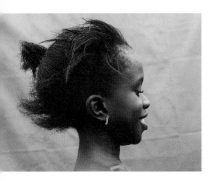

Children are always rewarding subjects for the camera and, in the more remote parts of the world, our interest in them is often matched by their fascination with the magic of photography. These pictures were taken in Gambia, where children appeared, apparently from nowhere, and crowded around the camera as soon as it was taken from its case. This avid interest in a stranger's every move and an irresistible urge to pose as soon as the equipment appears makes it almost impossible to take candid shots. The only alternative is to exploit the circumstances, direct the children's poses, and hope to maintain a degree of control. Enlisting the aid of one or two little helpers is a great benefit; they can communicate your wishes to other members of the group and maintain some semblance of order, leaving you slightly freer to concentrate on the photography. If one or two youngsters catch your eye as being particularly good portrait subjects, keep it to yourself at first and take a selection of group pictures to ensure that everyone has had a chance to be included. Then, with the help of your young assistants, approach the individuals.

△ If you are staying in one place, it is simple to set up an outdoor 'studio' and take a series of posed portraits.

Pentax LX, 100 mm macro, Kodak Ektachrome 64, ¹/₁₂₅ sec, f8

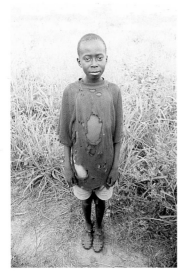

△ Wordlessly this boy pointed to the camera and stood to attention. His proud stance and unwavering gaze seem quite at odds with his tattered shirt. Overexposure by one stop revealed skin texture.

Pentax LX, 28 mm, Kodak Ektachrome 64, ¹/₆₀ sec, f8

▷ The intention was to photograph one child, but this group quickly assembled, waiting for a turn in front of the lens.

Pentax LX, 28 mm, Kodak Ektachrome 64, ¹/₁₂₅ sec, f11

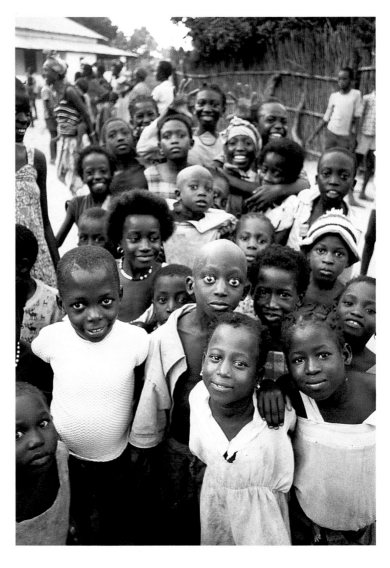

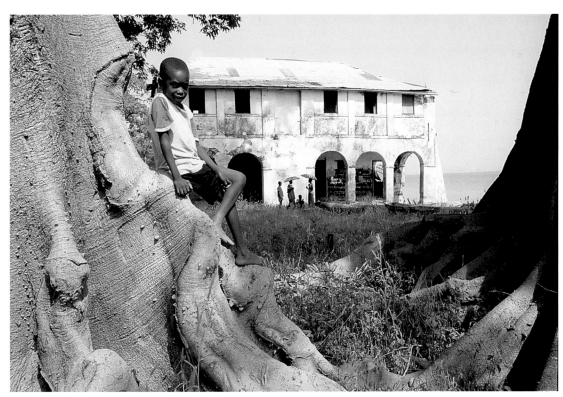

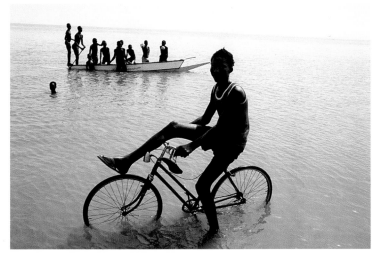

△ While this building was being photographed and the shot composed with the tree trunks either side as a framing device, a boy perched on one to watch. His intrusion has added an extra, human element that gives the picture increased interest and greater impact.

Pentax LX, 28 mm, Kodak Ektachrome 64, $^1/_{125}$ sec, f11

△ This picture also came about largely as a result of a child's curiosity about the picture-taking process. This time the boat and its crew were the subject, drawing him into the shot. A change of viewpoint to balance the two picture elements within the frame was all that was needed before setting the exposure to render them as silhouettes.

Pentax LX, 28 mm, Kodak Ektachrome 64, $^1/_{125}$ sec, f11

See also:
FRAMING THE SUBJECT pp20–21
CAPTURING ACTION pp48–49
DESIGN WITH FIGURES pp58–59
THE WEDDING ALBUM pp92–95

THE SIMPLE SETTING

Portraits of people taken in their own environments are greatly improved by selecting a background which reflects the subject. Backgrounds contribute in different ways but the most important is to provide a contrasting backdrop which adds to our knowledge of the sitter. The balance between subject and setting, which is particularly important with this kind of picture, is determined by the placing of the person in relation to the camera and background, taking into consideration colour contrast and lighting. People framed towards the centre and near to the camera dominate their setting, whereas people placed well into the room and framed off-centre become more a part of their environment. Bright, contrasting clothes draw the attention of the eye. If the room is dimly lit, localized lighting can be used to highlight a person's face or figure.

▷ For this portrait of a tea planter's wife, no arranging was necessary. With obvious pride and self-assurance she sat in the centre of the picture and looked straight at the camera.

Pentax LX, 28 mm, Kodak Ektachrome 200, 1/60 sec, f11

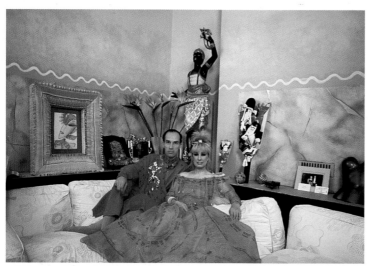

◁ Using bounced flash can be risky, since reflecting the light off colourful surfaces can give it a colour cast. Fortunately, in this picture of fashion designer Zandra Rhodes and artist Andrew Logan, the ceiling was white, but had it been tinted, the solution would have been to bounce the flash off white paper.

Pentax LX, 28 mm, Kodak Ektachrome 200 1/60 sec, f16

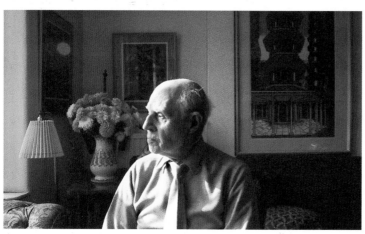

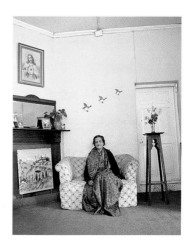

△ Tonal contrast through careful lighting is another way of selecting a balance between subject and background. In this shot of artist Edward Bawden, a shaft of sunlight spotlighted him.

Pentax LX, 28 mm, Kodak Ektachrome 200, 1/60 sec, f11

△ In this study of an Indian woman it was important to communicate her pride in her home. She sat in her favourite chair and the picture was framed to include much of the room.

Pentax LX, 28 mm, Kodak Ektachrome 200, 1/30 sec, f8

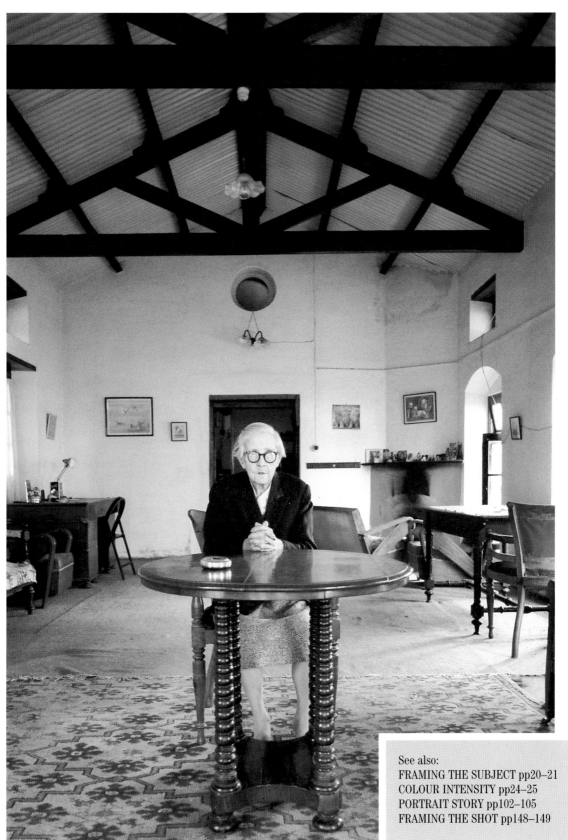

See also:
FRAMING THE SUBJECT pp20–21
COLOUR INTENSITY pp24–25
PORTRAIT STORY pp102–105
FRAMING THE SHOT pp148–149

UNUSUAL VIEWPOINTS

It is always a problem to keep your work fresh and lively when you attempt to tackle the same subject time and time again. For professionals the problem is even more acute, for if their work doesn't contain a flow of new ideas they will go out of business. Gimmicky filters, coloured gels, and distorting optics are the easy way out, but they are not always appropriate and can become repetitive. Presenting a subject in a realistic but unique way takes far more creative flair.

One approach is to approach the subject from an unusual viewpoint. Portraits, in particular, can be given fresh impetus when taken from an unusual angle. Naturally, you'll need the cooperation of the sitter, and you may need to persuade your model that he or she will not look ridiculous. For this reason, it's probably best to start your experiments with family and friends.

▷ Simply posing the girls with their heads upside down made these pictures quite different from conventional portraits, even though the features are not distorted and are clearly visible. But a visual puzzle is presented to the viewer and the temptation is always to turn the image upside down. But even when you do, the orientation remains disturbing.

Pentax LX, 28 mm, Kodak Ektachrome 200, ¹/₁₅ sec, f16

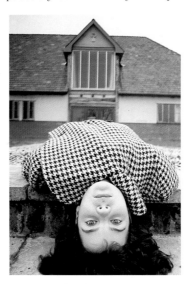

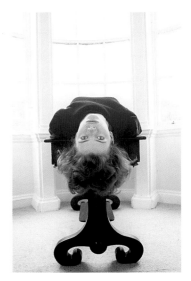

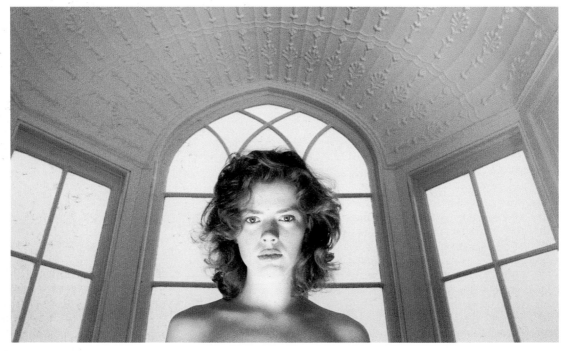

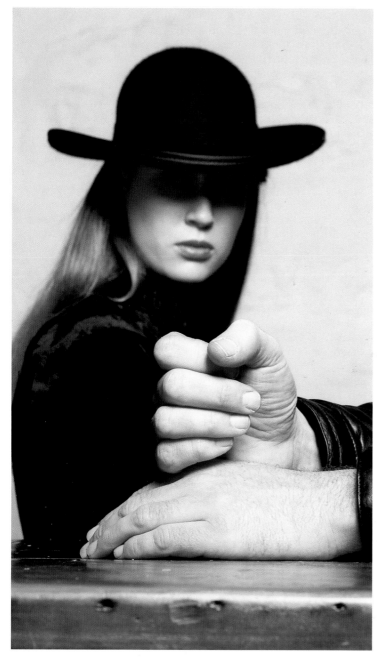

◁ A low viewpoint close to the hands has emphasized the element of mystery conveyed by their juxtaposition with the girl's face. Hands are an expressive subject in themselves, but their impact has been sharpened by the disproportionate sense of scale and by the posing of a clenched fist that echoes the outline of the girl's chin. The scene was lit by studio flash with umbrella reflectors, directed to throw a shadow over the model's eyes.

Hasselblad, 60 mm, Kodak Ektachrome 200, 1/125 sec, f22

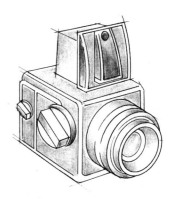

△ Medium-format cameras that use 120 or 220 rollfilm share some of the ease of handling of a 35 mm SLR camera but they offer the benefits of a much larger picture area.

◁ This window bay provided an attractive background but, from a normal height, the view outside proved too distracting. An answer to the problem was found by standing the model on a set of steps and taking the shot from below. A wide-angle lens was used to include the ceiling and to exaggerate the odd perspective created by a low viewpoint. The unreal atmosphere was further strengthened by providing tungsten foot-lighting and shooting on tungsten-balanced film to give the sky a cooler tone.

Pentax LX, 24 mm, Kodak Ektachrome 160 Tungsten, 1/30 sec, f8

See also:
EXPLOITING WIDE-ANGLES pp10–11
FRAMING THE SUBJECT pp20–21
DESIGN WITH FIGURES pp58–59

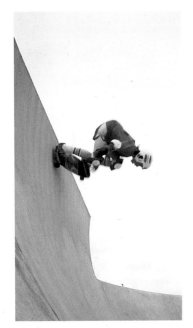

Children are ever-changing, ever-expressive subjects for the photographer, rarely remaining the same for more than a few minutes at a time. Their vitality is one of their most endearing characteristics, but it does cause problems when making pictures, whether candid or posed. The best approach has more in common with sport and wildlife photography than with straightforward portraiture. Exuberant children at play are rarely predictable, rushing madly about at one moment and stopping suddenly at the next. The photographer can be left with a bewildering choice of subject matter, with little or no time for making conscious decisions about framing and composition.

Indoors, the best light is bounced electronic flash that softly lights the whole room. Flash exposures are extremely short – down to as little $\frac{1}{30,000}$ sec in some flash units – and boisterous action shots, such as pillow fights, present no problems, as the soft, overall illumination allows you to change your viewpoint without having to change the lighting.

Outdoors, diffused directional light is best. It is strong enough to bring out the bright colours that children like to wear without casting distinct and heavy shadows. There is enough light to use fast shutter speeds and yet stop down to increase depth of field.

△ High-speed activities, such as skateboarding, are not always as difficult to capture on film as they may at first appear. Here, the skateboarder followed a regular path and all that was necessary was to pre-set focus and exposure, wait for his approach, then shoot at the appropriate moment. Skilled activities that take nerve and determination often attract extrovert characters who are more than willing to perform their most daring stunts for the camera.

Pentax LX, 135 mm, Kodak Ektachrome 200, 1/1000 sec, f8

▷ In the background, a group of cub scouts attentively surround their leader who is teaching them how to tie knots. By complete contrast, a precocious trio of noisy young tearaways let off steam for the benefit of the camera.

Pentax LX, 28 mm, Kodak Ektachrome 200, 1/60 sec, f16

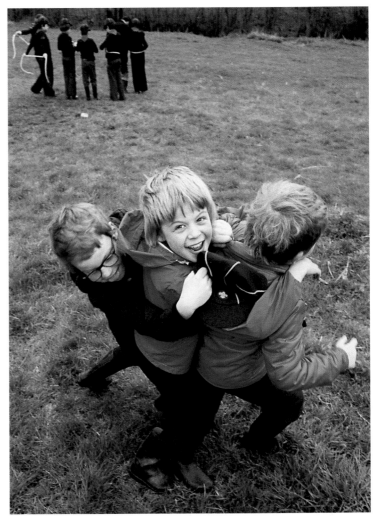

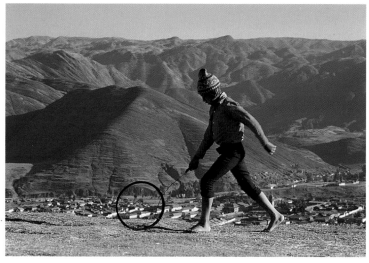

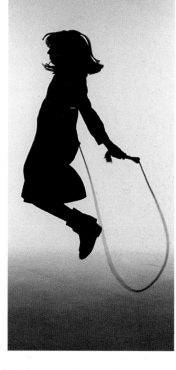

△ High above Cuzco in the Peruvian Andes, a boy trots along playing with a homemade hoop and stick. He is clearly outlined against the backdrop of the barren mountain range that is his homeland. In any photograph of a child it is important to try to capture that magical, elusive, and innocent quality that we call the spirit of childhood.

Pentax LX, 85 mm, Kodak Kodachrome 64, ¹/250 sec, f16

△ This picture is one of a series depicting children's games, made as silhouettes in the studio. For this skipping picture, a shutter speed was selected that would freeze all motion in the girl but give a touch of blur on the rope, providing a sense of movement.

Pentax LX, 50 mm, Kodak Ektachrome 160 Tungsten, ¹/250 sec, f8

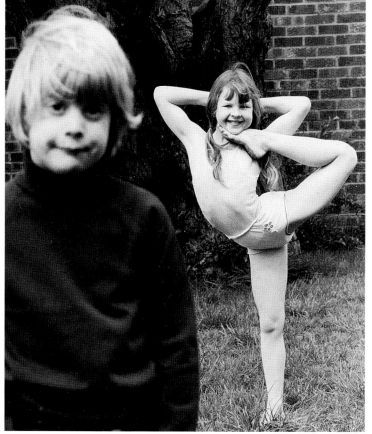

◁ Child prodigies not only amaze adults, but their abilities are sometimes regarded by their peers as beyond belief, as here, when the boy chanced on this extraordinary acrobatic feat.

Hasselblad, 80 mm, Kodak Tri-X ISO 400, ¹/250 sec, f8

See also:
SOFT AND HARD LIGHT pp18–19
POSED PORTRAITS pp42–43
SPORTING EXPRESSIONS pp130–131

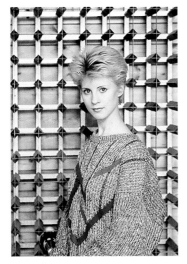

△ Empty wine racks in a cellar create a rigidly symmetrical background of squares against which the face is clearly seen.

Pentax LX, 150 mm, Kodak Ektachrome 200, ¹/₆₀ sec, f8

W hile the studio provides a controlled environment where the background is constructed to suit the portrait, there are times when ready-made backgrounds encourage the photographer to experiment. Then the photographer is inspired to choose appropriate props, to select a model, and to decide on the lighting to be used. This may appear to be creating a portrait around the least important part of the picture but backgrounds are a vital element and this way you won't find that you've created an unsuitable one. Such an approach often casts the background as an element that underlines the importance of the subject.

The background can serve as a contrasting backdrop, or one that harmonizes with the general atmosphere or mood. A dark background will highlight a brightly dressed person, a textured one will emphasize a smooth skin, a blue background will accentuate a tanned complexion. Shape can also be used to provide contrast. The curved outline of a figure is set off effectively by an angular background. Harmony can be enhanced by, for example, echoing a shape in the subject's pose with one in the background or by matching colour and tone. By selecting the background carefully before shooting, the photographer can avoid the very common pitfall of using one which does not complement and enhance its subject.

▷ A wall of filing cabinets form the background, their colour and pattern harmonizing with the soft, winter sunlight. The inclined head and odd darker drawer interrupt the strict symmetry.

Pentax LX, 135 mm, Kodak Ektachrome 200, ¹/₂₅₀ sec, f11

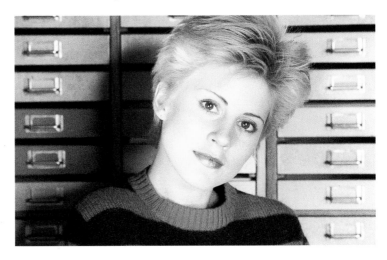

▷ A strongly patterned carpet produced too brilliant a contrast with the girl's leotard. In order to mute the colours of the carpet, a board was placed between the carpet and the light source – a window. The girl was lit by uninterrupted window light.

Pentax LX, 85 mm, Kodak Ektachrome 200, ¹/₂₅₀ sec, f8

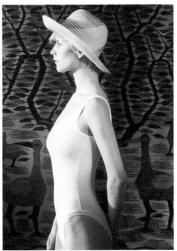

▷ A set of bedsprings hanging in an outhouse provided the background here. Their shape echoes the curly hair of the girl.

Pentax LX, 135 mm, Kodak Ektachrome 200, ¹/₆₀ sec, f16

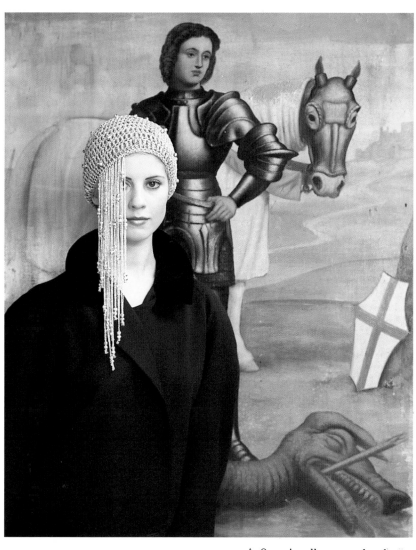

△ Occasionally, unusual and striking backgrounds are to hand, like this George & Dragon pub sign. Originally, the model was dressed in bright clothing, but black proved to be more appropriate to the mood.

Hasselblad, 150 mm, Kodak Ektachrome 200, 1/60 sec, f11

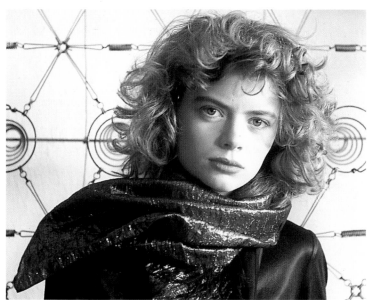

See also:
FRAMING THE SUBJECT pp20–21
PATTERN AND PORTRAIT pp40–41
THE HUMAN FORM pp174–175

GARDEN SETTINGS

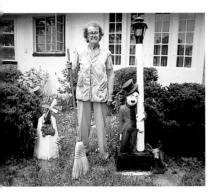

△ Garden gnomes are popular in many parts of the world and these novel designs are part of a collection that inhabits a garden in Long Island, New York. Like many gardeners and collectors of these 'little folk', this lady was very proud of her pieces.

Pentax LX, 50 mm, Kodak Ektachrome 200, 1/125 sec, f8

▷ The garden was the obvious setting for this portrait of Father Simplicity, a master gardener who practised his craft in an English monastery. His produce has been arranged with a good sense of design and the strength of the composition is enhanced by the positioning of the mass of flowers in the foreground. It is evident from his expression that he is justly proud of his produce.

Hasselblad, 60 mm, Kodak Ektachrome 200, 1/125 sec, f16

Gardens are created to be enjoyed. They are places of rest and relaxation where people can simply enjoy the smell and beauty of the surroundings, or can stroll, play games, or have picnics. As well as being places of recreation, gardens are also a source of pleasure for their owners. A great deal of time and energy is invested in the creation of beautiful gardens, and photographers should not miss the opportunity of using them as settings or as subjects in their own right.

A garden may be seen as a natural studio offering a wide variety of backgrounds and a selection of fine settings to suit almost any mood. A large garden, planted with large shrubs and trees, provides a range of different lighting moods from the warm, atmospheric light of evening to bright sunlight.

Owners and gardeners will often allow the photographer to use a small area – especially early or late in the day, when there are no other visitors – for a portrait session or for a wedding group. The results are likely to be more exciting than the more conventional churchyard and register office pictures. Many professional photographers regularly make use of public and private gardens as colourful backdrops for fashion and advertising, often at little or no cost.

A white reflector such as a sheet or a large piece of cardboard is very useful. So, too, is a tripod for the camera. If you use a garden setting sensibly you will find that you will not require any other special equipment.

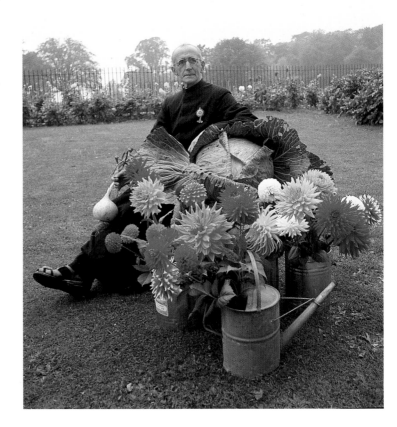

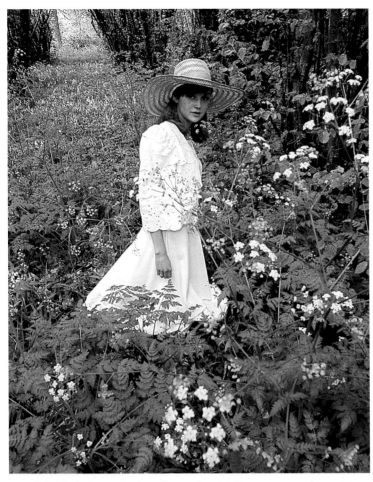

◁ Many large gardens contain semi-wild woodland areas which are ideal for romantic portraits and fashion pictures. For professional or lengthy portrait sessions it is always wise to seek permission, which is usually given gladly. The best time of year is mid-spring to early summer, when flowering is at its peak, the vegetation is lush, and the heady atmosphere of the new year's growth is at its height.

Pentax LX, 28 mm, Kodak Ektachrome 64, ¹/₆₀ sec, f11

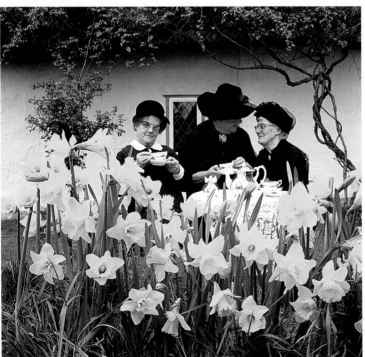

◁ A time-honoured English tradition is to take afternoon tea in the garden, a tradition that is the subject of this picture shot for a magazine feature. Early spring daffodils make a fine foreground with their especially 'English' quality, and the elderly ladies chattering over cups of tea create perfectly the peaceful, genteel atmosphere.

Hasselblad, 60 mm, Kodak Ektachrome 200, ¹/₁₂₅ sec, f16

See also:
THE WEDDING ALBUM pp92–95
WEDDING COUPLES pp96–97
GARDEN ATMOSPHERE pp108–109
IN THE GARDEN pp114–115

LAMPLIGHT SCENES

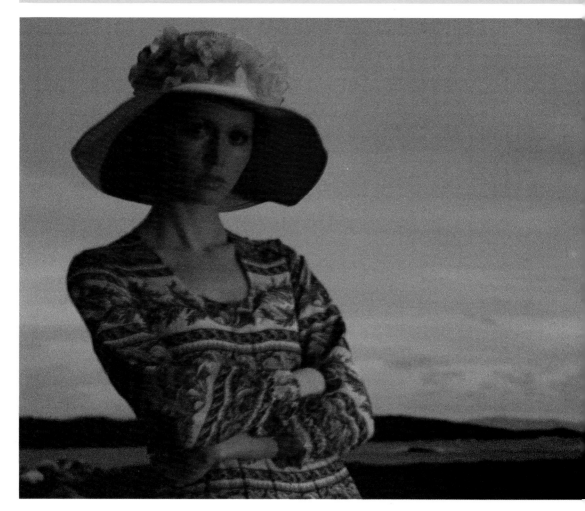

△ For this moody and romantic picture it was necessary to balance three exposures: the ambient light of evening, the car headlamps and the torchlight on the girl. In fact, several combinations and variations were tried, including the use of a second car's headlamps deflected on to the girl via a small mirror. But this subdued picture captured the right atmosphere. The use of tungsten film retained the warmth of the artificial lights, which contrasts well with the cool rendition of the sky.

Hasselblad, 80 mm, Kodak Ektachrome 160 Tungsten, ¼ sec, f16

A good torch is a useful light source for photography. It may be used as a main light to recreate the harsh, melodramatic illumination found in pantomime and old-fashioned theatre; it can produce soft, warm fill-in light without the fuss of setting up reflectors and studio flash; or its light can be included in the picture as part of the composition.

Until recently, photography by torchlight was made difficult by troublesome considerations such as the need for long exposures, which lead to reciprocity failure. But advances in technology have brought faster lenses, faster and finer-grained film, and reliable exposures from automatic cameras, quite apart from more powerful and compact torches. If you own a good compact camera, it's virtually a matter of pressing the shutter button, switching on the torch, and letting the camera sort out the exposure. But for pictures with the added atmosphere of the ambient glow of twilight, torchlight and natural light have to be balanced properly.

If you have a selenium-cell exposure meter in your camera you will find that it is slow in responding to low light levels, and, if this is the case, a hand-held CdS meter is useful for estimating exposures. When balancing torchlight with the much more powerful light from a flash, you can use slower speeds than the X-sync speed with focal-plane shutters.

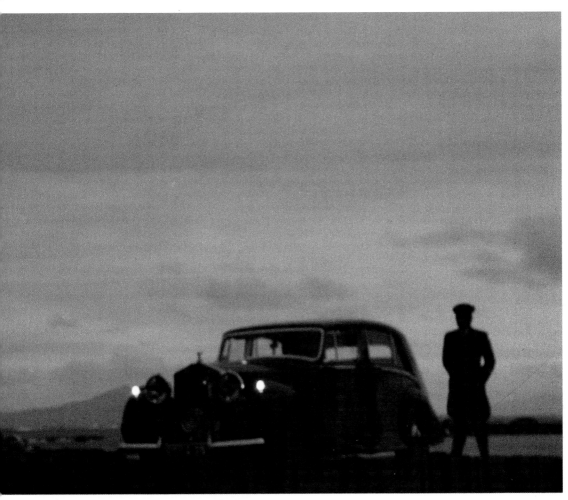

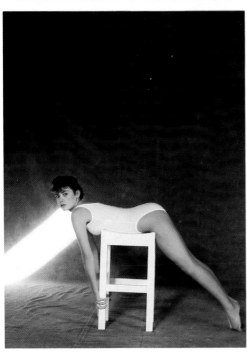

◁ The eye seizes on the light in this picture before it explores the rest of the image. The dazzling streak of white was made by reflecting the beam of a handheld stormlight off a tall mirror on to the background, as if with a spotlight. The model was lit by balanced studio flash.

Hasselblad, 80 mm, Kodak Ektachrome 200, 1/8 sec, f11

See also:
CREATIVE EXPOSURE pp16–17
EVENING LIGHT pp78–79
ARTIFICIAL LIGHT pp88–89

INSTANT IMAGES

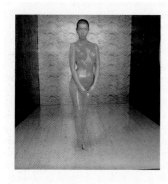

△ Strong colours can be introduced by fitting filters over the camera lens. For this shot a blue 85B filter was used.

With Polaroid instant-picture cameras such as the Supercolor 600 Series or the older Autofocus 660, the finished print appears within seconds. The way the image appears never fails to delight, involving everybody in the picture-taking process. As well as providing instantaneous fun, these cameras can be used for another, perhaps more serious, purpose. Many professionals find them invaluable as an instant check that all the elements for a studio session are correctly balanced before shooting begins, thus avoiding expensive and time-consuming errors and a possible re-shoot later.

The cameras are simple to use, but the very simplicity of the system's operation invites carelessness. Often backgrounds are overlooked, lighting not finely adjusted, props left out, or pictures shot indiscriminately. The cameras lack the sophisticated features such as viewfinder accuracy, exact exposure control, and sensitivity to subject brightness that many SLR users take for granted, but the advantages of the medium often outweigh the disadvantages. Polaroid prints offer no scope for cropping, so the image has to be carefully composed to fill the frame, but other unique forms of image manipulation can make Polaroid preferable to conventional film.

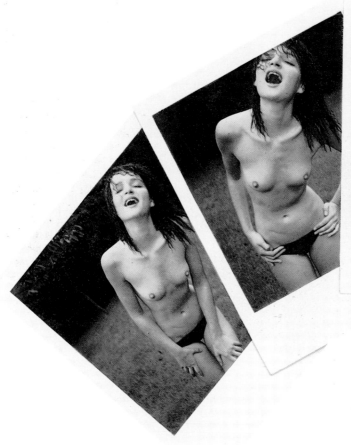

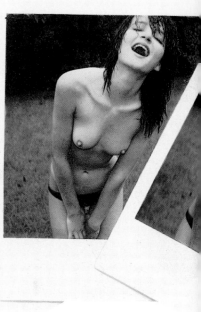

△ Polaroid prints taken originally for reference or experimental shots sometimes have potential as sequences. Each successive exposure was made from a higher viewpoint. In good light these prints give strong tones that can be enhanced by warming the film beforehand.

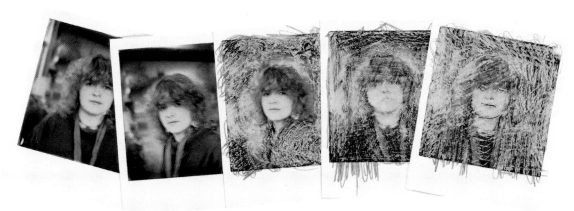

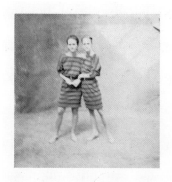

△ These pictures were taken in low light. The first two in the sequence suffer from softness caused by camera shake. In the other prints the background has been manipulated by moving the emulsion with a spoon handle immediately after the image became visible. The final picture in the series has also been drawn on with a ball-point pen, to enhance the effect.

△ Soft-focus effects can be achieved by conventional means – filters, gauze, and Vaseline – or you can fool the ultrasonic autofocus system by shooting through a sheet of glass. The camera then focuses on the glass, not the subject beyond, the degree of softness depending on the relative positions of camera, glass, and subject. The slight double imaging and diffusion combine to create an atmosphere of nostalgia and romanticism.

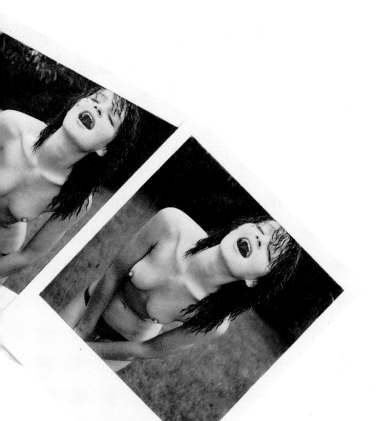

DESIGN WITH FIGURES

▽ In these two photographs, the quality of the light has lent a mellow illumination to the models' faces. In the shot immediately below, the red dress brings the girls closer to us, for emphasis, but the result could still be improved on. In the accompanying shot a more exciting arrangement has been found that makes much more use of the environment.

The man is smaller this time but his effect on the design is far greater. The exposures were based on the flesh tones and the lens was opened up by a half a stop to retain detail in the black clothing.

Hasselblad, 60 mm, Kodak Ektachrome 200, 1/15 sec, f11

The reasons why a picture works are complex, but good design is undoubtedly a fundamental element in its success. Without it, the photographs below would constitute a straightforward but uninspired record of a portrait group. However, design has given the viewer an extra insight into the feelings and emotions being communicated. It is essential that from the outset you understand and isolate what stimulates you in the subject, and, just as important, identify those elements that you do not like. The latter can then be excluded.

Photographing several friends together is a good way to start the exploration of composition with figures. Being relaxed in each other's company dispels any feeling of awkwardness and, when you work as a group, ideas usually abound. With three or four people the combinations of arrangement and poses are endless, and the results are as varied as they are numerous. If the group are young, creative people – as these were – then the session is likely to prove even more exciting and productive. Changes of clothing will add an extra dimension to the proceedings but try not to overdo it as too much choice can be a hindrance. Choose a setting which will complement the subjects without dominating them, since the background is as much a part of the image's design as the subjects themselves.

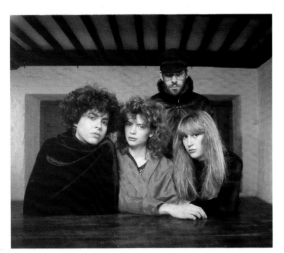 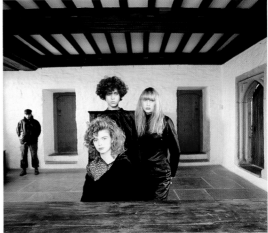

▷ For this shot, each model was carefully positioned to include all the elements and make maximum use of the background. The drama is heightened by balancing the tension and energy of the girl's brightly coloured legs with the other forms in the shot. The contrast of the available light – which comes from a window to the left and behind the camera as well as from the window in the background – has been balanced with reflectors.

Pentax LX, 28 mm, Kodak Ektachrome 200, 1/30 sec, f16

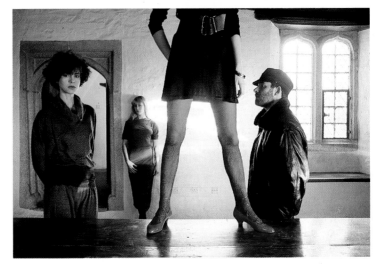

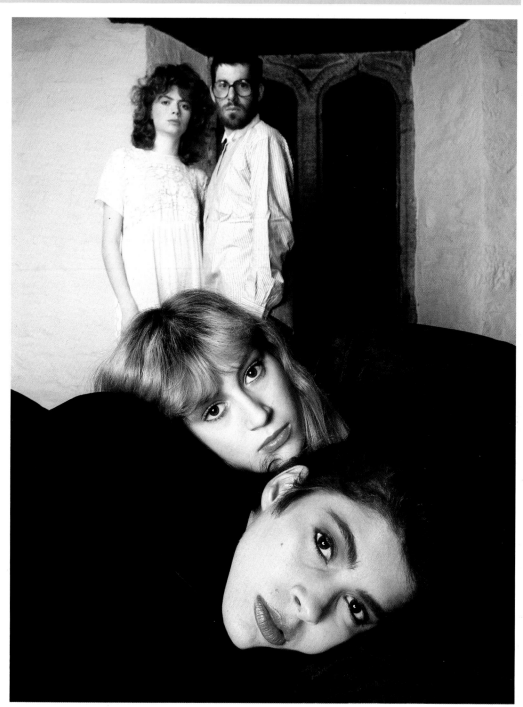

△ As the session progressed, stronger ideas on design and mood evolved. This proved to be one of the most powerful images of the series. A change of clothing and of viewpoint, and the careful placing of the figures – those in the background are over 2 m (6 ft) away – all add to the feeling of depth. This was further stressed by the perspective drawing of the wide-angle lens used at close range and the pale faces contrasting with the dark clothing.

Hasselblad, 60 mm, Kodak Ektachrome 200, ¼ sec, f22

See also:
PORTRAIT GROUPS pp36–37
POSED PORTRAITS pp42–43
ADVANCED COMPOSITION pp132–149

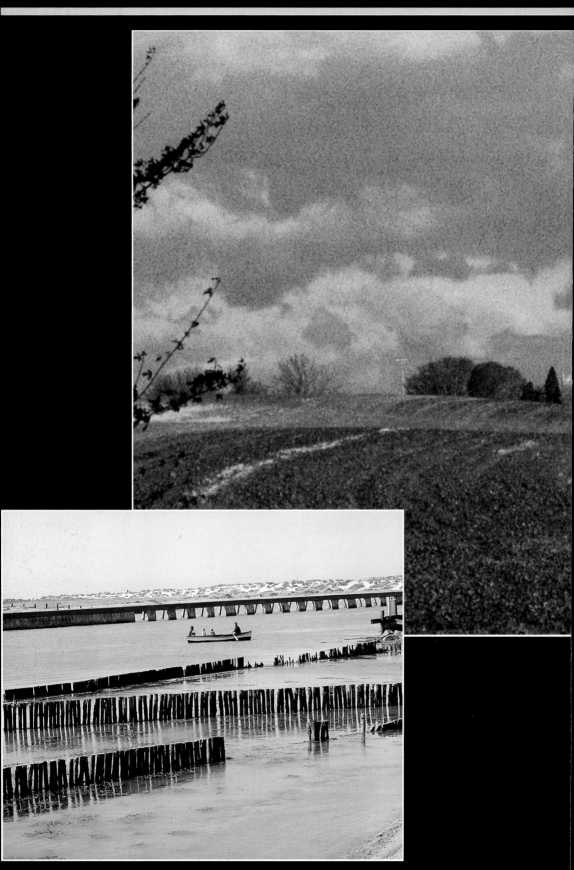

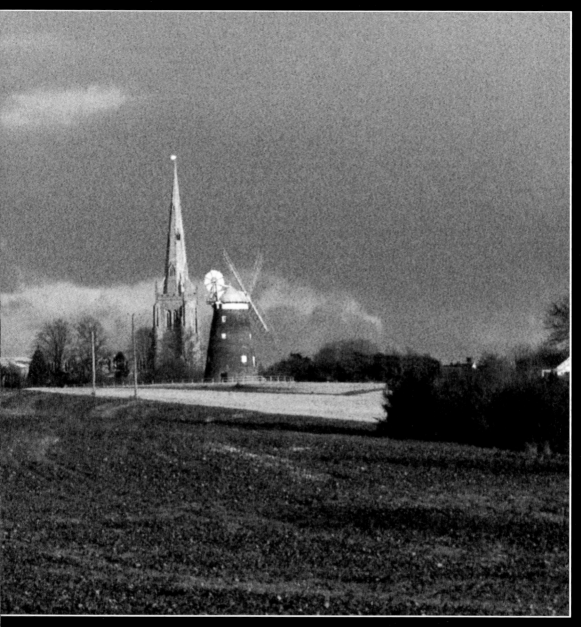

L andscape is a challenging subject. It is not easy to select a single, telling image from the mass of different visual impressions of any one scene. A landscape photograph may be a traditional vista that describes a sense of great space and the quality of changing light; equally, the same scene may provide countless, intimate close-ups of rocks and plants with images rich in texture and detail. Whatever approach you favour – representational, where the image is an accurate depiction of a scene or interpretative, where atmosphere takes precedence over physical likeness – the chief attributes of the landscape photographer are keen eyes, and an intuitive sense of composition.

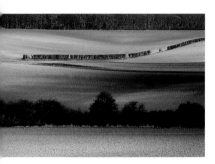

△ Under uniform light these fields appeared uninteresting. But, with broken cloud cover, the pattern of diffuse light and shade complemented the gentle undulations of the land and suggested this simple landscape shot.

Pentax LX, 85 mm, Kodak Ektachrome 200, 1/250 sec, f11

▷ The bolt of lightning in this picture was captured by fixing the camera to a tripod, fitting a neutral density filter to the lens, and directing the camera towards the area where previous flashes had occurred. The filter, combined with a small aperture and the use of slow film, allowed an exposure long enough to include the lightning flash to turn the rain into mist.

Pentax LX 85 mm, Kodak Ektachrome 64, ×2 ND, 4 sec, f32

▷ This landscape in Norway gradually changed under the influence of evening light from a cool, crisp mountain scene into one of warmth and tranquillity. The distant mountains, which were a wall of black rock in semi-silhouette, are now full of detail and soft colour. The impressive sense of scale and depth is a result of strong aerial perspective, where the tonal values become progressively weaker with increased distance.

Pentax LX, 85 mm, Kodak Ektachrome 64, 1/60 sec, f11

Landscape is one of the most challenging types of photography, mainly because the photographer is reliant on the vagaries of the weather when trying to capture the essential qualities of the scene. What, on one day, may appear as a dull and uninteresting ploughed field, can be transformed the next into an exciting pattern of textured soil. Such dramatic changes in mood depend too on the quality of light – its colour, intensity, and direction. Frequent storms and strong winds bring with them fast-changing light and a wide repertoire of moods. Heavy cloud from approaching showers brings about a sense of foreboding. Bright, hard light from clearing skies throws strong shadows and produces a fresh, crisp atmosphere. Misty mornings soften contrast, the water-laden air scattering the light, obscuring detail, and muting colour to create an air of tranquillity. Snow, mist, rain, fog, heat haze, clear air – all have unique properties that contribute to the mood of a landscape at any given time. Often you may discover a scene which you feel has strong photographic possibilities, only to be disappointed that the results are not quite what you had hoped. It may require several different visits in different weather conditions before you can capture a successful, expressive image.

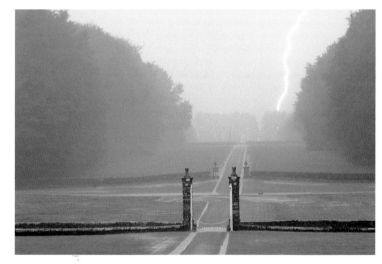

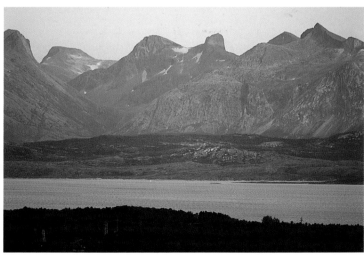

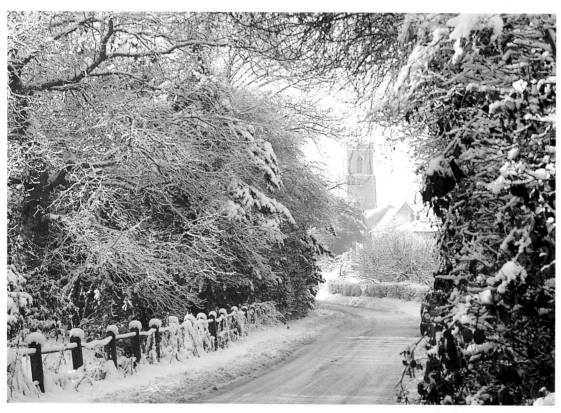

▽ Moonlight creates a characteristic atmosphere that is not easy to capture on film. This is largely because, although we expect to see a soft, cool luminosity, moonlight is in fact much the same as sunlight. Also, long exposures lead to colour shifts that lead to unconvincing rendition of night-time scenes, so the best time to make natural-looking moonlight pictures is in late twilight, when exposure can be shorter and the sky is still blue. The full moon, the cottage with a welcoming light, and the snow on the ground, all help to create a convincing atmosphere in this classically simple composition.

Pentax LX, 50 mm, Kodak Ektachrome 64, 1 sec, f6.3

△ The effect of sunlight on snow evokes a special emotional response in the viewer. Exposure must be exact to capture the sense of freshness and tranquillity.

Pentax LX, 28 mm, Kodak Ektachrome 64, 1/125 sec, f16

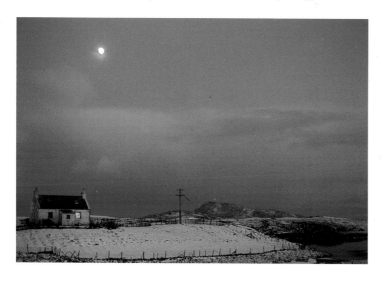

See also:
SOFT AND HARD LIGHT pp18–19
FLEETING LIGHT pp68–69
FILTERING EFFECTS pp72–73

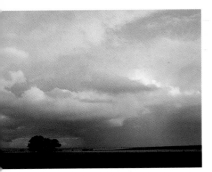

△ A storm gathers over the flat landscape of Lincolnshire. The contrasting play of shape and tone is a momentary event, and so there was no time to attend to the niceties of composition.

Pentax LX, 35 mm, Kodak Ektachrome 64, $^1/_{125}$ sec, f11

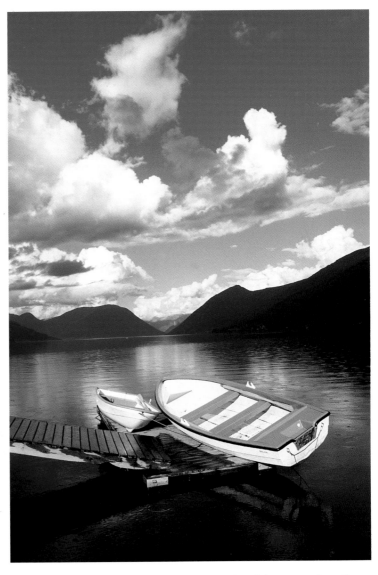

▷ Crisp Scandinavian air has an unreal quality that allows us to see for miles. This characteristic effect has emphasized the airy perspective of the Norwegian fjord seen here.

Pentax LX, 28 mm, Kodak Ektachrome 64, $^1/_{125}$ sec, f11

Considering that clouds are made up of nothing more than tiny transparent water droplets, they exert a powerful influence on any land- or seascape. Many pictures would be lifeless without the relief of a few white wisps in an otherwise blank sky. Clouds come in many different guises, but are most often in a constant state of flux, their mutations providing a wealth of subject matter. Because each water droplet refracts the sun's rays, clouds can create a dazzling array of light effects that colour the land below. In black and white photographs cloudscapes can be dramatized by using a red, orange, or yellow filter to darken the blue of the sky and increase the tonal contrast within the cloud mass. Red tends to cause extreme darkening, so yellow and orange are most useful. With colour film, a polarizing filter will enrich blue skies, the impression being strongest away from the sun, while a half-coloured neutral density (ND) filter can reduce the level of contrast between sky and land so that detail in both will be recorded. Most useful are the 0.3 and 0.6 NDs, because the exposure difference may be as much as four stops.

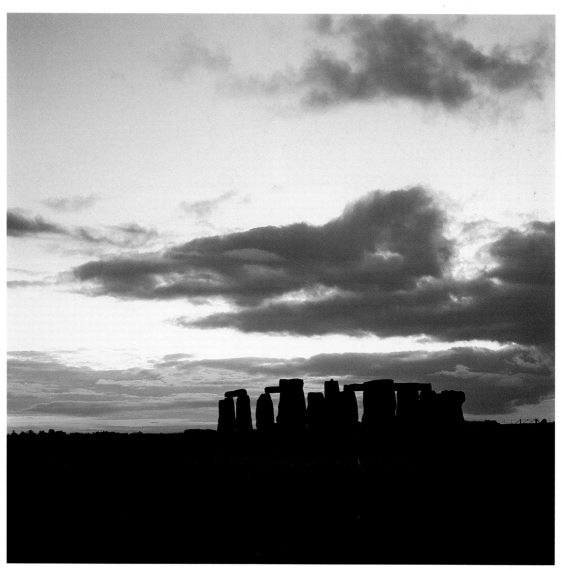

△ The ancient religious site of Stonehenge in the middle of Salisbury Plain is silhouetted against a pale sky. The clouds, too, are in partial silhouette, which strengthens the mood, their cool grey creating a tonal counterpoint to the pallid sky.

Rolleiflex 6×6, 80 mm, Kodak Ektachrome 64, $^1/_{250}$ sec, f11

When framing the picture, it is important to achieve a balance between the compositional weight of the sky and that of the land or sea below. A straightforward fifty-fifty division seldom works well – the effect is too well-ordered and contrived. A greater sense of drama can be injected into a composition by adopting extremes – for example, by showing very little land beneath a vaulting mass of cloud and sky, shot with a wide lens to increase the effect. The nature of the landscape is also important: flat, empty countryside such as that found in East Anglia calls for a different treatment from mountainous scenes, where cloud-masses and hills constantly interact and contrast with one another.

THE CLOUDSCAPE

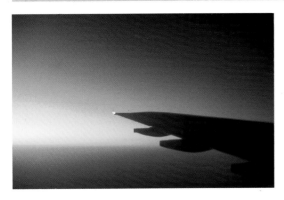

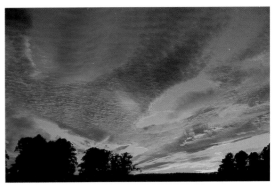

△ Sunrise over the top of a cloud mass is a sight familiar to air travellers. Often, the colour display is varied and dramatic. Photography through an aircraft window is not conducive to high-quality images, so settle for bold colour and shape and check interior reflections.

△ Lit from below, the clouds of late-summer sunrises provide a unique display of vivid colour. Taken in New Hampshire at first light, this shot illustrates the advantages of being an early riser. The air is cleaner at dawn, giving colours a clarity not seen at sunset.

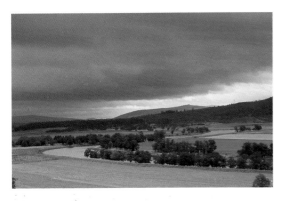

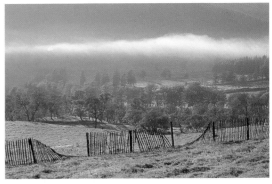

△ These storm clouds over the Scottish Lowlands seem to compress the light and deepen the colour. Summer storms often provide dramatic light effects.

△ Early morning rays of sunlight sidelight this strip of cloud in the sky over the Welsh Marches, lending a penetrating luminosity to the scene.

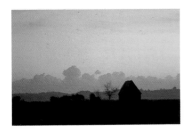

△ Twilight has tinted the low cloud a delicate shade of purple and the wispy altocumulus a vibrant shade of cerise.

▷ A Hebridean shepherd is silhouetted against a clearing sky, forming a counterpoint to the airy cloud-masses.

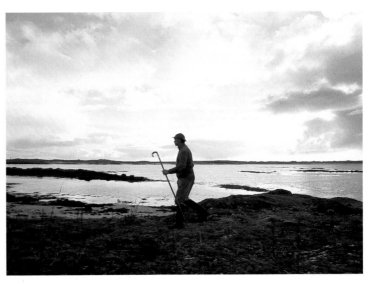

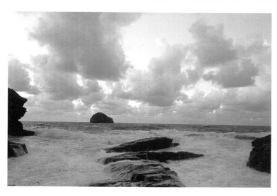

△ Scurrying cumulus at dawn heralds the start of a showery day off the North Cornish coast. The darker clouds set against a bright sky increase the sense of space and perspective.

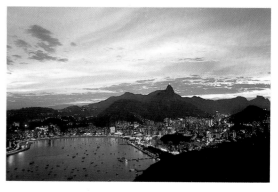

△ Dusk over Rio de Janeiro. Cool water and green street lights offer a strange, artificial colour mix that is heightened by the muted pastels of the sky.

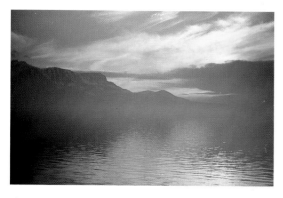

△ Lake Geneva in a mystical, opalescent light. High cirrocumulus – formed of ice crystals – is lit from beneath by a setting sun and throws its bright reflection across the lake's surface. Land, air, and water blend in an ephemeral combination.

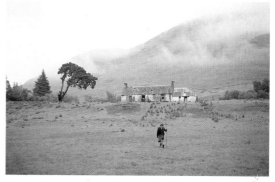

△ In the Highlands of Scotland, low cloud over high ground acts like a studio light tent, giving a soft, even light of great delicacy. The cool tones deepen the impression of isolation.

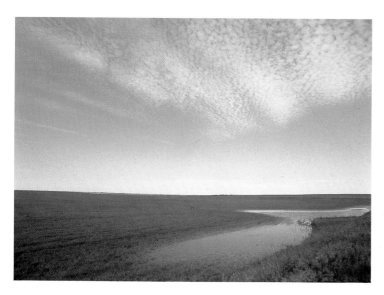

◁ Rippled altocumulus often gives rise to vivid cloudscapes of great beauty. These are pictured above the head of the Thames in Gloucestershire, their forms looking as if they have been created by a painter.

See also:
CREATIVE EXPOSURE pp16–17
COLOUR INTENSITY pp24–25
FLEETING LIGHT pp68–69
FILTERING EFFECTS pp72–73

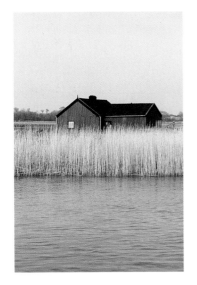

The ways in which light affects a landscape vary enormously, from the subtle to the dramatic. At dawn and at sunset, the speed of the sun's ascent and descent can transform the lighting quality in minutes – altering its colour, intensity, and direction – so the photographer must be acutely aware of the changes. Shortly before or after storms, when cloud cover is broken and the wind still strong, fast-moving patches of light pass across the scene, illuminating small areas as they travel. Light intensity fluctuates – wildly, if the sun bursts through – varying from soft to hard, and subtly altering colour.

In such situations landscape photography is not the tranquil art some believe it to be. The photographer has to be alert, anticipating how the light will play on the land, being aware of the changing formations of cloud patterns, and gauging wind speed to judge the exact moment when the picture elements come together. Timing is as crucial to producing good results in this field of photography as it is in the more obvious disciplines required to take sports and action pictures.

△ The soft, directional sunlight broke through the cloud for this picture of a scene on the Norfolk Broads, but it lasted only a minute or two, highlighting the golden reeds.

Pentax LX, 85 mm, Kodak Ektachrome 64, $^1/_{125}$ sec, f8

▷ Towards the end of an overcast day in Morocco, the sun broke through just long enough to bathe the landscape in warm light.

Pentax LX, 50 mm, Kodak Ektachrome 64, $^1/_{125}$ sec, f8

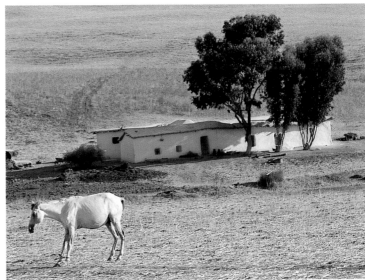

▷ Turbulent mountain air frequently leads to stormy skies with briskly moving clouds that create a fast-changing play of light and shade on the land below. Mood and atmosphere can alter by the minute, creating many different opportunities for good pictures. Try to judge when the shifting play of the elements makes the best shots. Stay and watch carefully, be prepared to make many exposures, and exercise fine judgements in timing.

Pentax LX, 100 mm, Kodak Ektachrome 64, $^1/_{250}$ sec, f8

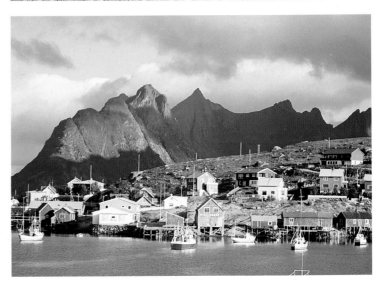

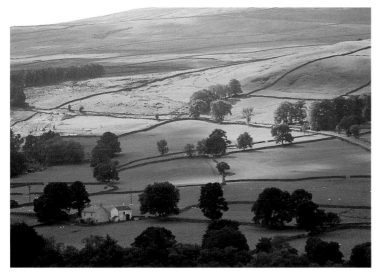

◁ Low cloud scudding across the uplands of Northern England laid a constantly changing pattern of subtle light and tone over the land. To make a success of this type of picture it is important to wait for a pleasing balance between light and shade before making the exposure. Sometimes this entails discomfort and patience.

Pentax LX, 135 mm, Kodak Ektachrome 200, 1/125 sec, f8

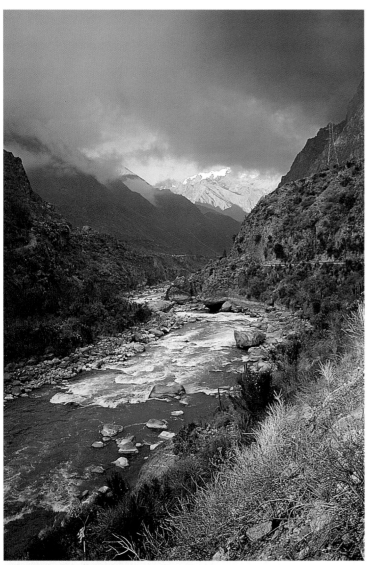

◁ This gorge in Norway looked best through a wide lens, but the overcast sky destroyed the sense of grandeur and of depth that were needed for a successful picture. Distant breaks in the cloud indicated that waiting for a chance shaft of light might be worthwhile – and it was. The bright foreground, lit by a fleeting splash of sun, arrests the eye and leads it deeper into the scene, towards the horizon.

Pentax LX, 28 mm, Kodak Ektachrome 200, 1/125 sec, f16

See also:
SOFT AND HARD LIGHT pp18–19
COLOUR INTENSITY pp24–25
LANDSCAPE MOODS pp62–63
A TOUCH OF LIGHT pp82–83

LIGHT ON WATER

Water is a mercurial reflector. At times it can be absolutely flat, like a lake at dawn, and reflect the land and sky as though it were a mirror. Then, with the slightest breeze, the reflection is broken into tiny fragments of shape and colour that form an endless sea of pictures. When it is airborne mist or spray, water refracts light in displays of splendid colour that change by the second, providing a subject well worth exploring.

Light is reflected off the surface of water at the same angle that it is incident upon it. When the sun is low in the sky, its reflections are oblique and extended far from the observer. At midday the overhead sun makes a compact reflection that is close to the observer. At sunrise and sunset the surface of a lake or the sea is coloured with golds, reds, and yellows but at midday the predominant colours are those of the sky: blue, white, or grey. Bright days are ideal for photographing the reflections of objects by or on the water and you can easily spend several hours in a harbour making a range of totally different pictures of this one subject. It is best to underexpose by about half a stop to increase colour saturation, but perfectly good images can be made with up to one or two stops overexposure. The colours will be much diluted but, because the pictures are abstract, this result can be very agreeable.

Even if you live miles away from the sea, it is still possible to use this technique. Reflections of neon signs, for instance, make colourful abstract patterns when seen in a puddle on a rain-soaked pavement. Also, you can double the impact of floodlit buildings at night by also including their reflections, from a river perhaps, in the foreground of the picture.

On occasions reflections can spoil a picture, distracting from the main subject, or preventing you from seeing how clear the water is. A polarising filter can come to your aid here – reducing or eliminating the reflections. By rotating the filter on the front of the lens, and changing your angle of view, you can maximise the effect seen in the viewfinder.

▽ Close-ups of abstract reflections provide colourful and very varied images. Rays of the setting sun just catch the rippled surface of the water. A relatively large area was selected in order to emphasize pattern.

Pentax LX, 50 mm, Kodak Ektachrome 64, 1/250 sec, f16

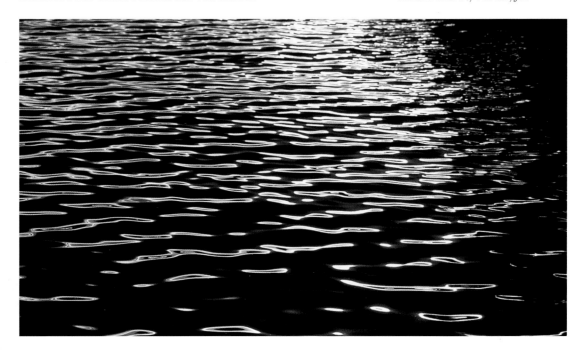

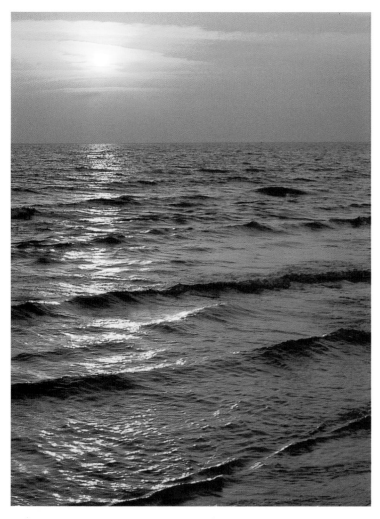

◁ A setting sun over a gilded sea – probably one of the most photographed scenes, but one that yields as many disappointments as it does delights. The prime cause of failure is gross underexposure, but this can be avoided by metering off the water and waiting for the sun to be obscured by cloud. This reduces flare and contrast, while deepening colour. Remember to compose the shot with the horizon away from the picture's midline.

Pentax LX, 50 mm, Kodak Ektachrome 64, ¹/₂₅₀ sec, f16

▽ Bright sun, an azure sky, and a gaudily painted boat are melted into one another by innumerable surface reflections to make a brightly coloured abstract.

Pentax LX, 50 mm, Kodak Ektachrome 64, ¹/₂₅₀ sec, f16

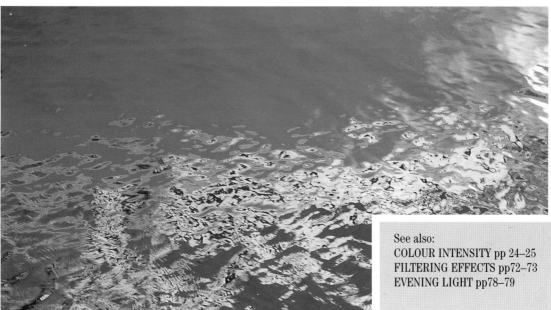

See also:
COLOUR INTENSITY pp 24–25
FILTERING EFFECTS pp72–73
EVENING LIGHT pp78–79

FILTERING EFFECTS

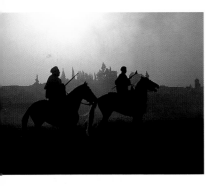

△ Using a graduated orange filter for this shot taken in Morocco has turned this silhouette shot into a sunset study.

Placed in front of the lens, filters can have a dramatic, and even extravagant, effect on the image. To the landscape photographer, the most useful of these accessories are the ones that have a less-profound effect on the result — making the use of trickery look less noticeable to the viewer.

Of all the filters that you can buy, the polariser is the one with the most all-round appeal. Its ability to selectively darken areas of the picture, by eliminating or reducing reflected highlights, means that it can add depth of colour. It can also be used to reduce reflections on water. As the effect the filter has is variable, by rotating the filter itself, you can pick the angle where it has the maximum, or desired, effect.

Graduated filters are of particular use in landscape photography, as they allow you to darken the sky without affecting the foreground. This reduces the contrast of the picture to a level the film can cope with. A grey graduate is a sensible option, as it does not affect the colour of the sky — it just darkens the colour that is already there; but blue and orange graduates can often work well.

UV filters are often left on lenses all the time by photographers, as the filter can act as a low-cost protection for the front element of the lens. They also useful at high altitude and by the sea, as they cut down the blue light that can affect pictures taken in these locations.

▷ One of the most versatile filters, the polariser cuts down reflections from water and glass. In this shot, the reflections of the overhead clouds have been eliminated from the frame, deepening the blue of the waves and allowing the breaking peaks to become the only highlights in the foreground. A polariser must always be rotated whilst you look at the image through the viewfinder, ensuring that you set the filter to the angle where it has the maximum effect.

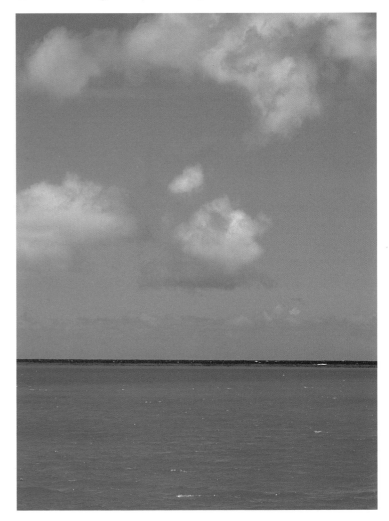

△ The bluey haze of mountain scenes and seascapes can be particularly galling to the photographer. An ultraviolet filter can reduce much of this, by reducing the amount of unwanted UV light from reaching the film. For a slightly more dramatic effect, you can use a skylight filter, which is slightly amber in colour, thus correcting the blue wash over the picture.

▽ A graduated grey filter was used for this shot to reduce the contrast between the sky and the foreground. Without it the exposure used would either leave the picture with an insipid, washed-out sky, or the main subject would be too dark. Square graduate filters are best, as you can adjust the filter's position to that of the skyline. The smaller the aperture you use, the more marked the graduation in colour becomes.

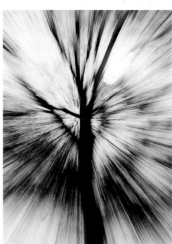

△ Special effects filters generally are unwelcome in landscape photography. However, here a radial zoom filter has created an interesting abstract from a shot of a silhouetted tree.

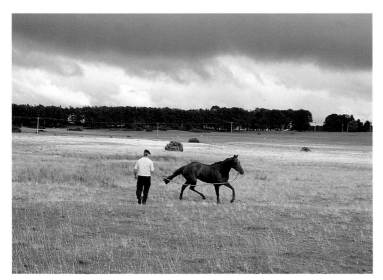

See also:
COLOUR INTENSITY pp24–25
THE CLOUDSCAPE pp64–67
LIGHT ON WATER pp70–71
MONOCHROME VIEWS pp74–75

Black-and-white film is particularly well suited to landscapes. This is not just because of its graphical quality, and its reliance on lighting to create mood, but because the photographer has so much control over the final image.

Landscapes can create a contrast problem, with skies that are much brighter than the foreground. With black-and-white film, contrast can be reduced in the darkroom by using softer grades of printing paper, or by giving the sky more exposure under the enlarger, to 'burn' in detail.

When using black and white film you will notice that blue skies are recorded much paler than you recollected — so much so that clouds may not even show up. To capture dramatic-looking skies, a red filter should be placed over the lens; an orange filter gives a slightly subtler effect. The disadvantage of red and orange filters is that they also darken foliage; if this presents a problem a green filter can be employed, as this darkens skies but lightens the tone of grass and leaves. A yellow filter portrays both sky and foliage in natural tones.

A dark red filter is essential when using infrared black-and-white film. This emulsion is capable of giving a ghostly appearance to foliage and jet-black skies. The film is difficult to handle — it must be loaded and unloaded in total darkness, and accurate focusing is not possible visually — but its curious portrayal of the world around us makes it worth the effort.

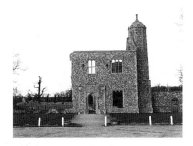

△ Unfiltered shot sees blue sky much brighter than in reality, so that white clouds disappear.

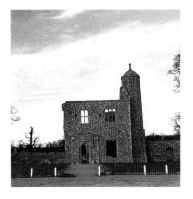

△ Using a yellow filter over the lens restores the natural tone to blue sky, so the clouds become visible.

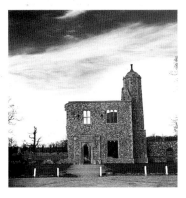

△ A deep red filter deepens the tone of blue skies, accentuating the cloud formation.

▷ An orange filter was used to add mood and drama to the sky above these sand dunes.

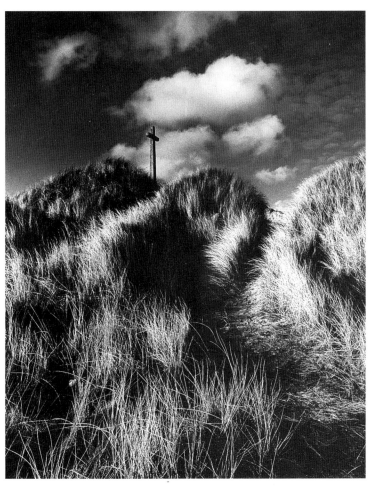

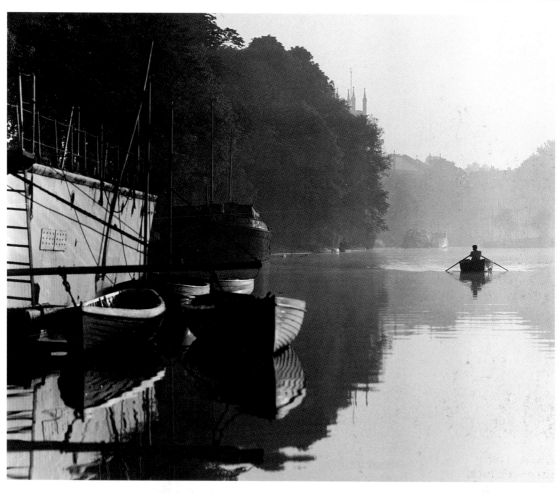

△ A soft grade of printing paper was necessary when printing this exposure so that some detail was still retained in the hazy river backdrop.

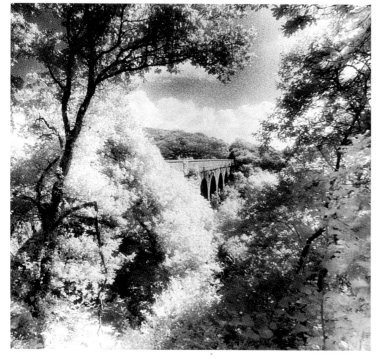

◁ Black-and-white infrared film produces a characteristically grainy image, with snowy foliage and dark skies.

See also:
BLACK AND WHITE pp22–23
THE CLOUDSCAPE pp64–67
FILTERING EFFECTS pp72–73

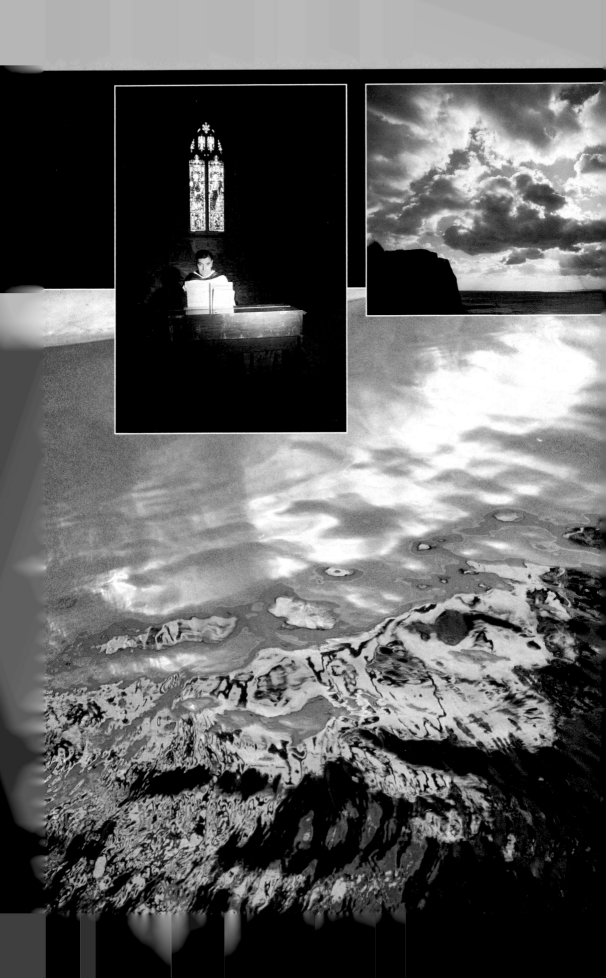

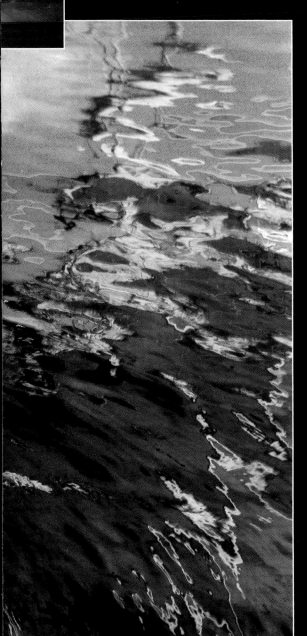

Photography is dependant upon light forming the image on film, but the photographer's understanding of light must go far deeper than that. Light has a fundamental influence on the character of a photographic image in ways that, at first, are not always obvious. It can bring surprising results which are quite different from what the eye may have seen. Learning to see light, experimenting with it, and making pictures of it should be the aim of every serious photographer. Light makes a fascinating subject, but it is not always easy to capture its essential qualities in a single image. Colour, brightness, the pattern of shadow and highlight, or the source itself need to dominate the scene, making light the pictorial theme and placing objects in a supporting role.

EVENING LIGHT

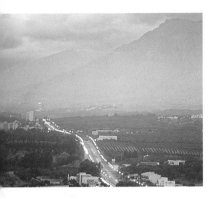

As sound is to music, so is light to photography. And just as there is a whole range of notes from which to compose a tune, so there are many different qualities of natural light with which a photograph can be made. Of these, evening light is probably the richest, as it envelops the landscape in a glow of colour that changes with each passing minute. Rich rewards await the photographer who is prepared to take advantage of the many different moods that this light can create. It is important not to concentrate on a favourite view, for doing so restricts picture possibilities at a time when small changes in viewpoint bring dramatic changes in colour and illumination. So, stay alert and alter your camera position as often as you can.

When the sun finally sets and disappears, the lighting is further softened, bringing more delicate hues to the sky. This is the moment when many photographers, suddenly deprived of sunlight, mistakenly pack their bags and leave. The colours that remain might appear pale and muted but the film will enrich them, while the concentration of a landscape on to a small piece of film further intensifies the results. Twilight, in the early morning or evening, presents a completely new set of possibilities, although the fading light of evening requires the use of faster film – ISO 200 or higher – and sometimes a tripod to steady the camera. A further problem can be the excessive brightness difference between sky and foreground, which is often too great for the film to record detail and colour in both. Some sacrifice has to be made in order to favour highlight or shadow, but there is no 'correct' exposure level – just different degrees of emphasis and a change of balance.

△ Taken near Marbella, in Spain, this shot depends as much on the hazy atmosphere as on the colour and quality of the evening light. The strong aerial perspective that the haze created gives the photograph a feeling of depth, for we see pastel tones as being more distant. Bright streetlights arrest the attention, drawing the eye to the subtler detail in the scene. A camera with semi-automatic exposure was used and exposure was based on an overall reading with no modification.

Canon AE-1, 90 mm, Kodak Ektachrome 200, 1/250 sec, f8

▷ A kilted piper and, in the background, Glamis Castle's 15th-century tower, bring together all the elements that are needed for a strong image of the Highlands of Scotland. Everything is bathed in the golden glow of a late winter afternoon's sunlight, which shares many of the characteristic effects of sunrise and sunset. Not least of these is the low lighting angle, which casts long, graphic shadows, throws small detail into relief, and emphasizes texture.

Rolleiflex 6×6, 80 mm, Kodak Ektachrome 200, 1/125 sec, f8

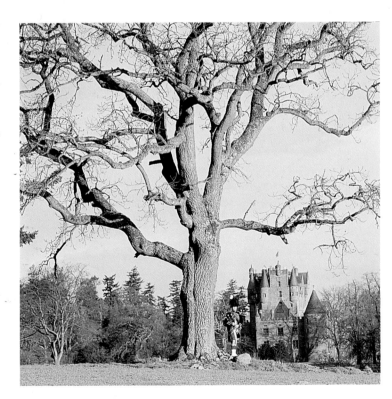

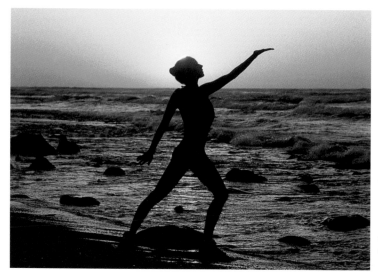

◁ After a full day on the beach shooting swimwear in bright sunlight, the the model was encouraged to play around, striking a series of dramatic poses. This is one of the last shots taken. Her body has blocked out the sun as it dips below the horizon. Its exclusion has reduced overall contrast, cut out any flare, and intensified the already crude colour. A straight exposure was made from an average reading of the scene.

Canon AE-1, 50 mm, Kodak Ektachrome 64, semi-automatic exposure, 1/60 sec

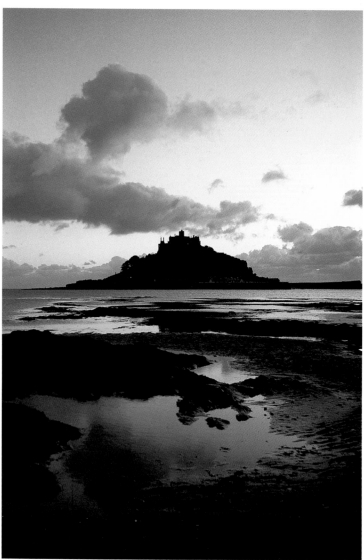

◁ A Cornish legend has it that the Archangel Michael visited local fishermen here and, as a consequence, a monastery was founded. The place is now known as St Michael's Mount. Twilight was chosen as fitting to picture this romantic castled isle, and served to enhance its mysterious beauty. After the sun set, the viewpoint was selected to take advantage of the mirror-like pools. An added bonus was the appearance of a brilliant full moon, which gave a subtle lift to shadow areas. Balancing the exposure to capture the island in silhouette has intensified the muted colour of the sky and its reflections in the bay.

Hasselblad, 80 mm, Kodak Ektachrome 64, 1/15 sec, f8

See also:
SOFT AND HARD LIGHT pp18–19
FLEETING LIGHT pp68–69
FILTERING EFFECTS pp72–73

SHADOW DESIGNS

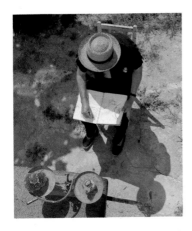

△ The shadows in this portrait of Graham Sutherland create intricate links in the picture's composition.

Rolleiflex, 80 mm, Kodak Ektachrome 64, ¹/₂₅₀ sec, f8

The shape of an object usually provides our first impression of it and is our primary means of identifying the things around us. Consequently, shape is a powerful design element in pictures. One of the richest sources of interesting shapes is shadows. All photographs are created by a combination of highlight and shadow, but compositional shadows must be much more than mere tonal variation. They need to be bold to create a strong visual impression and hold the viewer's attention. Shadows are particularly effective in providing strong picture elements. Not only do they form a design of their own, but they give vital clues about the object that cast them: its outline, where it is located, and its relationship to other elements in the scene. Sometimes shadows that are not linked to the object that cast them become abstracted. This strengthens the sense of mystery often associated with shadows, a feeling that is heightened if they become distorted by falling across an oblique or uneven surface and they can have a powerful influence on the mood and atmosphere created. Incorporating strong shadows into the composition of a picture can create striking visual impressions, and it is important for photographers to realize that shadows can have as powerful an influence in a photograph as light itself, and to accord them the same degree of care and attention.

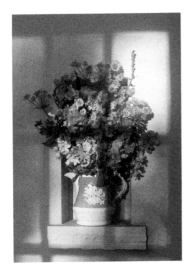

△ Late-evening sun casts the shadow of a lattice window across this vase of flowers. Trees outside soften the effect.

Pentax LX, 100 mm macro, Scotch (3M) 1000, ¹/₆₀ sec, f16

▷ The strong shadow thrown by the girl's body has created a double portrait – one in profile, the other full face.

Pentax LX, 35 mm, Kodak Ektachrome 64, ¹/₂₅₀ sec, f11

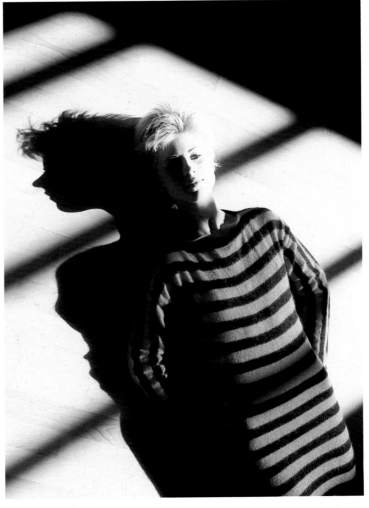

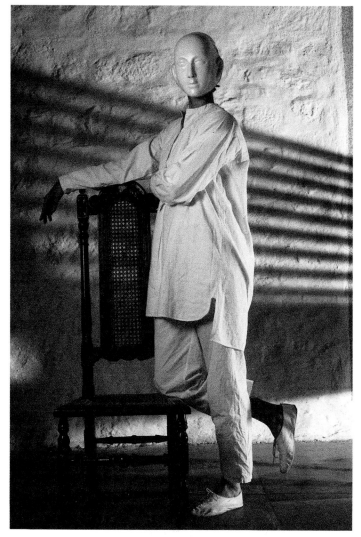

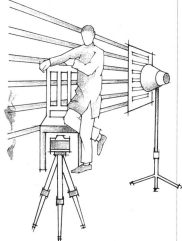

◁ A floodlight set up behind a screen with horizontal openings (see diagram above) was used to cast the shadows in this picture. The shadows themselves provide a strong compositional element and the sense of the melodramatic was heightened by the model's mask.

Pentax LX, 50 mm, Scotch (3M) 640T, 1/60 sec, f8

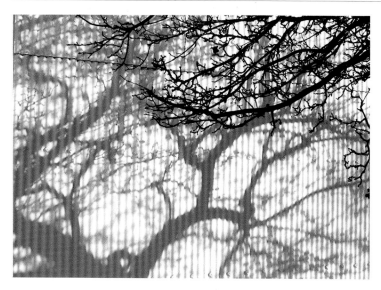

◁ This hideous corrugated-iron warehouse wall has been transformed into a fascinating design by shadows cast by an adjacent tree.

Pentax LX, 28 mm, Kodak Ektachrome 64, 1/125 sec, f11

See also:
CREATIVE EXPOSURE pp16–17
SOFT AND HARD LIGHT pp18–19
A TOUCH OF LIGHT pp82–83

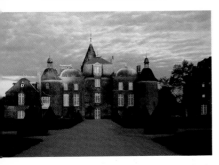

△ It was worth waiting for a shaft of sunlight briefly to highlight the top of this French château. What had been a sunless scene moments before was transformed into this atmospheric picture.

Hasselblad, 80 mm, Kodak Ektachrome 200, ¹/₁₂₅ sec, f11

Daylight, when it is carefully controlled, is capable of producing richly coloured low-key images, without the harshness associated with normal, direct sunlight. Such light is readily available indoors, particularly at the end of the day, but outdoors it tends to be most available in autumn, winter, and spring. In these seasons low cloud layers often act as a mask, focusing the rays of the sun into a golden spotlight that produces magical lighting effects on whatever it touches. In these conditions bright patches of warm light form a rich contrast with the darker grey backdrop of clouds. Almost inevitably, these golden opportunities are fleeting, disappearing even as they present themselves, so it takes a prepared and alert photographer to make use of them. If possible, select your subject in advance, and then wait for the right quality of sunlight and shade to appear.

▽ Shafts of sunlight occasionally burst through broken cloud to cast patches of light on the sea, as in this picture taken off Flamborough Head in Yorkshire, but it was some time before a beam finally highlighted the cliffs. The shot was taken quickly, before it vanished.

Pentax LX, 35 mm, Scotch (3M) 100, ¹/₅₀₀ sec, f16

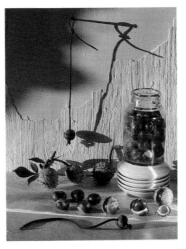

△ Following an afternoon storm, a sudden burst of sunlight caught this simple still life arrangement, which had been left out after use earlier in a session.

Pentax LX, 100 mm macro, Kodak Ektachrome 64, ¹/₃₀ sec, f16

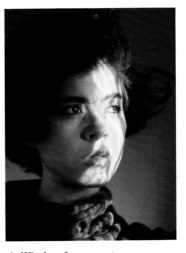

△ Window frames act as very good filters when sunlight needs focusing. This portrait was made in the late afternoon. Rich, directional light enhanced the colour and texture of the skin.

Hasselblad, 120 mm, Kodak Ektachrome 200, ¹/₆₀ sec, f11

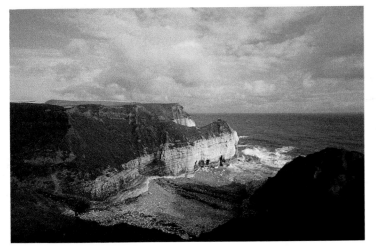

▷ After an autumn storm had passed, the setting sun appeared, casting a golden shaft of light across the field and church. It highlighted the corn stubble in the foreground and so led the eye to the tower and thence to the sky in the background.

Pentax LX, 35 mm, Scotch (3M) 100, ¹/₅₀₀ sec, f16

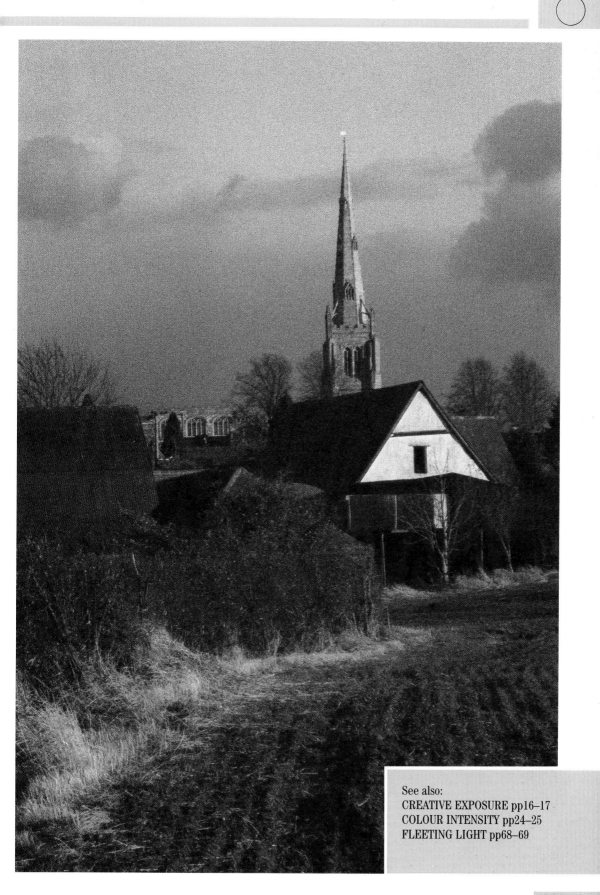

See also:
CREATIVE EXPOSURE pp16–17
COLOUR INTENSITY pp24–25
FLEETING LIGHT pp68–69

FLARE FOR EFFECT

lare occurs when the camera is pointed towards a strong light source such as the sun and, in the normal course of photography, it is something to be avoided, just like unintentional under- or overexposure. But used creatively as a compositional element it can produce interesting effects and strengthen the atmosphere of a picture. With the light source just outside the edge of the frame, the flare light spills in to bathe the image in a diffuse glow, while if the light is within the frame, a bright, radiant star-like effect is achieved.

Flare 'spots' are created when the incoming light is reflected off the interior lens components, the size and shape of the spots depending on the lens aperture used. Compose them within the frame as carefully as you would any other major picture element. More than any other type of shot, those taken facing a light source depend upon correct exposure for success, so take a number of exposures to cover the shot if you can.

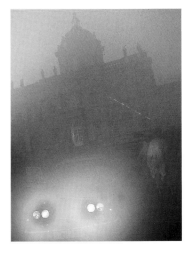

△ Haloed lights, a misted lens, and tungsten film create a twilight effect at Castle Howard.

Hasselblad 80 mm, Kodak Ektachrome 160 Tungsten, ¹⁄₃₀ sec, f16

◁ For this theatrical setting a broad swathe of flare has been used. Its source is a bare flash tube which radiates light in all directions. Notice how the effect is emphasized by its falling on to the black background of the model's cloak.

Pentax LX, 28 mm, Kodak Ektachrome 64, ¹⁄₆₀ sec, f8

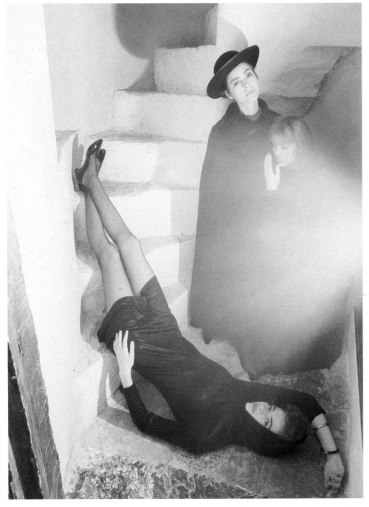

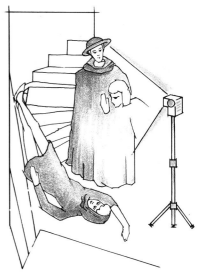

▷ The flash tube was placed just outside the frame, at a middle height to fall on the desired area of the shot.

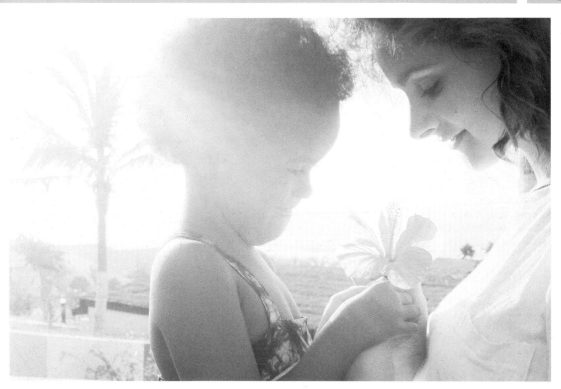

△ Here, an overall flare from outside the frame creates a warm, gentle light. The outlines of the two faces are highlighted, bringing them closer together, and the petals of the flower, lit from behind, form a natural focus for the image. Since atmosphere was important in the picture, the exposure was set to favour shadow – at about three stops over 'normal'.

Pentax LX, 100 mm, macro, Kodak Ektachrome 64, 1/125 sec, f11

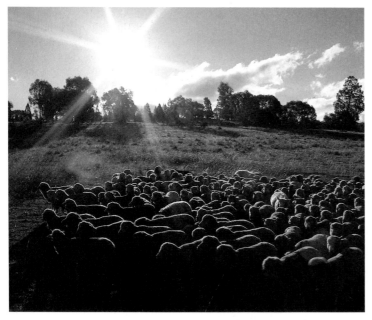

△ The intense heat and light of a Western Australian sheep farm is conveyed by the starburst effect of the sun. The flare is increased by using a small aperture. The scattered flare spots serve to enhance the diffused rimlight on the sheeps' backs.

Pentax LX, 50 mm, Kodak Ektachrome 64, 1/250 sec, f16

See also:
EXPLOITING WIDE-ANGLES pp10–11
CREATIVE EXPOSURE pp16–17
LAMPLIGHT SCENES pp54–55

OUTDOOR SILHOUETTES

Some of the very first photographs were silhouettes made by Thomas Wedgwood of leaves, insect wings, and the like. Today the silhouette is still the simplest image form and one of the best for creating evocative designs out of shape alone. Ordinarily, we read daily scenes from the most fleeting visual information and rely almost entirely on objects' outlines for our interpretation of what we see. A very effective way of exploring the impact of shape is through the two dimensions of a stark silhouette.

Many subjects make powerful silhouettes and it is a simple matter of using backlight and exposing for the highlights to make them stand out against the background. Appealing silhouettes of churches, castles, trees, people, and animals are easily made by choosing a viewpoint that places them against the sky or a particularly bright foreground. Bold subjects such as buildings make dramatic shapes, while complex ones – for example, trees – can create delicate traceries of black on white. The impact of focal length can easily be appreciated with silhouettes. The sides of tall buildings rapidly converge into pyramids when shot from below with a wide-angle lens. A long lens, by reducing steep perspective, will produce a normal-looking image.

▽ Brooklyn Bridge's suspension cables form a delicate pattern of parallels set against the skyscrapers in the distance. The misty air softens the severe rectilinear shapes of both.

Pentax LX, 135 mm, Kodak Ektachrome 64, 1/250 sec, f8

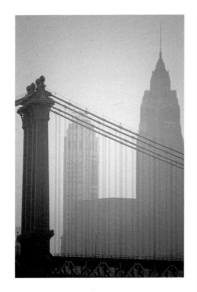

▷ A languid evening rest against the backdrop of an Indian dusk. A low viewpoint gave a clear silhouette and the exposure was set for the sky.

Pentax LX, 135 mm, Kodak Ektachrome 64, 1/250 sec, f8

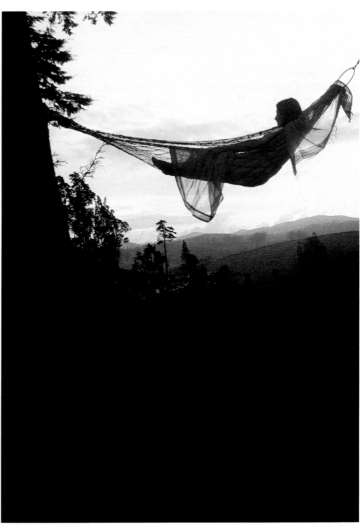

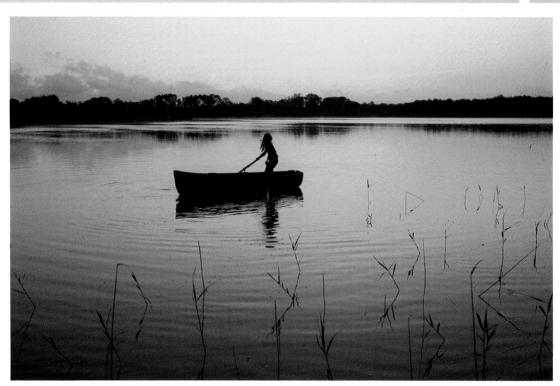

▽ Silhouettes can be effectively mixed with a more conventionally photographed subject. The fantastic outlines of these weeping ash trees have an eerie presence that envelops the distant monolith of Edinburgh Castle, hinting at its sinister past. It is an unusual, if gruesome, treatment of a subject that is more often depicted in summer sunlight.

Leicaflex, 28 mm, Kodak Ektachrome 200, ¹/₃₀ sec, f11

△ Normally the flatlands of the Norfolk Broads, lying by the exposed North Sea coast, are buffetted by stiff breezes, but here, in the quiet of a summer evening, a lake lies unruffled. The colours and placid atmosphere are heightened by the presence of a simple horizontal silhouette.

Pentax LX, 50 mm, Kodak Ektachrome 200, ¹/₂₅₀ sec, f11

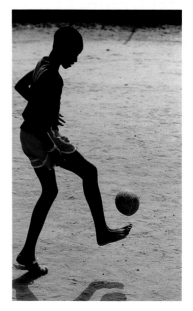

▷ A young boy in Guadeloupe displays his prowess with a ball. Almost in complete silhouette, his figure shows just a hint of colour and there is enough detail in the profile to convey his obvious pleasure.

Pentax LX, 135 mm, Kodak Ektachrome 64, ¹/₂₅₀ sec, f8

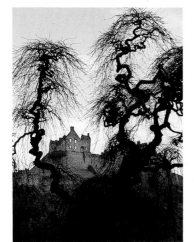

See also:
EXPLOITING WIDE-ANGLES pp10–11
EXPLOITING TELEPHOTOS pp12–13
CREATIVE EXPOSURE pp16–17
STUDIO SILHOUETTES pp166–167

Today, with fast lenses and ultra-sensitive film emulsions, the photographer has no need to wait for strong sunlight or use flash or studio lighting to exercise his creative freedom. Low-level artificial light sources can be used to create striking images that are full of atmosphere. Naturally, longer exposure times will be required to make the shot successful.

Any type of light can be used – candles, firelight, small lamps and torches, even a single match. Naturally, the light should be focused on the prime point of interest in the composition, leaving the rest of the image to fall into shadow and so strengthen the sense of mood created.

Equipment can be kept to a minimum, which makes life easier for the photographer. A minimum of equipment can also make the session less of an ordeal for the sitter, who will probably feel more relaxed in the intimate atmosphere created by a small pool of light.

Experimenting with unusual light sources does not, of course, guarantee successful or innovative photographs, and there are just as many pitfalls as when using any other light source. The image may be simple, but it takes imagination on the part of the photographer to make it effective.

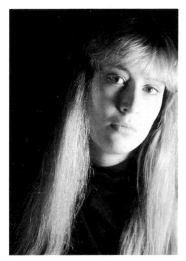

△ For this ethereal effect a small fluorescent torch was placed to the right and a little below the girl's face. The shadows thrown upward increase the sense of theatre produced by the pallid complexion.

Pentax LX, 85 mm, Kodak Ektachrome 160 Tungsten, 1/15 sec, f5.6

▷ Most of us associate candlelight with evocative, magical events such as childhood birthdays and romantic suppers. Typically, photographs of such events would include the light source, but a sense of atmosphere can still be retained by concentrating on the subject alone (here the candles have been included for reference). The equal balance between the two light sources has produced soft, even lighting for the portrait.

Pentax LX, 28 mm, Scotch (3M) 640T, 1/15 sec, f5.6

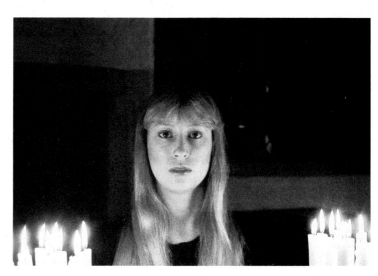

▷ The feeling of mystery and portent generated by the figures of the man and woman is heightened by the strong composition. The scene was lit with two desk lamps placed on tables behind the camera, one at either side. An unshaded standard lamp to the right produced the striking highlights in the woman's hair and face.

Pentax LX, 28 mm, Scotch (3M) 640T, 1/15 sec, f8

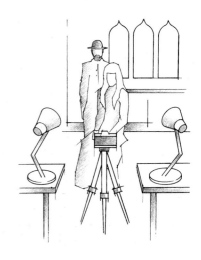

See also:
CREATIVE EXPOSURE pp16–17
SOFT AND HARD LIGHT pp18–19
LAMPLIGHT SCENES pp54–55

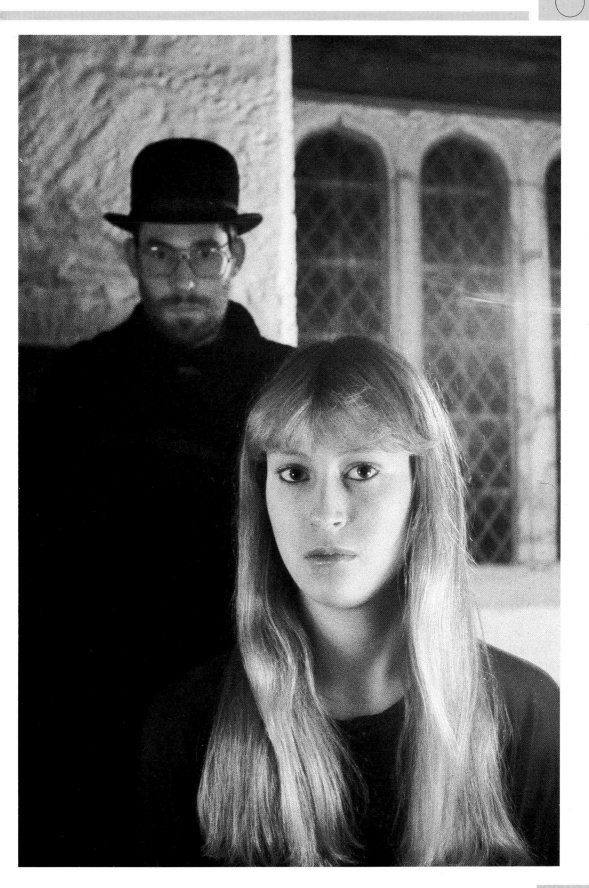

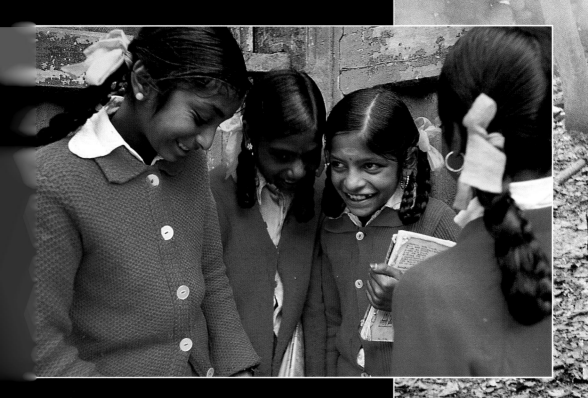

The importance of pictures in providing information in today's visually-aware society is paramount. Photojournalism is largely responsible for photography's pre-eminent role in factual communication. Many people hold the view that documentary photography should be an objective recording of people and events, but, in practice, the photographer's approach is coloured by his reaction to the situation. This reaction springs from his own experience and views, and influences his choice of subject, viewpoint and emphasis. These factors, far from being detrimental, are key elements in developing a personal style that is the hallmark of great journalistic photography.

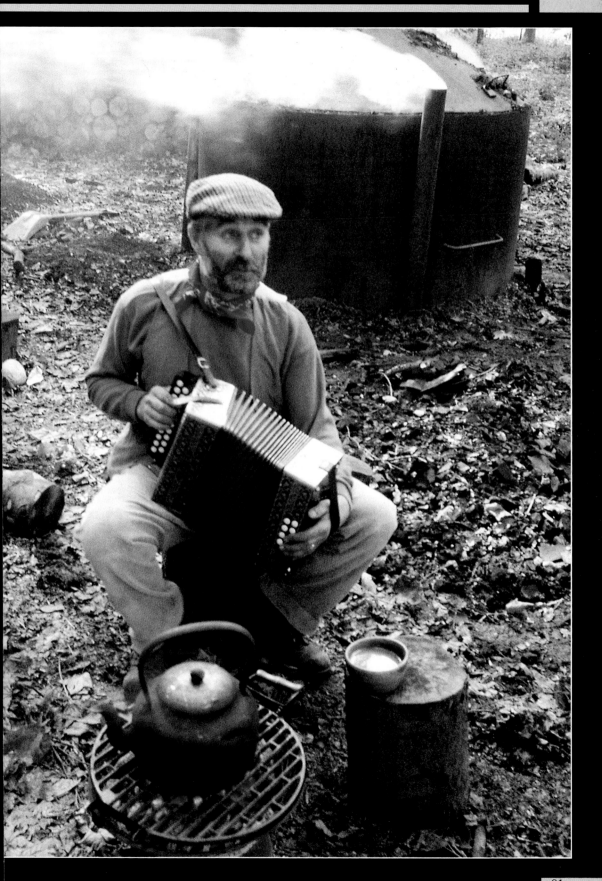

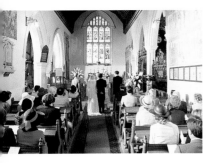

△ Check beforehand whether you are allowed to use flash inside the church. If not, you may have to switch to ISO 400 or 1000 film.

S uccessful wedding photography depends on careful planning and an ability to organize people. Shoot to a prearranged schedule so that nothing is missed out in a panic. In order to decide what pictures are wanted, make sure that you meet the families beforehand. In this way, you will know who is who and will be able to maintain the correct hierarchy in the traditional set pieces. Don't take it for granted that photography will be allowed in the church or in the grounds of the reception venue. Also, reconnoitre all locations to select suitable settings, remembering to allow for any special problems that space, backgrounds, and lighting might pose. Select the best viewpoints for each of your required shots at this stage. Check your equipment thoroughly, making sure that you have plenty of film and essential spares.

▷ If you are not the official photographer, you can concentrate on capturing those fleeting expressions that reflect the spirit of the occasion.

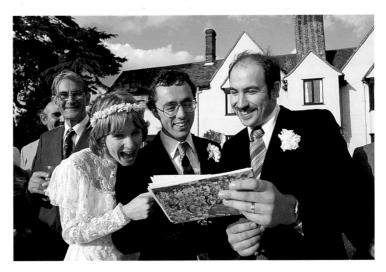

▽ The most effective way of posing a large group is in a half-circle. Make sure everyone gets a clear view of the camera, so that they will all be in the shot.

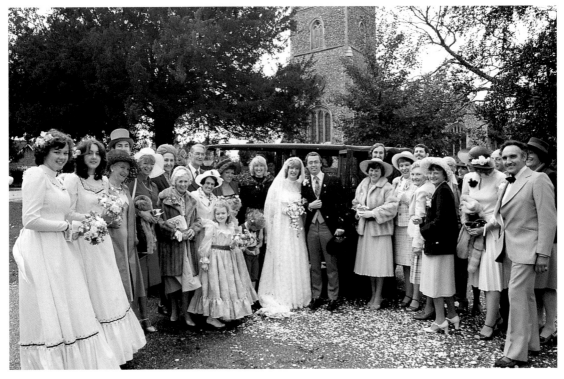

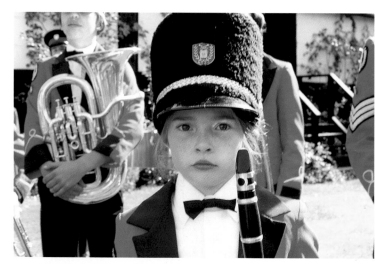

◁ Weddings often bring together a selection of people of all ages. Children make particularly fascinating portraits and are normally quite unconscious of the splendid clothes they have been dressed in for the occasion.

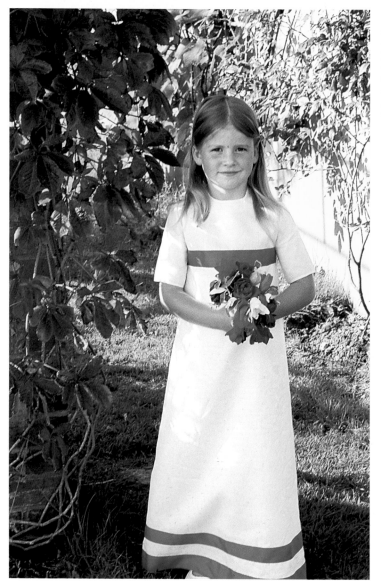

◁ Keep an eye out for opportunities to make individual portraits of important participants. A good setting, such as a large garden on a fine day, should be explored before the ceremony for possible backgrounds.

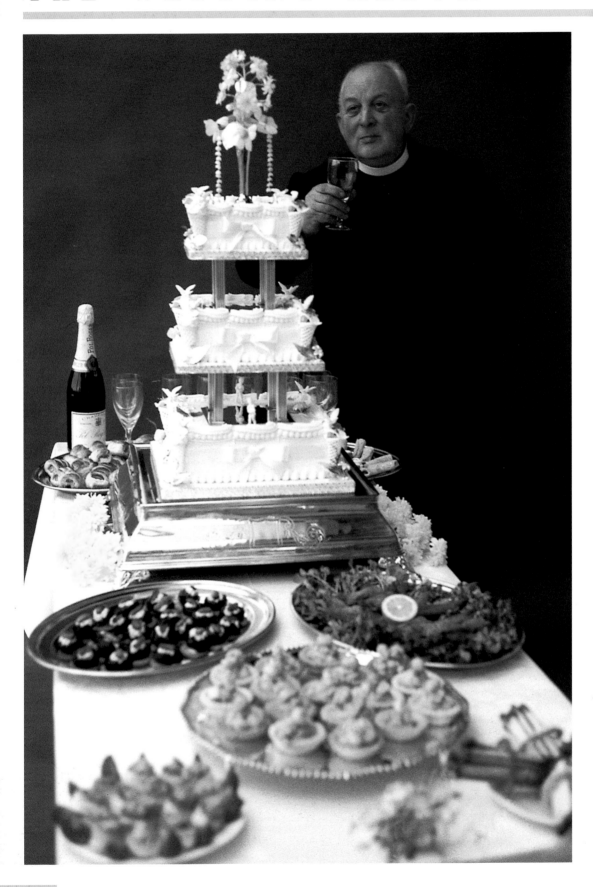

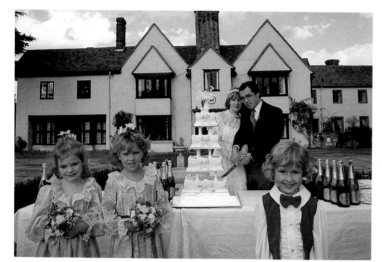

◁ Make sure you take the set shots: the bride, the bride and groom, the couple with their attendants, the couple with their families, all the guests, the couple cutting the cake, and their departure. Take a look at some wedding albums and make a list.

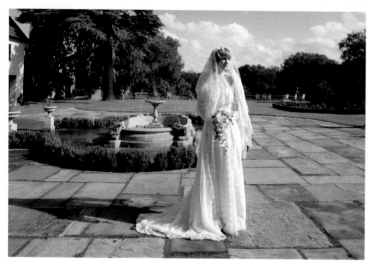

◁ Try to arrange an undisturbed photo session with the bride when she is in all her finery. A good half-hour or more in a beautiful setting will yield some of the best pictures of the day.

▷ Unusual shots like this overhead view of the reception help to give a set of wedding photographs an individual identity and make a change from the formal group shots.

◁ Indoor receptions nearly always lack sufficient ambient light for the use of normal (ISO 100) film, so take some high-speed stock to obtain candid shots without the need for flash.

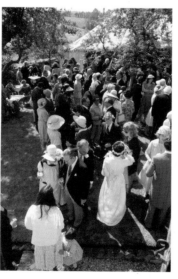

See also:
FRAMING THE SUBJECT pp20–21
PORTRAIT GROUPS pp36–37
GARDEN SETTINGS pp52–53
DESIGN WITH FIGURES pp58–59

WEDDING COUPLES

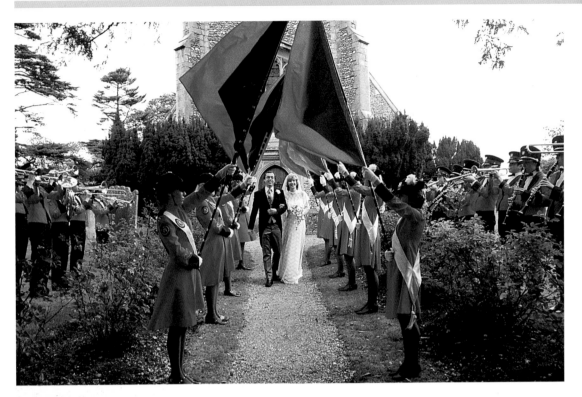

△ A shot of the couple leaving the church is traditional, but there is still plenty of scope for a creative approach. Try a high or low viewpoint, a long lens, or combining flash with ambient light for original results.

Pentax LX, 28 mm, Kodak Ektachrome 200, $^1/_{125}$ sec, f8

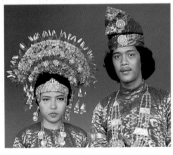

△ This Malayan couple have been posed so that groom's head is above the bride's, forming a triangular composition. Conventionally, it is the male who is made dominant, and this is achieved by his extra height and his direct gaze. The picture was taken with diffused flash.

Pentax LX, 50 mm, Kodak Ektachrome 64, $^1/_{60}$ sec, f8

See also:
FRAMING THE SUBJECT pp20–21
CLOSE ENCOUNTERS pp34–35
THE WEDDING ALBUM pp92–95

The couple are at the centre of events on their wedding day and it is natural that the most attention, photographically and otherwise, should be paid to them. If you plan to photograph the event successfully, you should meet the bride and bridegroom beforehand to discuss how they would like to be portrayed, any special requests, and to rehearse them in response to your directions. This will at the very least put you on first-name terms, which helps to cement a closer and a more productive rapport.

Photographs of the couple together should capture the atmosphere of a close and loving relationship, and it is important that the setting should complement this. All proposed locations should be inspected before the event so that the lighting direction can be taken into your planned images.

An intimate photograph of the wedding couple, arranged in a pleasing and balanced composition, demands a special approach not necessarily applicable to other pairs or small groups. Keeping their heads close together and maintaining a close physical proximity can present you with problems. The trick is to keep the couple on slightly different planes. Heads at the same level create an over-symmetrical effect, so arrange them so that one's head is higher than the other's. For more interest, take some shots with one or both partners looking away from the camera, so that you will capture the lighter moments of the day as well as the more formal poses. Above all don't be too obtrusive – it is the couple's wedding day after all, not a photo-session!

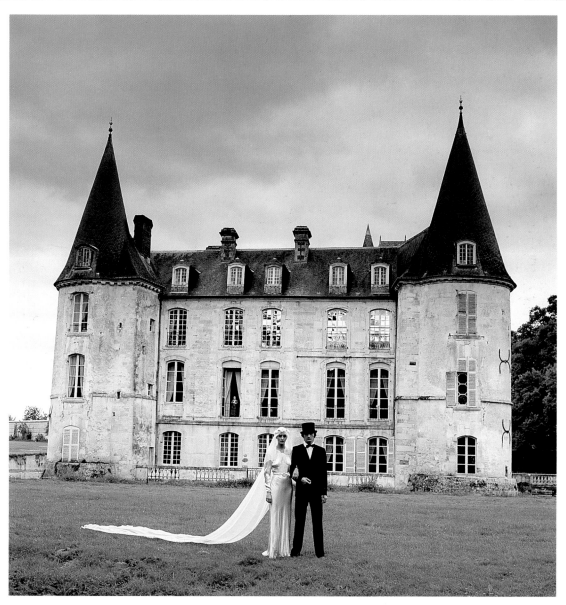

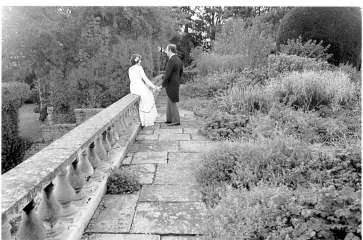

△ Unusual settings, such as this French château, are always worth using, especially if there is a location that allows you to separate the couple from a crowd of family and friends.

Hasselblad, 80 mm, Kodak Ektachrome 200, 1/60 sec, f8

◁ It is worth staying alert to the possibilities of taking candid shots at a wedding.

Pentax LX, 28 mm, Kodak Ektachrome 200, 1/125 sec, f8

Old photographs depicting life in years past are almost always fascinating. We like to see what streets and cities looked like, what changes have been made, and how people lived. Everyday objects such as letterboxes, signs and posters become fascinating as historical references and illustrate the value of recording ordinary aspects of daily life as we see it.

Most old and valuable photographs were not commissioned by authorities or patrons interested in making documentary records for future generations but were made as 'snap shots' by keen amateurs. Today it is especially important that photographers continue to document modern life in its infinite variety because our world is changing more rapidly than ever. Although much of what can be photographed will automatically gain in interest and, possibly, value as time moves on, documentary pictures should always be made with the same creative input and thoughtful approach as any other photograph. By careful selection of subject matter and sensitive treatment, photographs can be much more than straightforward visual records, revealing a great deal about our lifestyles, attitudes, social organization and, in many cases, our sense of humour.

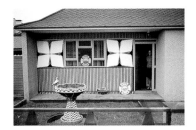

△ Most people who live in streets of identical houses decorate their homes to achieve a degree of individuality, painting the woodwork, replacing doors or windows, or using stone cladding. Sometimes decoration is more original. This family in Newcastle used old navy trophies in a bid to maintain an individual identity.

Pentax LX, 50 mm, Kodak Ektachrome 64, 1/125 sec, f8

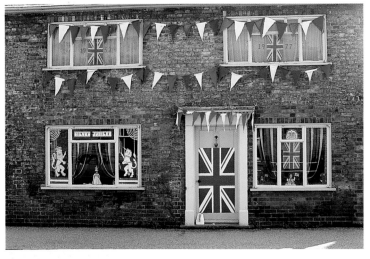

◁ Elaborate decorations such as this are a rare sight today, except for special occasions – when local football teams reach the Cup Final, for example, or during national celebrations. This modest home in Ely, Cambridgeshire, covered with patriotic emblems, shows the mood that swept Britain during the Queen's Silver Jubilee of 1977.

Pentax LX, 50 mm, Kodak Ektachrome 64, 1/125 sec, f8

◁ The modern equivalent of those 'dark, satanic mills', this Manchester scene contains much information that may prove to be valuable as historical reference. The photograph is also an expressive image depicting the grim character of the modern industrial suburb.

Pentax LX, 50 mm, Kodak Ektachrome 64, 1/125 sec, f8

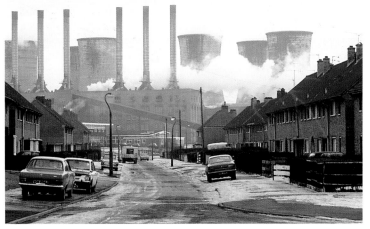

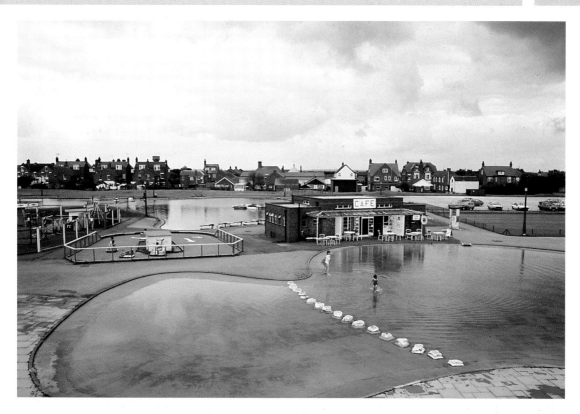

△ Rapid progress doesn't always lead to welcome change. This empty amenities park was part of open heathland that stretched to the sea. The heath was well used for picnics and had a flourishing community of wildlife. Now, the pool, playgrounds, car park, and café are seldom used, and the area is deserted for much of the time. The two lonely figures paddling in the empty expanse of water help portray the sense of change for the worse.

Pentax LX, 24 mm, Kodak Ektachrome 64, $^1/_{125}$ sec, f8

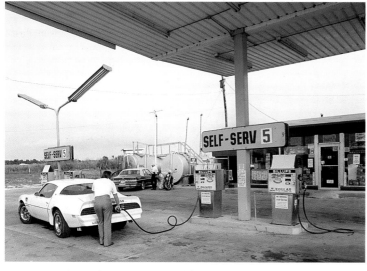

△ Some of the most telling images of the 20th century will show how our environment has been adapted to accommodate the car. Filling stations are a familiar sight everywhere, but look out for interesting regional variations.

Pentax LX, 28 mm, Kodak Ektachrome 64, $^1/_{125}$ sec, f8

See also:
FRAMING THE SUBJECT pp20–21
DOWN ON THE FARM pp100–101
ARCHITECTURAL THEMES pp150–159
FOUND STILL LIFES pp168–169

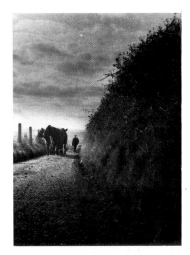

One of the most important tasks of a photographic essay, whether long or short, is to give the viewer a comprehensive picture of the subject. Although the narrative approach, with a beginning, middle, and end, is sometimes appropriate, it is not always the best, but, even so, each picture should support the series and give it a greater meaning. As a general guide, a picture essay will start with some 'establishing' shots that set the scene and introduce the viewer to the subject, followed by a selection of pictures showing different viewpoints, perspectives, and details to create variations in pace and style. Study the subject matter first and, if possible, visit the location and people involved to make yourself familiar with the features likely to make good picture material. Then list your proposed shots. This will be your 'storyboard', but do not stick to it too dogmatically. Adapt it as your knowledge of the subject develops during the course of the photography.

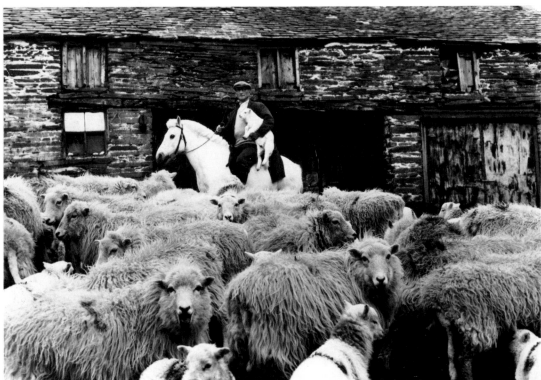

This small selection of photographs is taken from a series depicting the varying lifestyles and activities on some family-owned farms in England and Wales. When the documentary subject includes people, it is essential that you enlist their co-operation and support. It is their first impression of you and your work that counts, so take care to be polite and, if you promise prints, never forget to supply them. Farm life revolves around the seasons, so this series incorporates pictures made at different times throughout the year, mostly when important agricultural activities were taking place. To ensure that each shot was correctly used with the accompanying text, copious notes were made during each visit to the different farms and kept in the files with the contact sheets.

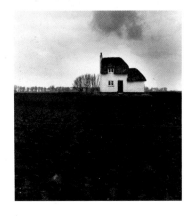

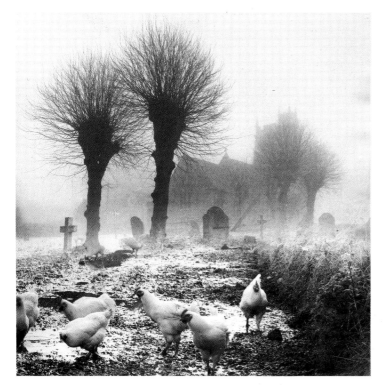

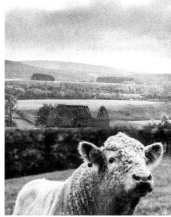

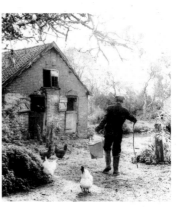

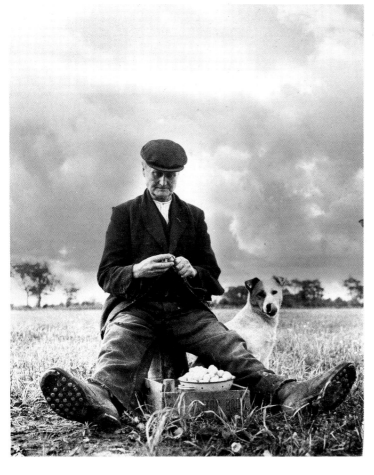

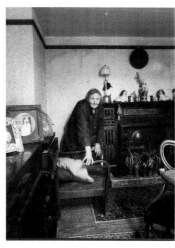

See also:
FRAMING THE SUBJECT pp20–21
BLACK AND WHITE pp22–23
THE WEDDING ALBUM pp92–95
PORTRAIT STORY pp102–105

PORTRAIT STORY

Most of us make portrait photographs to be viewed on their own, as a single entity. But there are many occasions when a series of pictures will combine to make a far more telling portrait than an individual one. Portrait stories or essays are normally the domain of photojournalists but they can be tackled by any photographer wishing to enlarge his scope. In fact many familiar portraits proclaimed as outstanding examples of the art were taken for an essay and are the product of the close rapport between photographer and subject that is built up over the long time spent together. Magazine editors need a selection of different images that together can make an essay, often in the form of a story spiced with variety, changes in pace, and with a beginning, middle, and end. Prior knowledge of the subject's personality, occupation, and tastes, forms an essential part of the portrait photographer's approach. Not only does this demonstrate to the sitter a genuine interest in his or her life, it also helps the conversation to flow, preventing it from faltering to a strained silence which can make the session uneasy. In addition to researching the subject's background, the photographer must make sure that all the equipment is ready for immediate use.

▽ The silhouette is one of the strongest and yet simplest forms of portrait. A profile is capable of revealing a great deal about character and strength of personality, as this shot of the printmaker shows. A large, sloping forehead, deep eyebrows, a prominent nose and chin, all indicate a man of independent spirit. Each of these features would be evident whether the silhouette was big or small. A stark silhouette forms a striking visual counterpoint to other more colourful pictures.

Pentax LX, 85 mm, Scotch (3M) 1000, 1/500 sec, f5.6

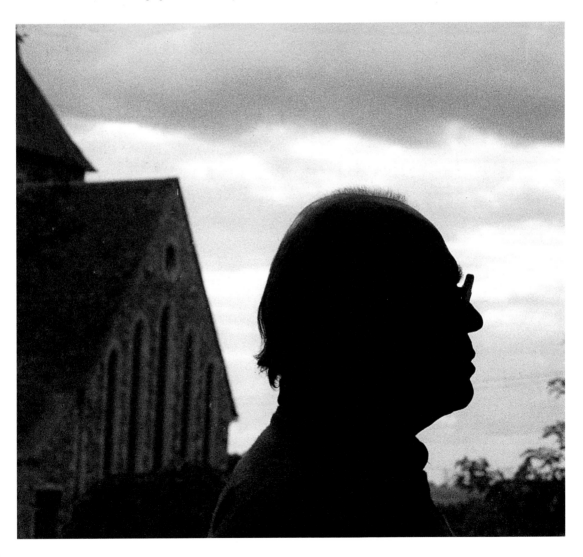

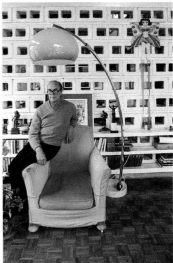

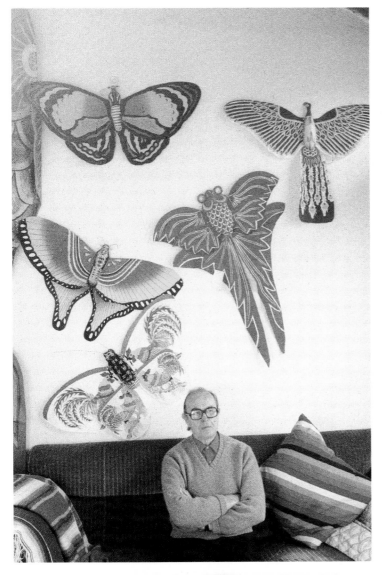

△ One of the most interesting
features of Rothenstein's modern
home was the use of utilitarian
building materials for the interior
finish. The white concrete lattice,
normally seen in the garden,
forms an effective contrasting
backdrop.

◁ Influences are an important
part of any portrait story,
especially stories featuring
creative personalities. Michael
Rothenstein's new work had been
inspired by these brightly-
coloured Japanese kites and
butterflies.

◁ For a more personal statement
about Rothenstein's home, he was
photographed in one of his
favourite rooms. A wide-angle lens
took in many intriguing objects.

*All three pictures taken with a
Pentax LX, 28 mm, Scotch (3M)
1000*

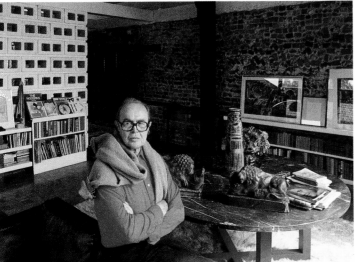

PORTRAIT STORY

Take only what is necessary when you go to shoot a portrait story. Most assignments of this kind can be handled with just a moderately wide lens, a standard lens, and a short telephoto. For lighting, a powerful hand-held flash and accompanying reflector will be adequate, and all that you need besides are a tripod, a cable release and film of different types and speeds. Never arrive late. When you arrive keep an eye out for suitable locations, always bearing in mind the editor's requirements. Prime among these are likely to be head and shoulders portraits; not one but several, including examples from the waist up and full length studies, with each shot showing the subject in a different setting. Other shots to include are some of the hands, which can reveal a great deal about the sitter. Readers can relate to the person more easily if they can see where he lives and works, what he likes to accumulate around him, whether he is tidy or lives in chaos, and what clothes he wears. Much time can be saved if natural and available light is used wherever possible. Superb results can be achieved with just window light and a large, white reflector for lightening the shadows. If artificial light is needed, try bouncing it off a neutral-coloured surface for a softer effect. Given time and a co-operative subject, most competent photographers can hope to make a success of a portrait session. It is important to stay relaxed under pressure. Diplomacy is of key importance during the whole of the session – while setting up, during shooting, and afterwards. It is particularly important to send prints if you have promised to supply them. You should, however, having expressed your gratitude, politely but firmly resist any request from the sitter that he or she approve the pictures before publication.

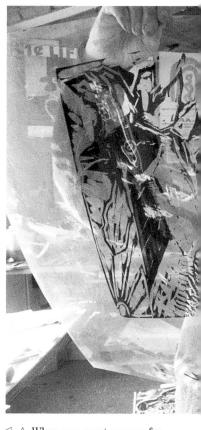

▽ To avoid repetition Rothenstein wore a different shirt and now blends in rather than contrasts with the surroundings. The strong foreground has been dramatized by making use of the exaggerated perspective of the wide-angle lens. Lighting was from a window.

Pentax LX, 28 mm, Scotch (3M) 1000, ¹/₁₅ sec, f8

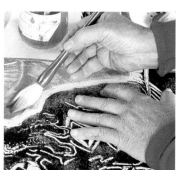

◁ △ When you meet anyone for the first time one of the first questions you will probably ask is what work he or she does. So it follows that few portrait stories are complete without a series depicting the person at work. Rothenstein's studio had many picture opportunities, most of them enlivened by bright colours, contrasts, comparison or scale, and varieties of form. To avoid any possibility of repetition, viewpoint, lenses, and poses were changed frequently and a good mix of vertical and horizontal shots was made both from close up and from a distance.

Pentax LX, 50 mm, Scotch (3M) 1000, ¹/₁₅ sec, f8

Pentax LX, 28 mm, Scotch (3M) 1000, ¹/₃₀ sec, f5.6

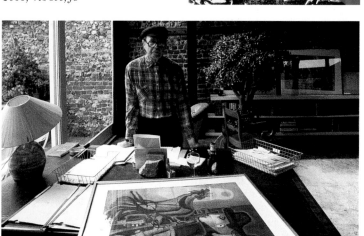

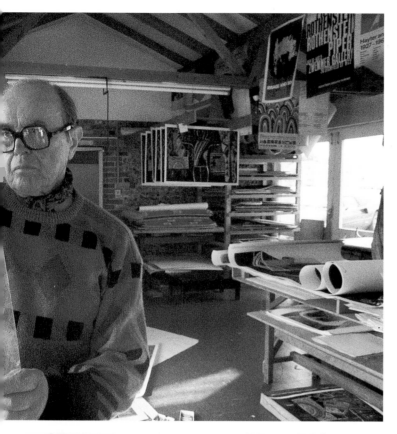

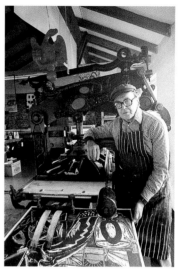

△ The artist with the printing press that is an indispensable tool of his craft.

Pentax LX, 28 mm, Scotch (3M) 1000, 1/15 sec, f8

◁ A further change of clothes keeps interest in the portrait series alive. The mass of plain tone in Rothenstein's jersey contrasts well with the intricately detailed background.

Pentax LX, 28 mm, Scotch (3M) 1000, 1/15 sec, f8

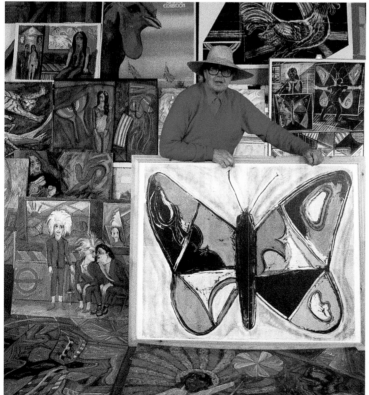

See also:
EXPLOITING WIDE-ANGLES pp10–11
CLOSE ENCOUNTERS pp34–35
BEHIND THE SCENES pp50–51
OUTDOOR SILHOUETTES pp86–87

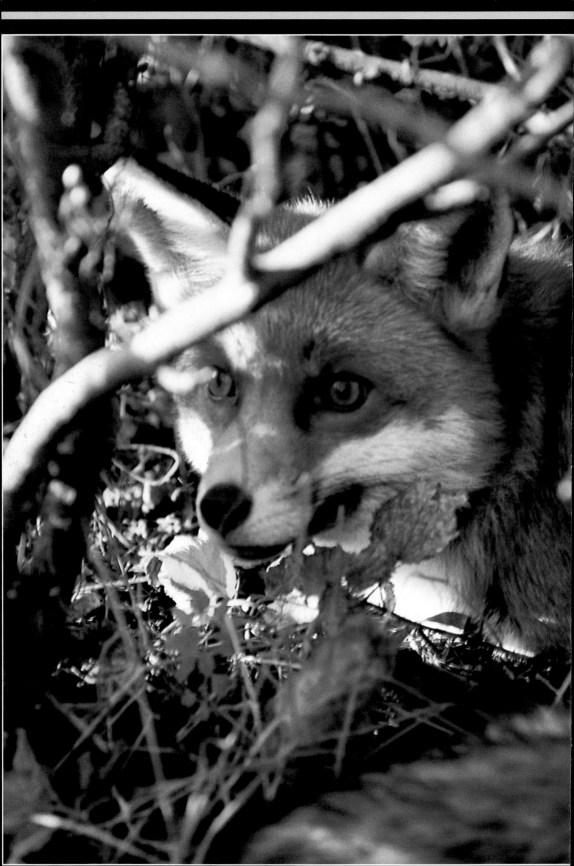

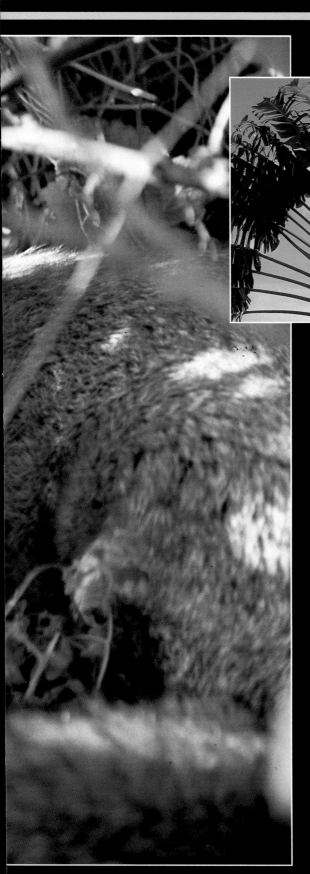

Photography is unique in its ability to reveal Nature's hidden secrets, illustrating relationships that might otherwise be missed. Recent developments in camera and film technology have brought the diversity and splendour of nature and wildlife photography within the bounds of any competent photographer. From sweeping panoramas taken in African game reserves to minute details of flora and fauna, the technicalities of obtaining dramatic, high-quality images no longer depend on the ownership of expensive, specialized equipment. But nature photography cannot be undertaken casually. There is no place for the photographer who does not already have a keen interest in wildlife and a sound knowledge of the subject.

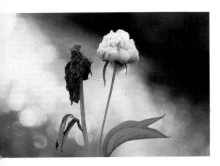

△ A crumpled peony shot against soft highlights produced by sunlight filtered through distant trees evokes a strong feeling of nature's beauty. A silver reflector positioned by the camera has lightened the shadows in the colourful flower.

Pentax LX, 100 mm macro, Kodak Ektachrome 64, 1/500 sec, f6.3

It is not easy to take a single shot that captures the overall atmosphere of any garden. The sheer quantity and diversity of the plants growing there and the great variety and range of garden designs only make the task more difficult. Since you cannot expect to photograph everything, you must be selective in your choice of subject. But the choice of subject is not the only consideration when you are trying to record the spirit of the garden and capture its quintessential feel. Probably the most compelling influence on a garden's atmosphere is light. Most people are familiar with the peace and serenity that are so typical of a still summer's evening when golden sunlight filters through the trees and long shadows stretch across the lawn. Light is a vital element in pictures that succeed in conveying the characteristic atmosphere of the garden, and it is the photographer's ability to recognize this essential ingredient and his sensitivity in appreciating the subtleties of natural light that leads to an expressive picture.

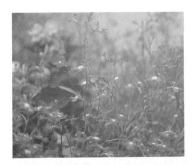

◁ Soft sunlight on a hazy day is best for flower photography. In this picture the light has been further subdued by the use of a soft-focus filter. The blurring of colour and tone adds to the romance of the image.

Pentax LX, 50 mm macro, Kodak Ektachrome 200, 1/125 sec, f8

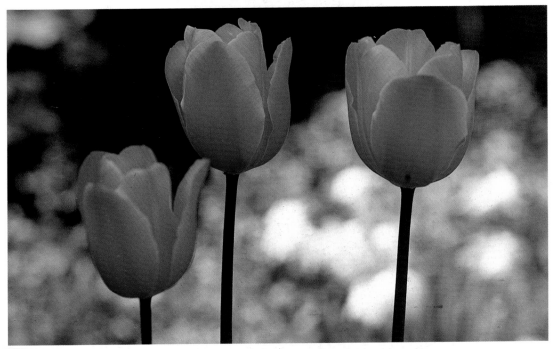

△ Extreme close-ups, such as this study of tulips, are very effective when you want to convey your strong impressions of a garden. The background was a confusing mass of colour, so a wide aperture was chosen to minimize depth of field and provide an unobtrusive backdrop.

Pentax LX, 100 mm macro, Kodak Ektachrome 200, 1/250 sec, f5.6

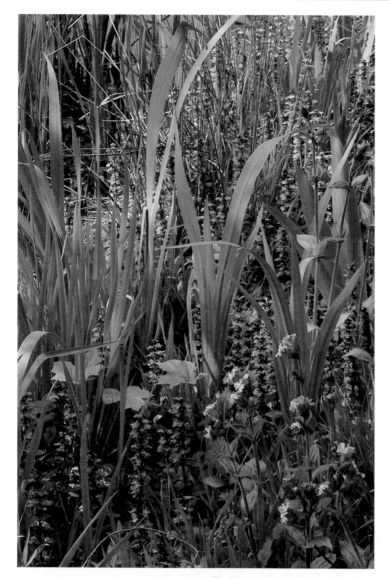

◁ Natural gardens have a special atmosphere of their own and enthusiasts often intermix wild flowers and garden varieties in an informal display. To capture the effect of this lakeside setting's luxuriant mass of plant life, an intimate view was chosen and the photograph was made when low light from late afternoon sun revealed shape and texture.

Pentax LX, 28 mm, Kodak Ektachrome 200, $^1/_{125}$ sec, f16

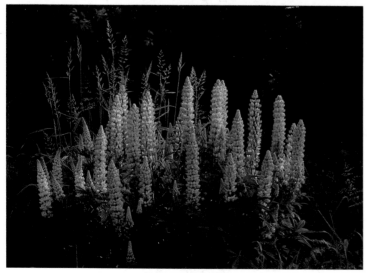

◁ These lupins were made more attractive towards evening, when a low-angled sun shone through an overhanging tree, illuminating them in a delicate oasis of warm golden sunlight.

Pentax LX, 85 mm, Kodak Ektachrome 200, $^1/_{125}$ sec, f16

See also:
SPECIAL LENSES pp14–15
SOFT AND HARD LIGHT pp18–19
A TOUCH OF LIGHT pp82–83
THE VERSATILE LENS pp116–117

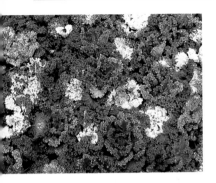

F lowers and shrubs are the most important element in any garden design, and deservedly attract attention. Special features of many British gardens are the luxuriant herbaceous borders and the wide variety of flower types, ranging from indigenous species to exotic imports. British gardens have exerted an influence all over the world.

There are many ways to photograph flowers. They can be shot as individual blooms in a manner similar to that of traditional portraiture, arranged in a display either formally or informally, in flower beds or borders, or in the wild. Naturally, if you are aiming for maximum impact in colour, shape and form, you should aim for perfect flowers in full bloom, but it's also worth photographing them when they are fading, dried, or even discarded – such images can be very striking and evocative.

Close-up flower photography is most successful with a macro lens – the short telephoto versions offering the best perspective rendition – and with the camera set on a tripod. A selection of white and silver reflectors help to control ambient light, while a collapsible windbreak will reduce subject movement. Concealed wires also help to keep the subject still.

△ Although not, in fact, using flowers, this display of exotic, floral-looking cabbages illustrates how exciting images can be made with an arrangement in a tightly packed mass.

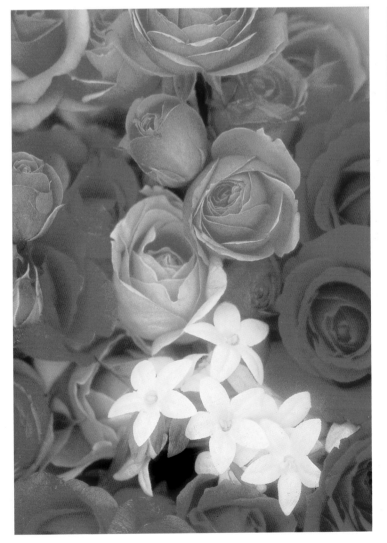

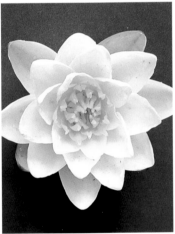

△ Damaged leaves in the background proved too distracting for this picture of a water-lily, so a card was placed underneath in order to hide them.

◁ These tightly packed rose blooms, with a mimosa as a counterpoint, have been made softer and more appealing and romantic by the use of a filter.

▷ These dried-up blooms still exhibit a subtle, if decayed, beauty. Soft, directional light from a north-facing window gives a richness to the faded flowers and reveals the texture of the fragile petals.

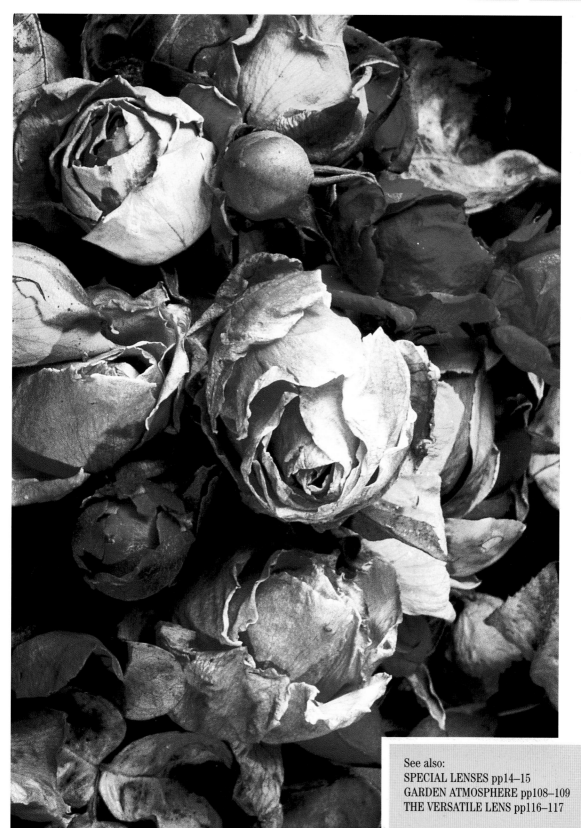

See also:
SPECIAL LENSES pp14–15
GARDEN ATMOSPHERE pp108–109
THE VERSATILE LENS pp116–117

NATURAL REPETITION

We have a natural tendency to seek order in our lives, so it is not surprising that we discern pattern in the built environment and in nature, which is particularly rich in examples. Spiderwebs, leaf skeletons, tree branches and annual rings, rippling sand, are just a few examples from the many to be found.

Often patterns are not obvious from a normal viewpoint but reveal themselves only from a distance or from close up. The strongest patterns, easily spotted by the naked eye, are made up of a single shape repeated many times in a regular design, such as the cells in a beehive, but more subtle ones can be made up of less regular elements – the arrangement of leaves and branches in a shrub, for example. These patterns are often enhanced by the two-dimensional nature of photographs.

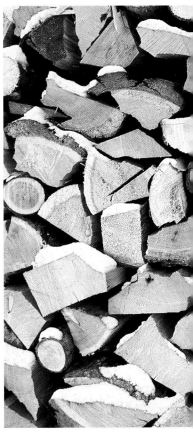

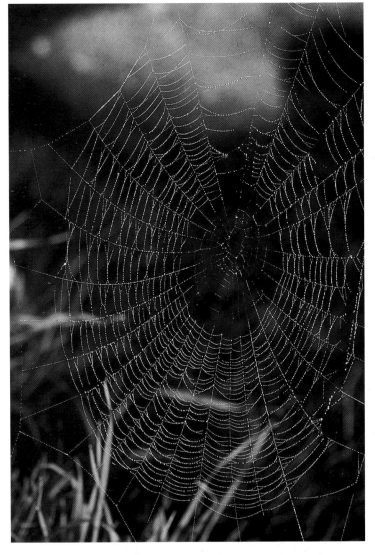

▽ Unlike the stack of logs, the delicately toned leaves of this succulent create a discordant pattern, given clarity because the third dimension has been subdued in the photograph.

Pentax LX, 100 mm macro, Kodak Ektachrome 64, ¹/₆₀ sec, f11

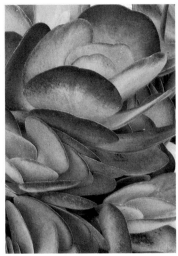

△ One of nature's most beautiful designs, the cobweb, is best photographed in the early morning, back-lit and moist with dew. It can be separated from the background by the use of a relatively wide aperture.

Pentax LX, 100 mm macro, Kodak Ektachrome 64, ¹/₁₂₅ sec, f8

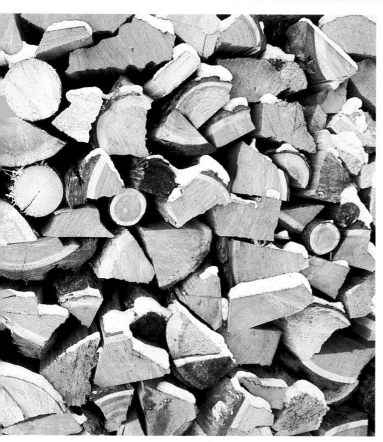

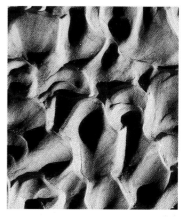

△ Just as the wind shapes snow into patterns, so the sea makes designs with sand. A gently sloping beach such as this is sculpted afresh with the ebb and flow of every tide.

Pentax LX, 50 mm macro, Kodak Ektachrome 200, ¹/125 sec, f16

△ From across the farmyard this stack of logs appeared as a regular pattern, but, in fact, no two logs are the same shape. The pattern is created by repetition of elements of similar size and tone.

Pentax LX, 50 mm, Kodak Ektachrome 64, ¹/125 sec, f16

▽ The most prominent pattern in this picture of rice fields is that of the terrace walls. Then there are the broader bands of the terraces themselves and, on a smaller scale, the rice plants.

Pentax LX, 150 mm, Kodak Ektachrome 64, ¹/125 sec, f16

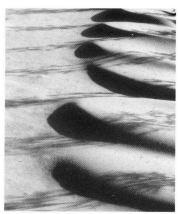

△ Wind-blown snow has eddied around these tree trunks, creating a pattern. Highlighted by weak winter sun, their shadows mingle with those cast by other trees.

Pentax LX, 50 mm, Kodak Ektachrome 64, ¹/125 sec, f16

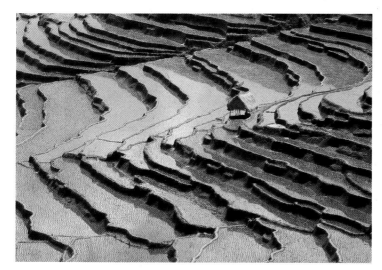

See also:
SPECIAL LENSES pp14–15
FRAMING THE SUBJECT pp20–21
SHAPE AND DETAIL pp152–153

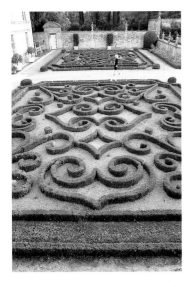

Gardens are a wonderful subject to photograph; they come in an endless variety of shapes and sizes and are located the world over. Arguably, Britain has the finest selection, ranging from the small cottage garden with its colourful herbaceous borders to the landscaped vistas that surround the great country houses. Other European countries have a different tradition, often tending towards more formal creations along the lines of the magnificent Versailles. Whatever the scale and style of gardens, they are usually fascinating and offer the photographer both a wide range of subjects and scope for a broad deployment of photographic techniques.

Start by exploring the garden. Many are planned as a series of different elements, although only a few will be in their prime at any one time. A quick tour will enable you to absorb the garden's broad concept as well as its notable features. It is worth remembering, for example, that suburban gardens are frequently designed as a setting for the house, and good viewpoints are likely to be from a distance. Gardens that surround a grand manor are often best viewed from near the house, or even from inside. Many larger gardens are laid out with the surrounding landscape in mind, with broad vistas over parkland and local woods, so look for the landscape shot as well as for detail.

Spring, early summer, and autumn are generally the best times to photograph gardens, as many plants are then at their most beautiful. Gardens open to the public tend to be crowded at these times, so it is best to arrive early or wait until evening.

△ Formal gardens are composed of strong geometric designs which can make graphic images. The severe and rather barren landscape created by such formality is relieved here by including the girl's figure.

Pentax LX, 24 mm, Kodak Ektachrome 64, 1/125 sec, f8

▷ Garden pictures sometimes lack a centre of interest, so it can be a good idea to include statues, a seat, or a garden building such as a gazebo, to provide a counterpoint to the plants.

Pentax LX, 28 mm, Kodak Ektachrome 64, 1/125 sec, f11

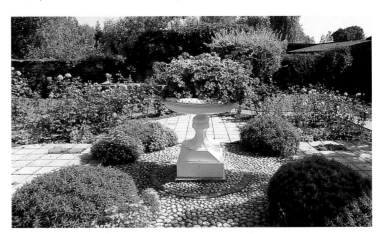

▷ Popular gardens hold a special problem for the photographer – crowds of people. Although a scattering of people is sometimes appropriate, too many will spoil the shot. For this shot of a Baroque garden in Tuscany it was necessary to wait until lunchtime for the crowds to clear.

Pentax LX, 24 mm, Kodak Ektachrome 64, 1/250 sec, f11

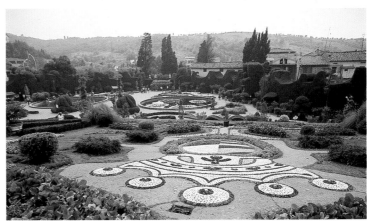

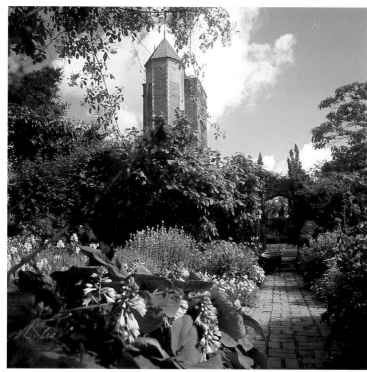

◁ Sissinghurst in Kent is one of the world's great gardens and typifies the English approach of combining a series of small, quite different gardens. The low viewpoint emphasizes the exuberant display of flowers and a feeling of depth is given by the relationship of the nearby plants and the distant tower.

Rolleiflex, 80 mm, Kodak Ektachrome 64, $^1/_{125}$ sec, f8

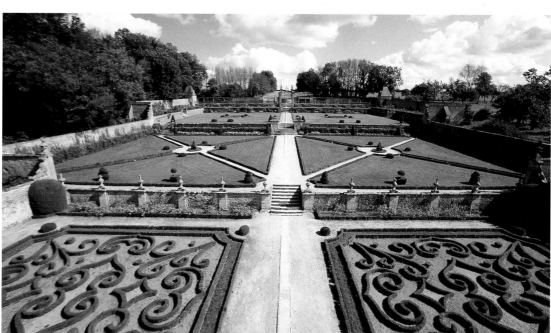

△ Many of the grander gardens of Europe, such as the one at Versailles, are based on the formal designs pioneered in the 17th and 18th centuries. The overall pattern is best seen from a high vantage point; in the case of this French garden the best view was from a room on the top floor of the château. A wide-angle lens was used to exaggerate perspective and make the most of the strong linear patterns.

Pentax LX, 24 mm, Kodak Ektachrome 64, $^1/_{250}$ sec, f8

See also:
LANDSCAPES pp60–75
EVENING LIGHT pp78–79
LINEAR PERSPECTIVE pp146–147
MANMADE PATTERN pp156–157

THE VERSATILE LENS

The macro lens was first developed as a specialist optic, designed for medical and scientific photography. It was not long before wildlife photographers recognized its remarkable potential for revealing nature in new ways, but these lenses were not widely used by other photographers until new designs improved the optical performance at more usual focusing distances. Modern macros are multi-purpose, capable of focusing from infinity down to very close distances.

Macros are available in many focal lengths, from wide-angle to mid-range telephotos, but the most useful are the standard (50 mm) and short-telephoto versions (85-100 mm) for the 35 mm format. The short telephoto is the pictorial photographer's favourite. The short-telephoto macro has an extremely wide focusing range – from about 0.5 m to infinity – and enables you to fill the frame with images up to half life-sized. Close-up photography demands an extensive depth of field, so these lenses are designed to stop down to f32 or f45. These small apertures can also be useful at more normal focusing distances.

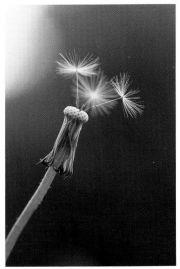

△ Photographing this dandelion's seed head against a dark background has accentuated the delicate rim light created by the last rays of a setting sun.

Pentax LX, 100 mm macro, Kodak Ektachrome 64, 1/60 sec, f8

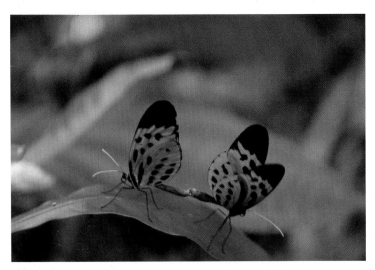

△ Insects are normally highly active, making them difficult to photograph in close-up. Choose a moment when they are still to maintain focus and framing.

Pentax LX, 50 mm macro, Kodak Ektachrome 200, autoexposure, f8

▷ Macro lenses are ideal for making selective images of subjects in the middle distance where surrounding detail would prove too distracting.

Pentax LX, 50 mm macro, Kodak Ektachrome 64, 1/125 sec, f8

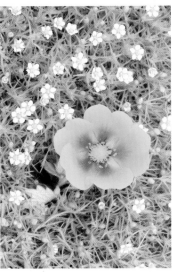

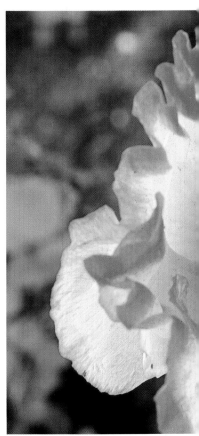

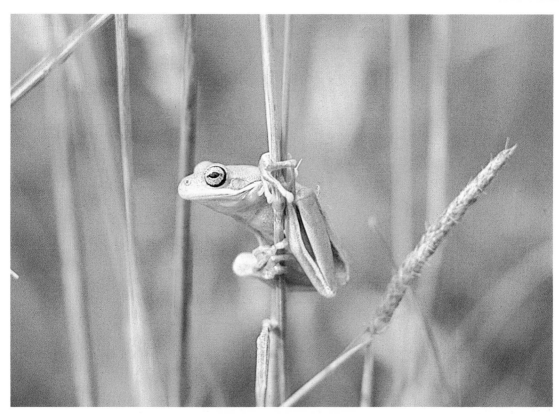

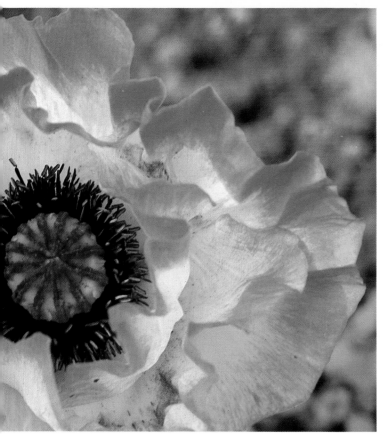

△ This well-camouflaged frog would have been lost against a background of sharply focused reeds. But, by using a wide aperture, they have been thrown out of focus to form a soft backdrop.

Pentax LX, 100 mm macro, Kodak Ektachrome 200, 1/500 sec, f11

◁ Even slight movement in macro photography will cause blurring so unstable subjects have to be supported. This flower was held steady by hidden wires.

Pentax LX, 100 mm macro, Kodak Ektachrome 64, 1/30 sec, f16

See also:
SPECIAL LENSES pp14–15
IMPACT OF FLOWERS pp108–109
NATURAL REPETITION pp112–113

BIRDS AND ANIMALS

Animals in the wild are wary creatures which treat the approach of any human with caution. Many, too, are small and difficult to spot because of their habitat or natural camouflage. These facts all add up to make fauna a difficult subject for the novice to tackle. Long lenses, well-thought-out hides, and hours of patience are all essential.

A good starting point for any would-be wildlife photographer are the birds and animals that are more used to having man as their neighbour. Your own back garden could attract several species of birds, for instance, but you can do far worse than to pay a visit to a local zoo, safari park or open farm.

Patience will still be necessary — captive creatures are not trained models. A long wait may even be needed for your target just to move to where your lens has a clear view.

Depth of field can be an acute problem with enclosed wildlife. Not only will you want unnaturalistic backgrounds to appear out of focus, but you will want the mesh or perspex that encloses them to vanish from your pictures too. The answer is to get as close to the cage as possible, pushing your lens into the fencing or glass if allowed. Then use a wide aperture to blur the backdrop as much possible, focusing on the eyes so that they become the focal point for your portrait.

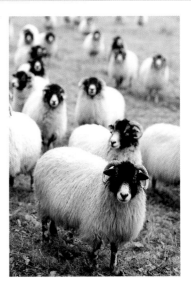

△ Farmyard animals can make easy subjects as they are reasonably used to humans, and can usually be found out in the open (so there is plenty of natural light, and no interfering backgrounds). This flock of sheep made an interesting pattern across the frame, as their inquisitiveness meant they were all looking at the camera.

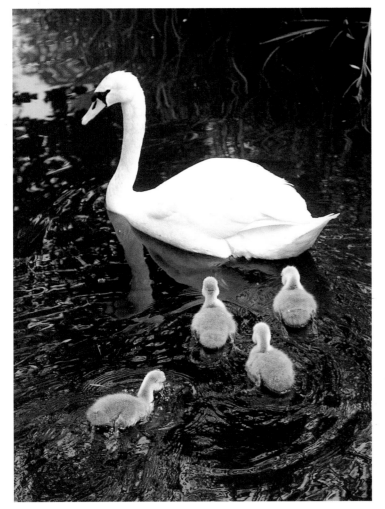

◁ It took a long wait, and several less-successful shots, to record this family of swans going for a swim. The young cygnets rarely stayed in formation behind their mother for very long. I had to be patient and remain ready for the right moment.

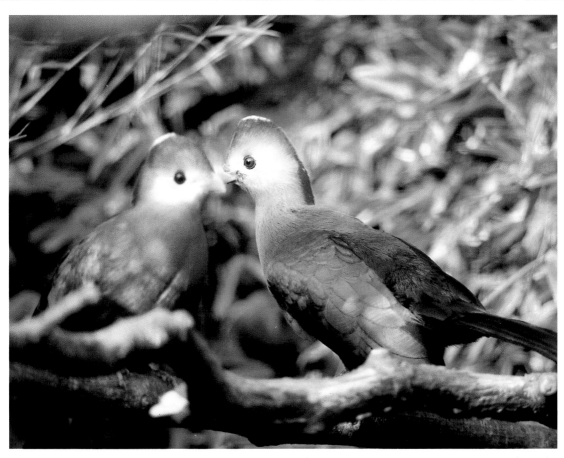

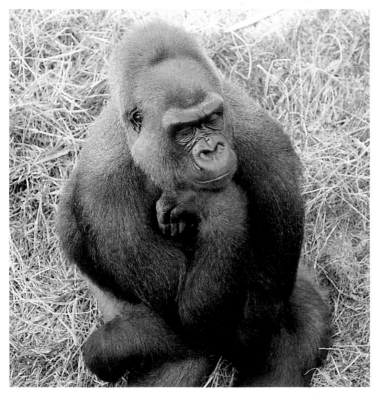

△ I needed to use my telephoto lens at open aperture for this shot, not only to ensure the background did not dominate the picture, but also to throw the mesh of the cage was so far out of focus it was not seen in the image. This also meant pressing the lens up against the wires. Note that the eye of one of the birds is critically sharp.

◁ Animals in zoos can sit for hours in one unattractive pose. It took a good, long wait to get this shot of a seemingly-sulking gorilla.

See also:
EXPLOITING TELEPHOTOS pp12–13
DOWN ON THE FARM pp100–101
THE VERSATILE LENS pp116–117
UNUSUAL ANGLES pp144–145

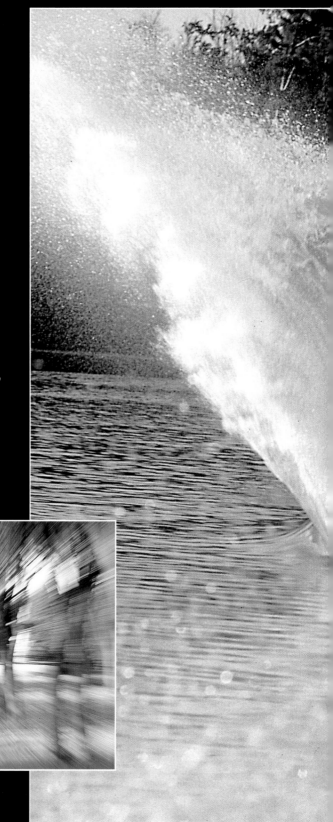

Sports are about people in action, spectators as well as competitors, and great sporting shots are as much portraits as they are photographs that capture the spirit of an event. The most photogenic moments are not always instances of high-speed action or the winner at the line; the creative sports photographer will look for situations arising out of conflict – the determined face of effort, joy at beating the odds, and the despair of failure. Good sports photography depends upon a thorough knowledge of the event, familiarity with the venue, and a flexible approach that enables you to exploit unforeseen incidents.

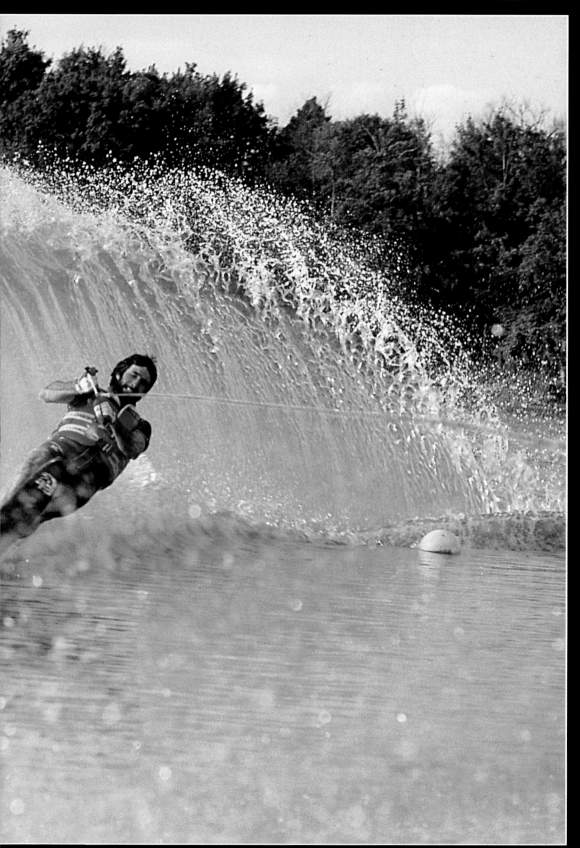

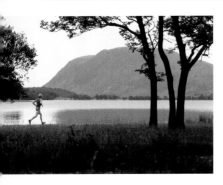

△ The viewpoint for this shot of a fell walker in the Lake District was carefully selected to silhouette the contestants as they passed. All camera controls were preset before the walkers arrived so it was just a question of waiting until they crossed the bright reflection on the lake.

Pentax LX, 85 mm, Kodak Ektachrome 64, 1/250 sec, f8

Almost any sporting event, from a school sports day to the World Cup Final, offers enough picture-taking opportunities to stretch the skill and satisfy the appetite of the keenest photographer.

Sport is about competition, about people pitting their prowess, skill and determination against each other. Raw emotion – excitement, elation, aggression, defeat, dejection, misery – gives rise to intense drama that is seldom encountered elsewhere. A wealth of exciting pictures is there for the taking.

A professional photographer working for a newspaper or magazine must concentrate on capturing the winner or the height of the action, but as an amateur you can simply look for the best pictures. Excited spectators, exhausted competitors, tension at the start line, and a proud parent's praise are aspects of a sporting event that may not be newsworthy, but nevertheless provide opportunities to take excellent pictures.

Light and weather can be crucial in sports photography, where fast action can be frozen only with high shutter speeds, while typical viewpoints often dictate the use of long lenses. You need good light, even with fast film, so an overcast day is often restrictive, forcing the use of wide apertures, as well as affecting the general atmosphere. This in turn leads to limited depth of field and greater demands on your focusing abilities.

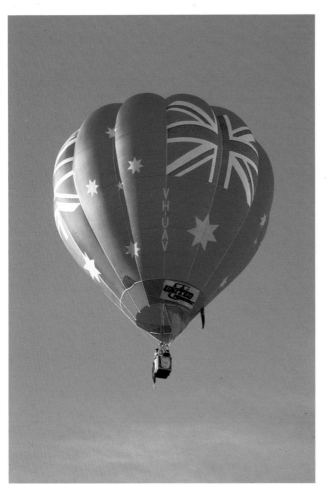

◁ Ballooning has its own special problems, especially if you are restricted to shooting from ground level. If you can hitch a ride, your chances of getting some really exciting images are greatly increased. Most events start in the early morning when rich, warm light and blue skies complement the bright colours of the envelopes. In competitions the balloons go up in quick succession, offering the chance of group pictures, but they soon disperse. This balloon was taking part in an international race.

Pentax LX, 85 mm, Kodak Ektachrome 200, 1/500 sec, f8

▷ The supporters' club frequently puts as much effort, energy and enthusiasm into urging the team on as the team do in playing the game. Turning the camera away from the event can pay dividends – the resulting pictures are often very revealing.

Pentax LX, 35 mm, Kodak Ektachrome 200, 1/500 sec, f11

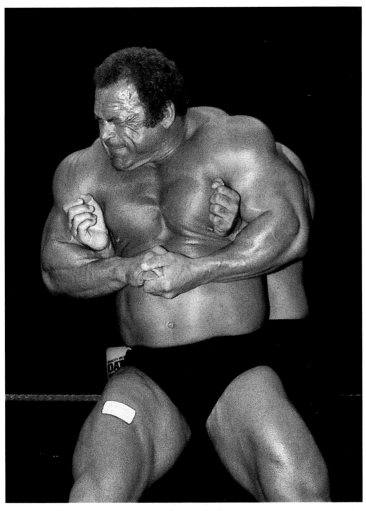

◁ Flash on camera is the best way to capture the rough and tumble of a wrestling match, but you should watch out for the ropes, as they can throw ugly shadows across the picture if they cross the flash beam. Hurtling bodies, animated expressions, and rowdy crowd scenes are all fair game for the photographer who is quick off the mark and is able to move around. Spectators at competition or exhibition matches may get annoyed if you take too much time for framing and composition, so more creative work is best left to training sessions at the local gym.

Pentax LX, 85 mm, Kodak Ektachrome 200, X-sync, f16

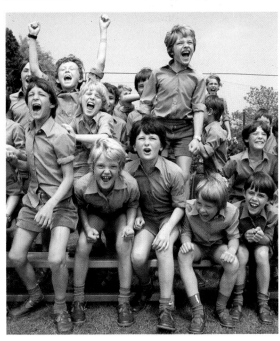

See also:
EXPLOITING TELEPHOTOS pp12–13
SPORTING EXPRESSIONS pp130–131
THE ESSENTIAL SHOT pp140–141

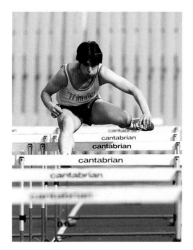

Whatever the sport, it is essential for the photographer to capture the winning moment and, if possible, to encapsulate the spirit of the event in the same shot. If you can add creative expression of movement, you have the ingredients for a truly dramatic sports picture. Despite the photographer's best endeavours, these elements rarely come together in one frame, but you should always aim to make a picture that records the vital moments and actions which decide the outcome of an event. In a horse-race, it might be the last part of the final straight, with the leaders running neck-and-neck, turf flying, a jockey throwing a quick glance at his rival, and the horses wide-eyed and with their necks straining for the winning post. Within a split second, it will all be gone. There is no need to frequent important national sporting events to capture such moments; local competitions and school sports events offer similar opportunities, the competitors showing the same elation or disappointment.

△ This telephoto shot of a hurdler does not give an accurate impression of the track, for the 'stacking' effect of the lens has brought the background forwards. However, this head-on camera position allows you to shoot several frames as the athlete approaches.

Pentax LX, 800 mm, Kodak Ektachrome 200, 1/1000 sec, f8

▷ The highpoint is when action changes direction and slows momentarily – an ideal time to freeze movement. Here it happened at the top of the goalkeeper's leap.

Pentax LX, 150 mm, Kodak Ektachrome 200, 1/2000 sec, f8

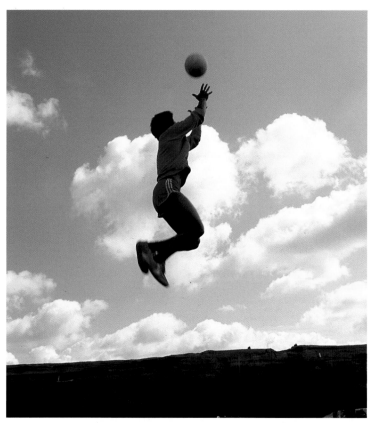

Guide to minimum shutter speeds for freezing movement

	Medium shot	Long shot	Panning	Diagonal movement
Walking (3mph/5kph)	1/250 sec	1/125 sec	1/30 sec	1/125 sec
Running (13mph/20kph)	1/500 sec	1/250 sec	1/125 sec	1/250 sec
Kicking ball	1/1000 sec	1/500 sec	1/125 sec	1/1000 sec
Car (50mph/80kph)	1/4000 sec	1/2000 sec	1/125 sec	1/1000 sec

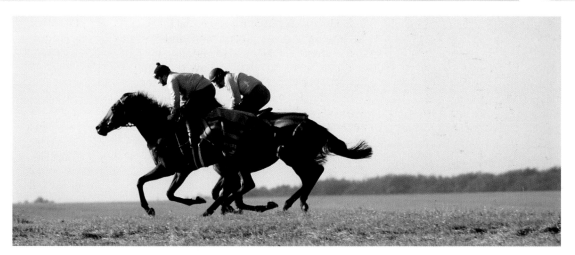

△ Training sessions are more relaxed than 'live' events and there are plenty of opportunities to take pictures that capture the spirit of a race. These two steeplechasers, galloping head-to-head during early morning exercise, are just as intent on beating each other to the end of the gallop as they would be in a race.

Pentax LX, 85 mm, Kodak Ektachrome 200, $1/1000$ sec, f8

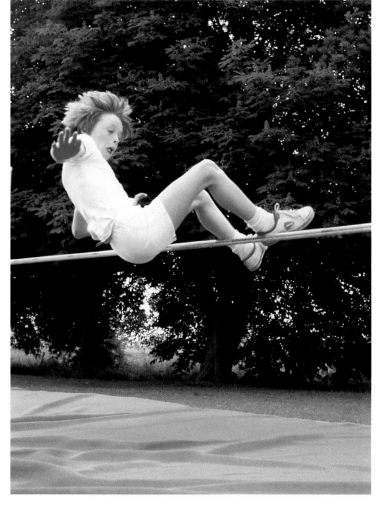

△ In this instant of time, frozen by the camera's fast shutter, a schoolboy achieves his ambition – a leap to clear the daunting barrier in a crucial high-jump final at the school's annual sports day.

Pentax LX, 85 mm, Kodak Ektachrome 200, $1/500$ sec, f8

See also:
EXPLOITING TELEPHOTOS pp12–13
CAPTURING ACTION pp48–49
SPORT AND WATER pp128–129

A SENSE OF SPEED

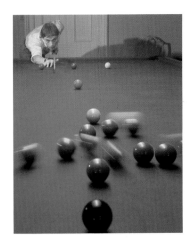

One approach to photographing fast action in sports is to attempt to freeze an instant of time by using a fast shutter speed. Results that are possibly even more exciting can be obtained by using a slow shutter speed and allowing the image to blur. You can either let the subject blur, or you can use panning, the result of which is that the subject is sharply focused but it is set against a streaked background. Make sure that you continue the pan after releasing the shutter. Stopping will cause camera jerk and spoil the image.

These techniques can be applied to almost any action in any sport. If you decide to use blur, make sure you use colour film, since successful shots rely on subject movement creating sweeps of tone across the frame, and their impact depends on contrast differences within the blurring.

Colour contrasts are commoner and have greater visual power than pure tonal contrasts that will need to be very marked to stop the picture tending towards a uniform grey tone. In the shot of the bike rider the blurred background created by panning is effective only because the bright highlights from light filtering through the trees contrasts against the dark trees.

△ Sometimes the speed of the action, in this case the moving snooker balls, is totally unpredictable and may move in many directions simultaneously. Selecting the correct shutter speed is largely down to experience – and a little luck! Try taking several shots at various speeds – for example, ¼, ⅛, ¹⁄₁₅ and ¹⁄₃₀ sec.

Hasselblad, 80 mm, Kodak Ektachrome 200, ¹⁄₁₅ sec, f16

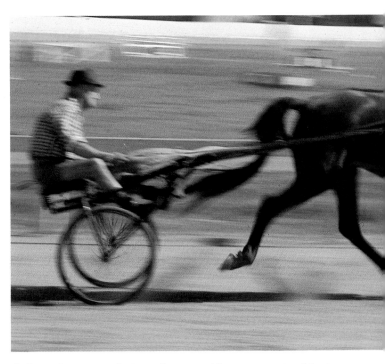

△ At track events a photographer can select a viewpoint, set up the camera, pre-focus on a section of the track and then wait for the competitors to approach before picking them up in the viewfinder to begin a pan. This shot made during a trotting race in Sydney, Australia, was taken when the horse passed directly in front of the camera. Note how its legs and the wheels are still very blurred and just some parts of the image are in fact sharp. This is because only those areas that travel in sympathy with the pan stay in one place relative to the film and are imaged sharply.

Hasselblad, 135 mm, Kodak Ektachrome 64, ¹⁄₆₀ sec, f16

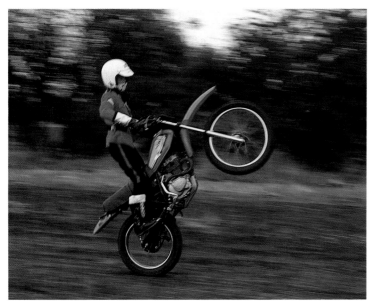

◁ Panning is the technique of following a subject with the camera and releasing the shutter as the subject passes in front of you. The smoothness and fluidity of the pan is a vital factor and it must continue for a short way after the shutter has fired. Sometimes a tripod with a panning head will help when the subject is travelling along a straight path such as a road. For this shot of a bike rider in a display team a telephoto lens was used and this had the effect of increasing the degree of blurring in the background.

Pentax LX, 135 mm, Kodak Ektachrome 200, ¹/₃₀ sec, f22

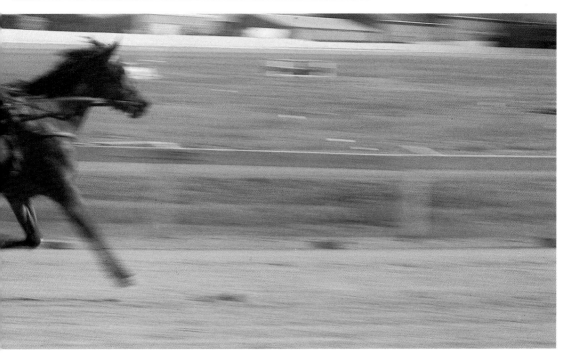

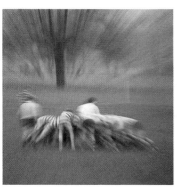

◁ Changing focal length during an exposure with a zoom lens also creates a dramatic blurring that suits some subjects. A tripod is usually necessary and zooming is most effective with a telephoto zoom lens and at shutter speeds of around ¼-¹/₁₅ sec.

Pentax LX, 70-210 mm, Kodak Ektachrome 200, ¹/₁₅ sec, f11

See also:
EXPLOITING TELEPHOTOS pp12–13
THE HIGHPOINT pp124–125
SPORT AND WATER pp128–129

Water sports such as swimming, diving, powerboat racing, sailing, canoeing, and water skiing offer a continuous spectacle to the photographer. Stunning images can be taken during the drama of race and competition, but the nature of the events often makes exhibitions and practice sessions a better bet. There are relatively few climactic moments, so the more relaxed atmosphere away from competition will not lower the quality of your work. You may also be lucky enough to hitch a ride with a participant or use a marshal's boat as a floating camera platform. Shooting from a boat takes a degree of expertise to cope with being tossed about and still keep the camera steady and the horizons straight. You must also be careful that your equipment does not get wet, particularly when photographing saltwater events, as salt is particularly corrosive.

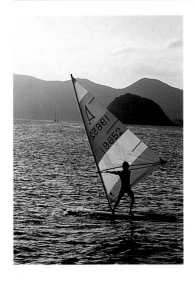

△ Not all sports pictures need to be dramatic action shots – there is plenty of scope to shoot images that set the scene and capture the spirit of the sport. Windsurfing conjures up images of exotic islands in the sun. This image contains the right evocative elements – sun, sparkling seas and bright light – to depict the sport as an exhilarating and pleasurable recreation.

Pentax LX, 85 mm, Kodak Ektachrome 64, 1/250 sec, f8

▽ The stern of the tow launch is the best place to capture images of the plumes of spray thrown up by water skiers. The most effective pictures are produced when the spray is back- or side-lit, especially by a low sun.

Pentax LX, 75-150 mm, Kodak Ektachrome 200, 1/500 sec, f8

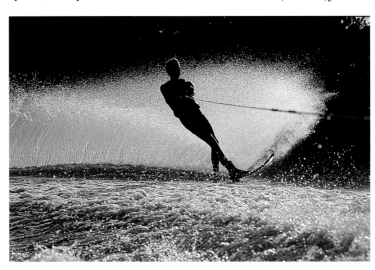

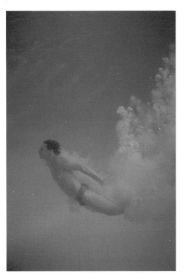

◁ Some international-standard pools have glass ports below the water level which provide a view that allows you to take shots of divers with a difference. This diver was one of a group practising at Crystal Palace, London, for a competition, so there were plenty of chances to get good pictures. Even so, it required split-second timing to capture the exact moment when the diver's body was curved upwards, followed by a trail of streaming bubbles.

Pentax LX, 50 mm, Kodak Ektachrome 200, 1/125 sec, f5.6

▷ Capturing dramatic action shots depends very much on viewpoint. For this shot, taken during a canoe slalom race in the turbulent waters of a Welsh river, a temporary bridge erected over the rushing water proved an excellent vantage point. From there, it was easy to see approaching competitors, anticipate their course, and isolate them from the confusion of tree-lined banks. Combined dull light and high-speed action called for a fast film.

Pentax LX, 50 mm, Kodak Ektachrome 200, 1/250 sec, f5.6

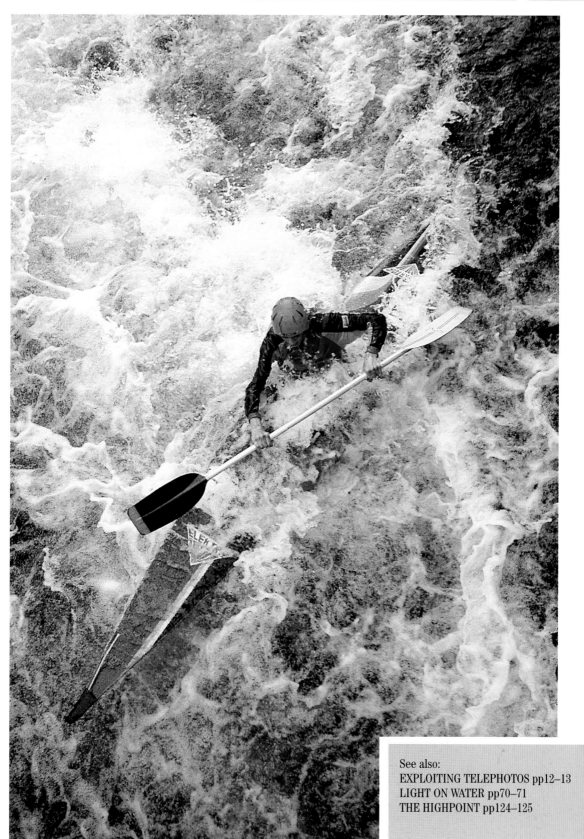

See also:
EXPLOITING TELEPHOTOS pp12–13
LIGHT ON WATER pp70–71
THE HIGHPOINT pp124–125

SPORTING EXPRESSIONS

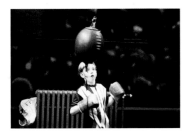

△ When shooting in lowlight it is essential that you focus so that the eyes of your subject are pin-sharp.

▽ The faces of onlookers can be as telling as those of the players themselves.

To master sports photography you need to understand the sport you are covering well. With only brief moments from a match or event to show for your efforts, it has hard to convey the full drama and action that has gone on. It is harder still to show the outcome — who won, and who lost.

Capturing the right facial expressions to match the result is a key to success. In every football match, each player will look angry, dejected, elated and in pain at some point or other. It is choosing the pictures that suit the circumstances that show whether the photographer really appreciates what is going on. A look of victory on a player which happens to be on the losing side will look incongruous after the event.

To get the right look on the players, therefore, you need to have your lens trained on them all the time — making sure that at least your subject's eyes are in focus. When that telling face shows, you must be completely ready to squeeze the trigger.

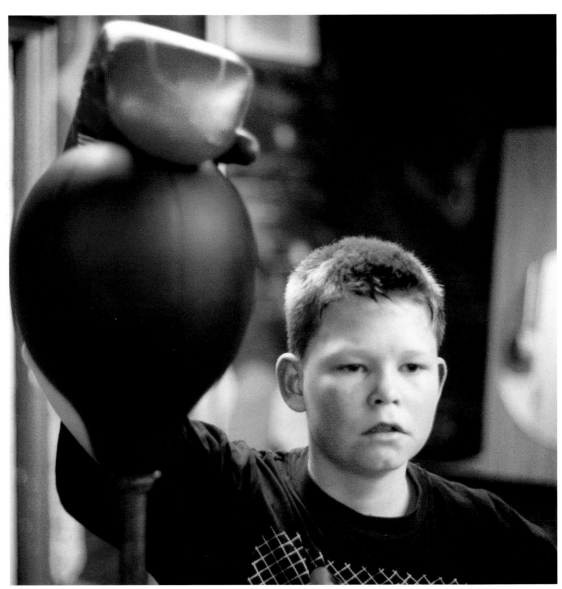

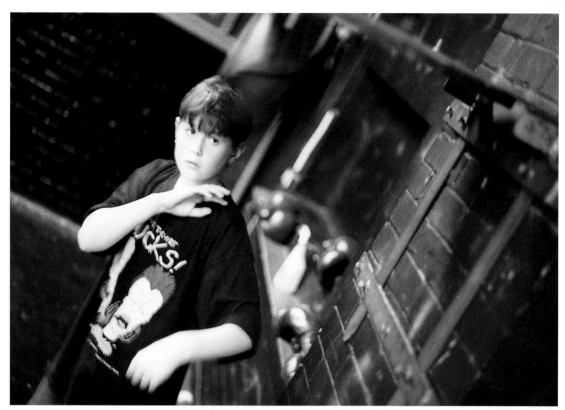

△ The concentration on this young boxer's face shows how seriously he takes his training.

▽ These two shots capture a lighter moment during training. A boy first braces himself to spray himself with water, and then we see his facial reaction.

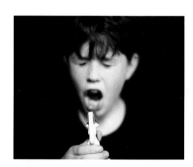

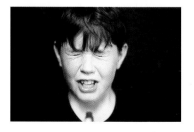

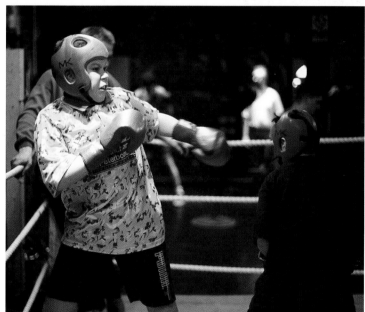

△ The expression on the boy's face shows that he is in danger of losing the round to his smaller opponent.

See also:
EXPLOITING TELEPHOTOS pp12–13
CAPTURING ACTION pp48–49
THE SPORTING LIFE pp122–123
THE HIGHPOINT pp124–125

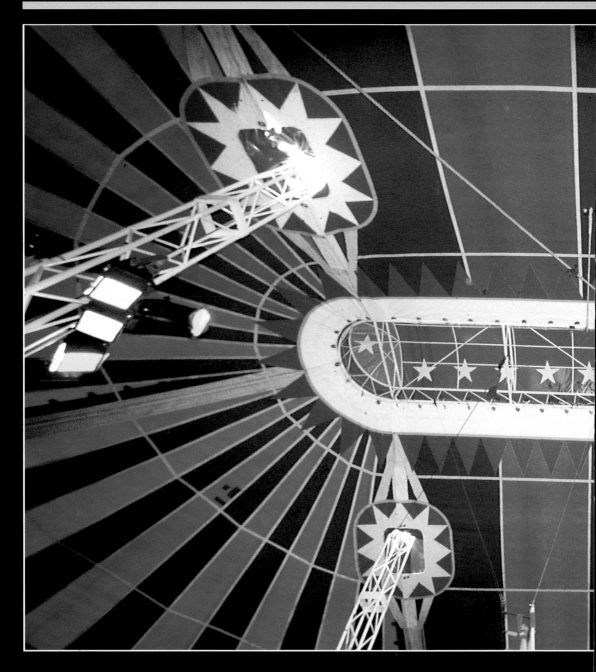

Composition is the organization of picture elements in to a purposeful relationship to enrich the visual experience and simplify the understanding of an image. Attention to lighting quality, viewpoint and subject properties does not assure success. To be more than ordinary, a photograph needs compositional finesse. You can use perspective, line, or pattern to lead the eye and create balance within the frame. Mood and atmosphere may benefit from abstracting the image to a simple form of tone and line. Alternatively, you can exploit the medium with multiple images and montage.

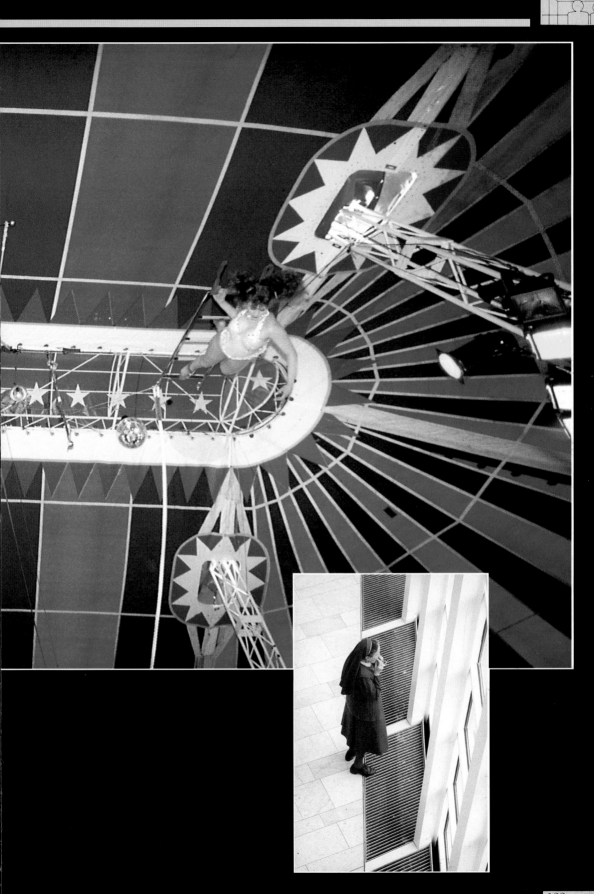

DIAGONAL DESIGNS

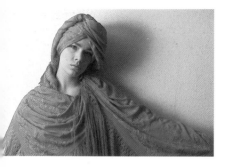

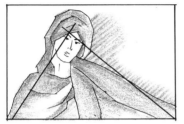

△ The framing in this picture was arranged in order that the model's pose should create three triangles. Intersecting diagonals lead the eye to the face, which is tilted to add emphasis.

Pentax LX, 50 mm, Kodak Ektachrome 200, ¹/₃₀ sec, f11

Most of the time we compose pictures to create a sense of order. They exhibit balance, have a single centre of interest, and make use of horizontal and vertical lines for framing and division. But there are times when a subject needs to be made more dynamic, to portray tension and imbalance. Using the diagonal is one of the simplest ways of achieving this.

Diagonals have to be emphatic. It is no use employing a slightly sloping line in an effort to enliven a classical composition; the line needs to be obvious. The most effective diagonals extend from corner to corner – a division which, of course, creates two triangles. In terms of composition, the triangle is among the strongest of shapes and evokes different emotional responses, depending on its orientation, from one of stability, when the apex is uppermost and the base is horizontal, to tottering imbalance when it is standing on a corner. It is possible to create a diagonal by angling the camera but there are many times when the result is unconvincing, for it is not simply a matter of tilting the camera. Often it is more productive to explore the subject more thoroughly and frame the shot in different ways.

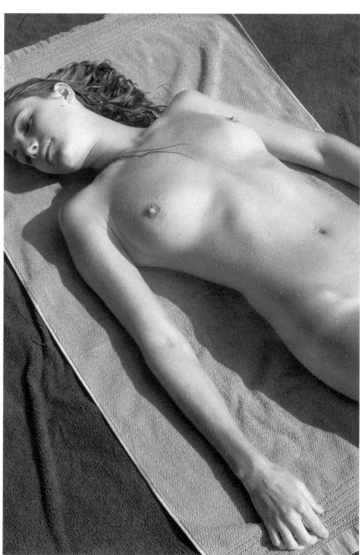

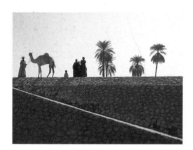

△ Early morning in Egypt. This composition in silhouette has had its graphic element dramatized by the highlighted diagonal. It cuts across and breaks up the dark mass of the wall, leading the eye to the figures.

Pentax LX, 135 mm, Kodak Ektachrome 64, ¹/₂₅₀ sec, f8

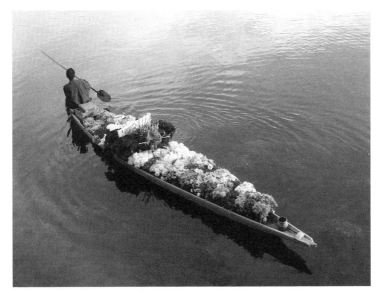

◁ Long, thin subjects such as this flowerseller's canoe on Lake Dal in Kashmir invariably benefit from diagonal framing. Conventionally framed from ground level, the boat would appear as a thin line, but a high viewpoint has isolated it and ensured that the flowers achieve maximum impact.

Pentax LX, 85 mm, Kodak Ektachrome 64, $^1/_{125}$ sec, f11

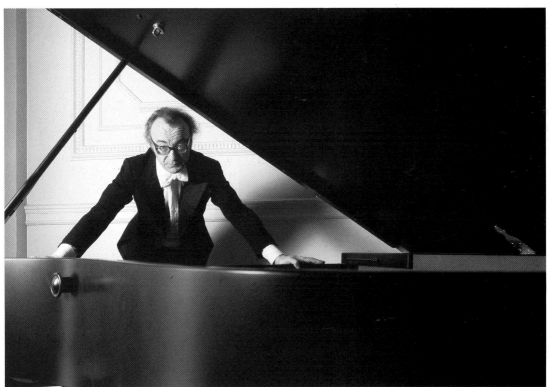

◁ The background tones contrast with the girl's tanned skin, to emphasize the diagonals and create the compositional interest. Had she been framed horizontally or vertically the result would have been much more pedestrian.

Pentax LX, 50 mm, Kodak Ektachrome 64, $^1/_{125}$ sec, f11

△ Pianist Alfred Brendel's portrait was made in a very confined area. But the piano with its diagonals and triangles offered the perfect setting. The strong flash lighting and tonal contrast enhance the effect.

Hasselblad, 80 mm, Kodak Ektachrome 64, $^1/_{125}$ sec, f16

See also:
FRAMING THE SUBJECT pp20–21
SPORT AND WATER pp128–129
FRAMING THE SHOT pp148–149

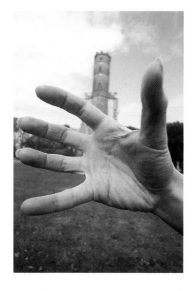

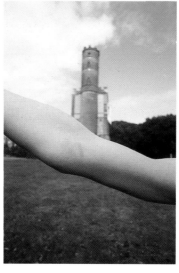

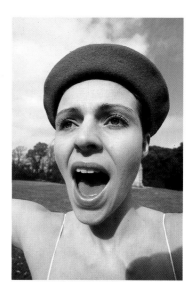

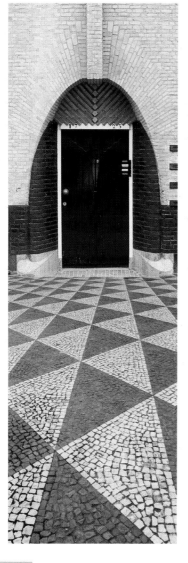

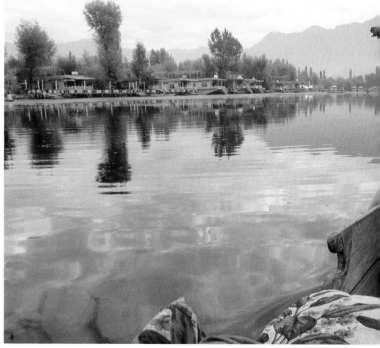

◁ Synthesis, rather than fragmentation, is another technique available to the creative photographer. This scene is created from two entirely separate images, taken at different times in two different places – the mosaic pavement in Rio de Janeiro and the doorway in Amsterdam. Together, they form a satisfying and convincing whole.

Doorway: Pentax LX, 50 mm, Kodak Ektachrome 64, $^1/_{125}$ sec, f8

Pavement: Pentax LX, 28 mm, Kodak Ektachrome 64, $^1/_{125}$ sec, f11

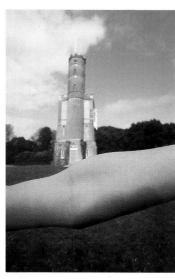 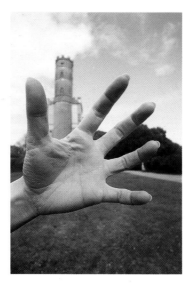

◁ When the subject is appropriate, loosely planned fragmented images can result in some amusing pictures. Here the distortion of the wide lens has been used to good effect by photographing a girl at very close range. The camera was moved between each exposure, describing a slight curve to increase the bow effect.

Pentax LX, 18 mm, Kodak Ektachrome 64, autoexposure, f5.6

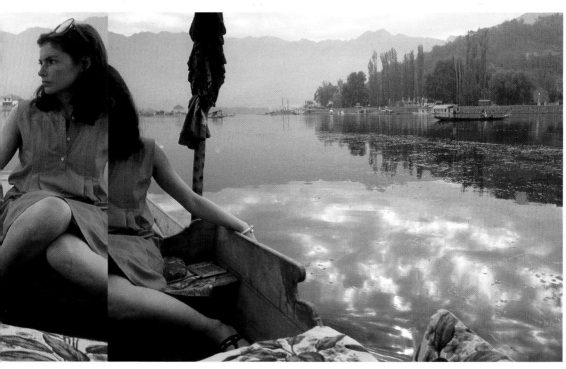

△ One of the commonest uses of joining a number of images together is to create a panoramic view, often to emphasize the expanse and tranquillity of a particular landscape. In many cases, there is no need to be ultra-precise when framing the shots, as long as some degree of overlap is allowed for. Using a wide lens, a broad vista can usually be included in just two shots. This picture was made on Lake Dal, Kashmir.

Pentax LX, 28 mm, Kodak Ektachrome 64, 1/125 sec, f11

SPLITTING IMAGES

Fragmenting an image by means of multiple exposure can be a very fruitful method of making your images transcend the bounds of reality. The technique is very simple, needing no special equipment and no complex image manipulation, but the results can be fascinating, breaking up what would normally appear on a single frame into pieces and giving a unique view of the subject, like a dismantled jigsaw puzzle. The whole image can be composed of many parts – from two to hundreds – formed by moving the camera slightly between exposures. There is no need to use one subject or to keep the movements in the same plane. Different figures can be mixed together, or the same one can be rebuilt. Moving images can be mixed with static ones, backgrounds can be changed, and so can lenses. Even film edges can be trimmed to suit whatever effect the photographer is looking for. No special lighting is needed and no extra space is necessary. It is usually best to work with the camera on a tripod so that each change in viewpoint can be selected with accuracy. Tape markers can be placed at the corners of the viewed area to help align the next exposure in the series.

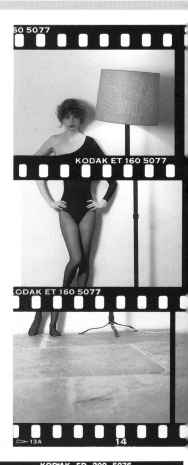

The three examples here were built up in a similar way, using just a camera and a tripod. The backgrounds have been kept plain in order to simplify the result. Complex backgrounds can create a confusing effect when split up and reassembled. Each picture was carefully planned, since one misplaced shot may ruin the whole image. A visualization can be done first in the form of a sketch.

Pentax LX, 100 mm macro, Kodak Ektachrome 160 Tungsten

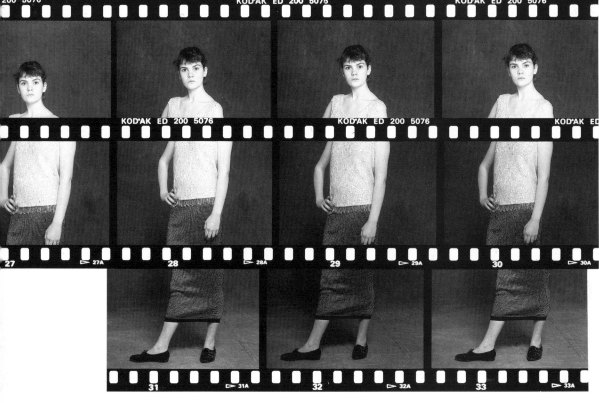

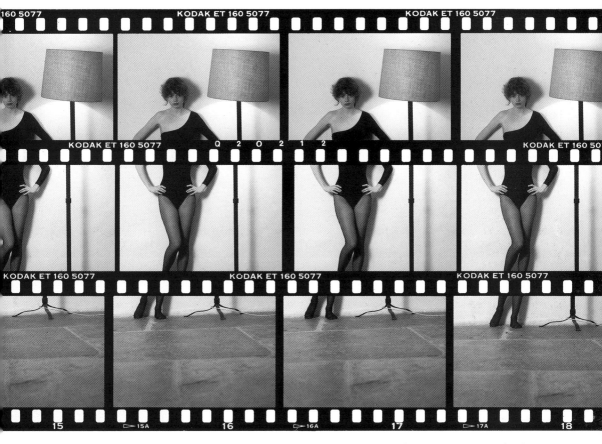

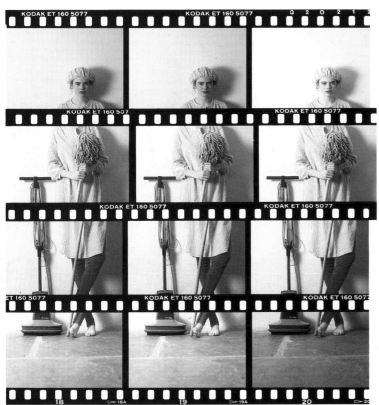

△ The camera was tripod-mounted and, starting from a height of about 2 m (6 ft), it was lowered for a fixed amount for each successive exposure sequence. Tape markers were used to assist in the repositioning of the camera.

See also:
FRAMING THE SUBJECT pp20–21
COMPUTER MANIPULATION pp26–31
STUDY IN MOSAIC pp158–159

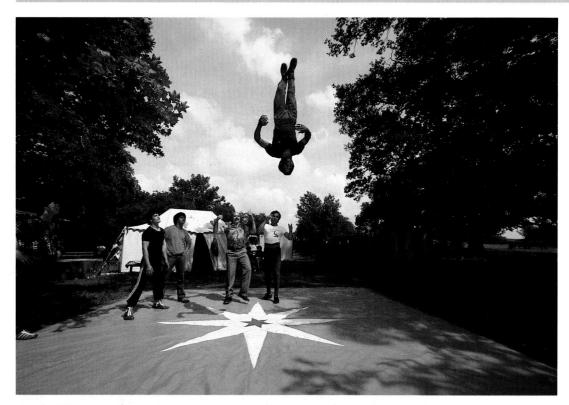

△ These acrobats were practising in a field without the benefit of a trampoline; one mistake in their split-second timing could have been fatal. Anticipating that the climax of their show would be when the acrobat was in mid-air, the picture was taken from ground level, with the acrobat framed dramatically against the sky.

Pentax LX, 28 mm, Kodak Ektachrome 200, $^1/_{1000}$ sec, f8

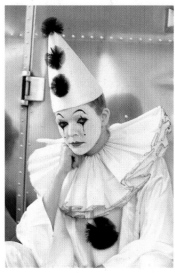

△ This poignant image of a melancholy clown is a portrait of the performer and gives considerable insight into his character. The soft light of open shadow and the muted tones ensure that there are no harsh contrasts to destroy the mood.

Pentax LX, 135 mm, Kodak Ektachrome 200, $^1/_{125}$ sec, f8

A photographer must, every time a subject is framed in the viewfinder, choose a moment in time and select a view from a multitude of possibilities. Even modest success depends on an ability to understand, either intuitively or consciously, what makes an image work. But to achieve excellence, to capture something of the precise moment, requires more.

With all subjects – active or passive – there are certain qualities that do more than just describe their physical state of colour, shape and form. These qualities include time, tension, balance, rhythm, atmosphere and attitude. A photograph that captures these more elusive elements – the taut muscles of an acrobat poised for action, an expression of anguish or loss, the subtlety of light on a landscape, the quiet of evening – is almost assured of capturing the essence of the subject. The most successful sports photography depicts not just the decisive moment and the peaks of the action, but the effort, fatigue, and even failure involved. Sometimes it may not be possible to combine all the desired elements into a single image to describe a subject fully, but it should always be the photographer's ambition to do so. Acute observation, anticipation, quick reflexes, and a sympathy with the subject are as important as technique.

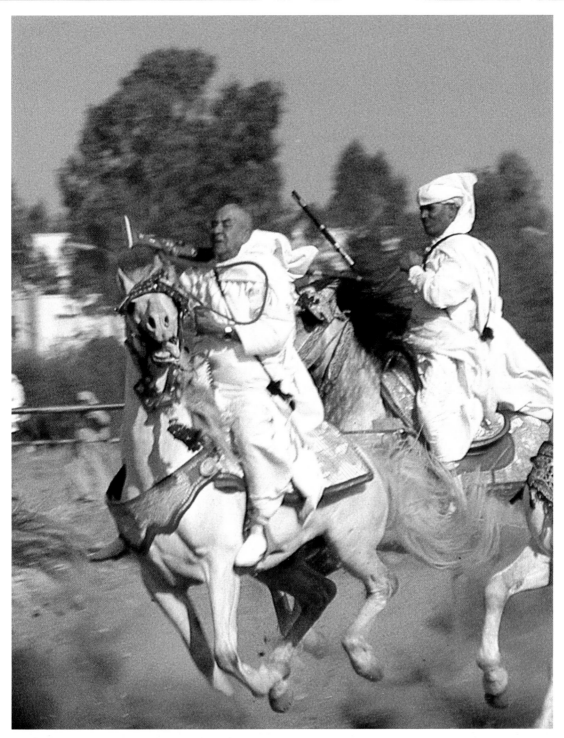

△ Events such as these races and displays of superb horsemanship in Morocco provide a continuous spectacle of skill and excitement. Precise moments that encapsulate the drama taking place amid the heat and frenzy of flying dust were numerous but fleeting, with the result that while many exciting moments were captured, many were lost.

Pentax LX, 200 mm, Kodak Ektachrome 200, $1/1000$ sec, f8

See also:
CLOSE ENCOUNTERS pp34–35
THE HIGHPOINT pp124–125
SPORTING EXPRESSIONS pp130–131

SELECTIVE VIEWS

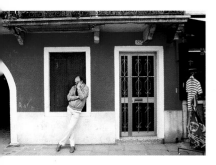

△ A man relaxes against a wall in a Venice street. His pose, the textures of the wall, and the geometric backdrop were all strong elements. The first shot includes them all but there is much distracting detail and more than one focus of interest, so that the eye tends to wander aimlessly around the picture.

▷ The second picture was taken with the same lens a few seconds later. The extraneous detail has been discarded and the image reduced to its key elements: the man and his pose, and the strong lines of the background. An added bonus was his positive reaction to being photographed.

Pentax LX, 28 mm, Kodak Ektachrome 64, 1/60 sec, f8

It is a fault of many photographers that they try to include too much in a picture, overloading it with superfluous detail. But this can be easily avoided by selective cropping. The simplest and most effective methods are to get closer to the subject or to use a longer lens. Moving in close simplifies the picture and makes the essential image area larger and so more significant. All too often, when the final print is viewed, you find that the key part of the image is lost, overshadowed by distracting detail. By cutting it out, you can reveal a much broader and deeper interpretation. The key to creative cropping is to experiment with framing and viewpoint. Ask yourself, for example, if a landscape is improved by using an 85 mm lens rather than a 28 mm. The final image may be distilled to just a fragment of the original view, but this can produce a far stronger visual statement.

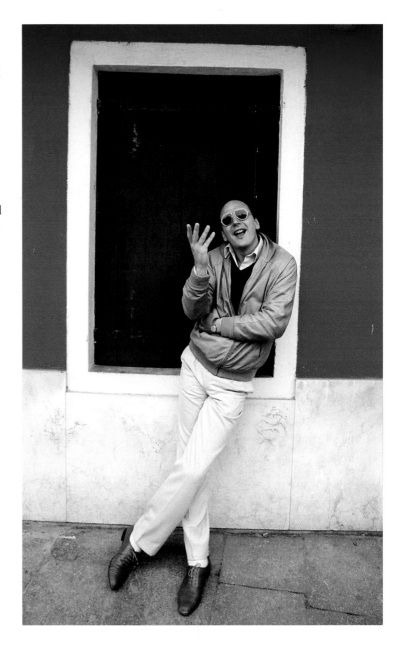

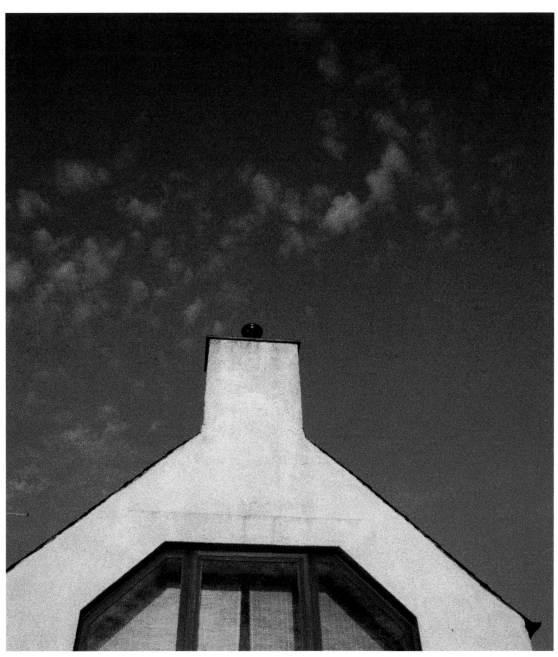

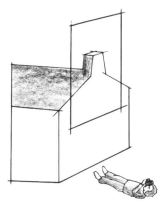

◁ △ An image of stark simplicity that is entirely the product of adopting a very low viewpoint. It is the top of an otherwise undistinguished building which was bathed in sunlight. Concentrating on a limited area creates an almost abstract image that is dramatized by the outlined shape.

Pentax LX, 28 mm, Scotch (3M) 1000, 1/1000 sec, f16

See also:
EXPLOITING TELEPHOTOS pp12–13
FRAMING THE SUBJECT pp20–21
CLOSE ENCOUNTERS pp34–35

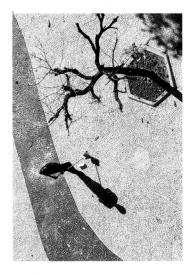

△ An overhead view, taken from a hotel balcony in Rio de Janeiro. The low, directional sunlight has cast strong shadows and highlighted textures. The viewpoint gives the composition a strong sense of design.

Pentax LX, 85 mm, Kodak Ektachrome 64, $^{1}/_{125}$ sec, f8

It is easy for photographers to fall into the trap of always taking pictures from eye- or waist-level. The inevitable result is a stream of images that are predictably dull, unless the subjects are very strong in themselves. Selecting an alternative view is one of our basic options when we want to add life to a composition, and often it is just a matter of departing from the two commonest shooting levels. In everyday life the normal angles of view change horizontally and we are used to seeing everything this way, but pictures taken from worm's eye or bird's eye viewpoints have an unusual quality of their own. Familiar subjects such as people, statues, and buildings become more imposing and acquire a sense of strength, towering above the viewer. Seen from above, these same subjects are diminished in relation to their surroundings and the viewer experiences a sense of domination. But raised or lowered camera positions are not the only alternative angles of view. Looking up from eye-level is perhaps the simplest change of all and often provides a refreshing perspective, especially from close range. The exploration of different viewpoints broadens the photographer's repertoire, and the aim should be for it to become second nature once conventional methods are familiar.

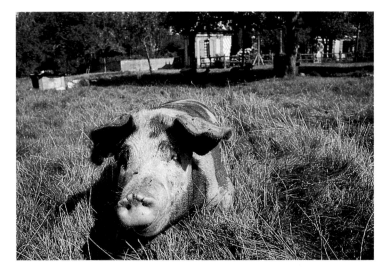

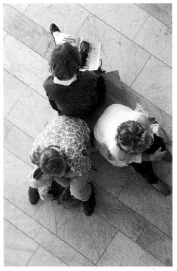

◁ Modern buildings often incorporate well-lit public spaces that can be viewed from a high vantage point such as a walkway or balcony. This picture comments on the planners' indifference to human scale and needs. Odd seats, uncomfortably spaced, enforced an awkward meeting of complete strangers. Naturally, people chose not to linger.

Pentax LX, 85 mm, Kodak Ektachrome 200, $^{1}/_{60}$ sec, f16

△ A piglet's eye view of mother. The pig's snout is an unmistakable feature, and the most important and sensitive part of its anatomy, so that it is natural to give it prominence. This was done by lying on the grass and taking the shot using a wide-angle lens to exaggerate perspective.

Pentax LX, 28 mm, Kodak Ektachrome 200, $^{1}/_{60}$ sec, f16

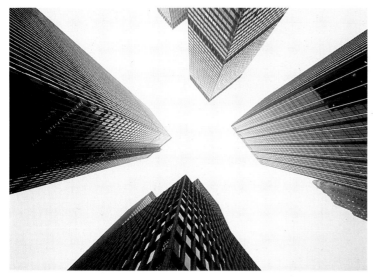

◁ An ultra-wide lens was used to capture this dizzy view of New York skyscrapers seen from the street, an almost compulsory view for the visitor. The perspective distortion characteristic of short-focal-length lenses emphasizes the towering dominance of the buildings. The best vantage point for these shots is usually the middle of the street, so the photographer needs to exercise great caution.

Pentax LX, 18 mm, Kodak Ektachrome 64, $^1/_{250}$ sec, f8

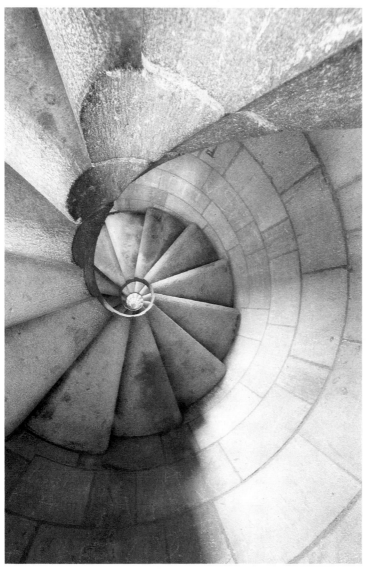

◁ Looking up a spiral stairway in the Catedral de la Sagrada Familia, in Barcelona, revealed a striking pattern and an attention to detail in an aspect of architecture that is often ignored. Searching out the alternative view helps to create good architectural photography and can yield exciting images.

Pentax LX, 28 mm, Kodak Ektachrome 200, $^1/_8$ sec, f22

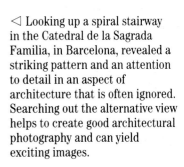

See also:
EXPLOITING WIDE-ANGLES pp10–11
UNUSUAL VIEWPOINTS pp46–47
SHADOW DESIGNS pp80–81
FRAMING THE SHOT pp148–149

LINEAR PERSPECTIVE

Perspective is an illusion that we are accustomed to accepting without question. In photography, a three-dimensional image is convincingly represented on two-dimensional film by making distant parts of the scene appear smaller than the nearer parts of the scene. Linear perspective – where parallel lines such as railway tracks appear to converge as they recede into the distance – is one of the most convincing forms of the visual deception characteristic of perspective.

Unlike draughtsmen and painters, the photographer has no need to learn the skills of shaping perspective – the camera and its lenses see to that – but it is important to know how to use it. The convincing portrayal of three dimensions is, however, a most demanding aspect of photographic composition.

Linear perspective is greatly enhanced by using wide-angle rather than long lenses, as they tend to enlarge foreground detail in relation to distant objects. The result of this is that parallel lines are seen to converge very sharply, so creating a strong illusion of great depth.

You can further dramatize the effect by choosing scenes that contain obvious linear elements, both near and far, and by placing them so that they run obliquely from the edges of the frame. Planes and lines that feature regular patterns in texture, form or tone, will also give an added sense of realism through the device of linear perspective.

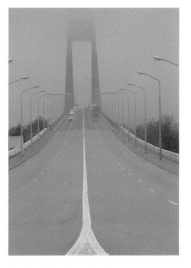

△ In this shot of a French suspension bridge, space and height are emphasized by the diminishing size and converging lines of the lamps. Use of tungsten-balanced film has added to the overall atmosphere.

Pentax LX, 28 mm, Kodak Ektachrome 160 Tungsten, 1/125 sec, f8

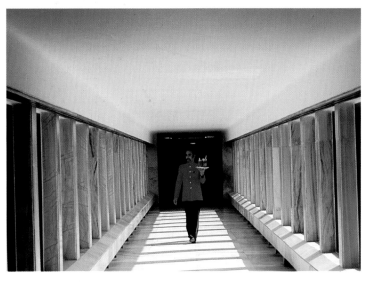

△ An advancing waiter in an Indian hotel hallway makes a simple picture taken on the spur of the moment. The linear elements leading to the one bright splash of colour were such a strong design that framing was entirely intuitive. The strong perspective depth is interrupted but enlivened by the repetitive pattern of sunlight and shade.

Pentax LX, 50 mm, Kodak Ektachrome 64, 1/125 sec, f8

▽ Linear perspective applied to three dimensions, such as the sides of a building, creates three vanishing points at the ends of three sets of converging lines.

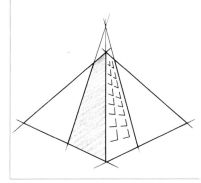

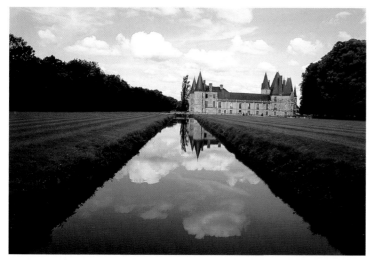

◁ The canal-moat has been dramatized by the effect of linear perspective, which has been heightened by the use of a wide-angle lens. The far château, which sits on the horizon, appears more distant than might be expected and the parallel banks of the canal widen sharply as they approach the foreground. The whole effect has been strengthened by adopting a landscape format.

Pentax LX, 28 mm, Kodak Ektachrome 64, $^1\!/_{125}$ sec, f16

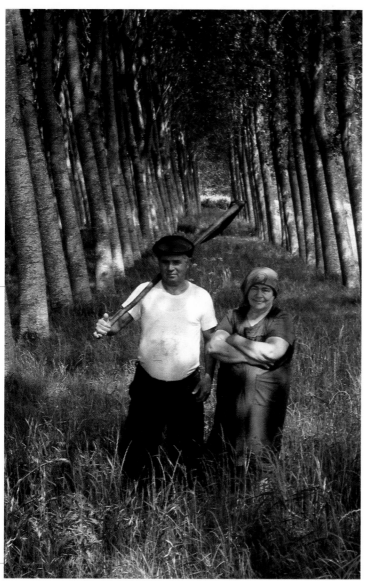

◁ The original intention was to photograph the receding avenue of trees but this couple of Portuguese farmworkers entered stage left and posed, evidently wishing to be part of the picture. In fact their presence has enhanced the feeling of depth by introducing a strong foreground image to contrast with the diminishing line of trees.

Pentax LX, 100 mm, Kodak Ektachrome 200, $^1\!/_{125}$ sec, f16

See also:
EXPLOITING WIDE-ANGLES pp10–11
FRAMING THE SUBJECT pp20–21
IN THE GARDEN pp114–115
DIAGONAL DESIGNS pp134–135

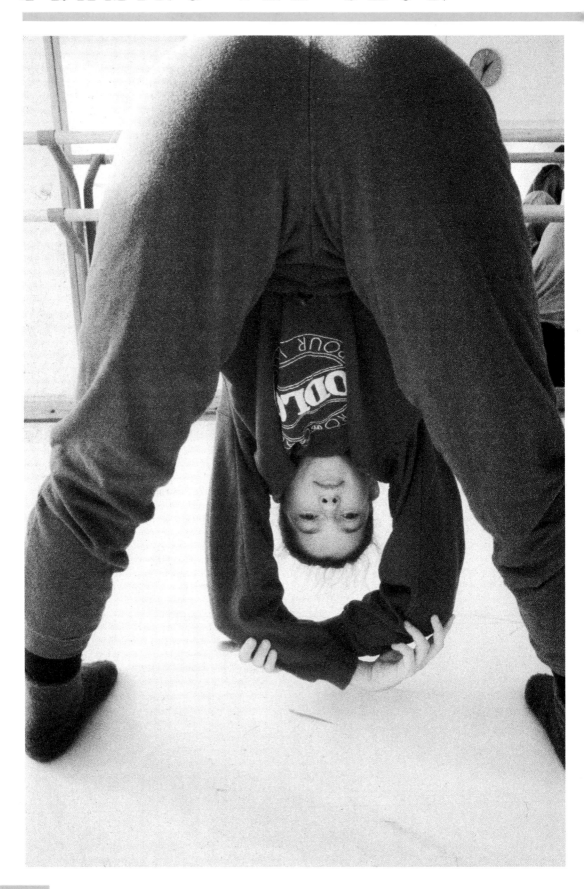

Very often, it is the way in which the photographer imposes the camera's framing on a scene that decides the outcome of the picture. The viewfinder is a cropping device, eliminating some shapes and detail while including others. What is included and how it is arranged within the picture are functions of the camera's format and the way the photographer uses the restrictions and division of its framing. But the borders of the viewfinder need not be the only way of framing a picture. It sometimes happens that part of the scene itself can echo the format, so that a picture within a picture is made. Although this frequently leads to a contrived image division, there are times when it can successfully draw the attention of the viewer to the more subtle qualities of the subject. Often-used examples are building details such as arches, windows, and doorways. They need an extra element – unusual shape, contrast, or colour – to make an arresting shot, but subjects that are not usually seen as a frame, such as hats, shafts of light, or people, may themselves supply impact. But shape is not the only compositional element that can be used as a frame. More subtle framing can be achieved by relying on colour or textural qualities.

▽ The stone archway frames and lends scale to this ancient tower in the Indian seaport of Madras, while the repetition of pointed forms strengthens the impression of soaring height.

Pentax LX, 28 mm shift, Kodak Ektachrome 200, 1/250 sec, f11

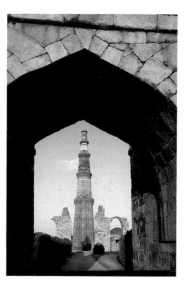

◁ The framing and the use of the shaving mirror accentuate the humour, with a hint of melancholy, characteristic of a clown's personality.

Pentax LX, 100 mm macro, Kodak Ektachrome 200, 1/125 sec, f8

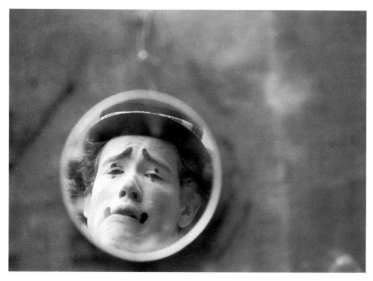

◁ It is not often that the subject provides its own frame, as this dancer has done. Her face clearly shows that she is unaware of the visual humour inherent in her pose, which has been emphasized by the choice of a wide-angle lens.

Pentax LX, 28 mm, Kodak Ektachrome 200, 1/60 sec, f11

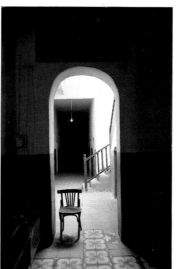

◁ Taken in a passageway in Luxor, Egypt, this picture's impact is entirely due to framing; the image is very simple and is in keeping with the style of dwelling.

Pentax LX, 28 mm shift, Kodak Ektachrome 200, 1/30 sec, f16

See also:
FRAMING THE SUBJECT pp20–21
FRAMING THE FIGURE pp180–181
MIRRORED IMAGES pp188–189

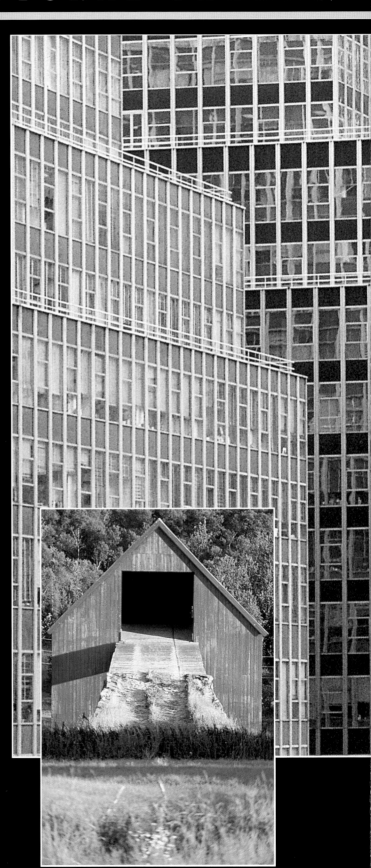

Architectural photography is fascinating and embraces a wide range of subject matter, from a straightforward record of an architect's creation in brick and stone to an abstract interpretation of a building's character. Buildings can be pictured singly or in groups, derelict and disused, or full of charm and vitality. This variety in subject matter, each aspect demanding a different kind of approach, is very challenging and it is easy to lose sight of what is really required of the image: it should display the essential character and form of a building through careful choice of viewpoint and the sympathetic use of light.

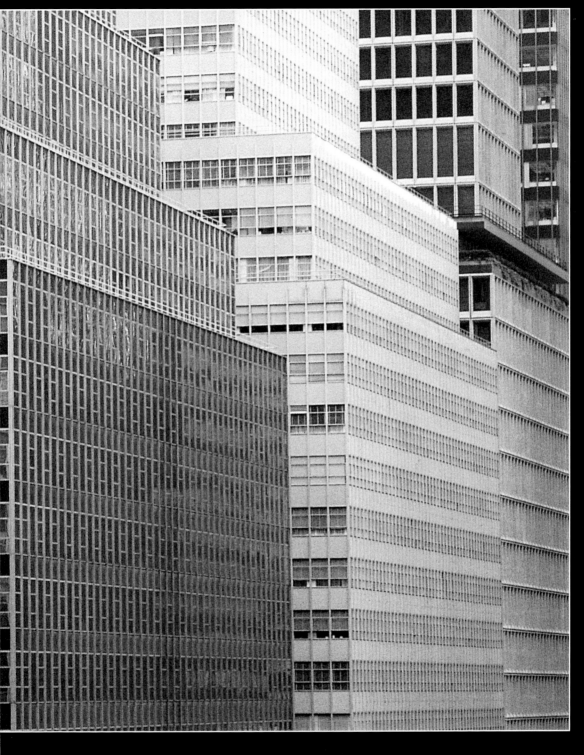

SHAPE AND DETAIL

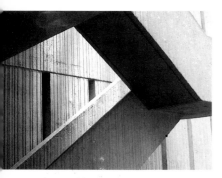

In architecture, interesting shapes and details abound and very often a photograph of a detail is more expressive than one of a whole building. Good architects pay attention to small details as well as to large, specifying furnishings and decor to fit in with their overall plan. It is in this way that individual parts can reflect the whole. To do justice to the architect's intentions, the photographer should select and frame carefully. The detail might show a good deal of the structure as a complete and coherent shape. Such pictures are best made in a sympathetic light. Rough stone or wood surfaces ought to appear textured; polished metal must gleam and reflect, and red brick or honey-coloured stone should have their warmth enriched. These qualities will be enhanced by the lighting conditions in different ways at different times of day, as the angle of the light and its colour change. This is particularly true of interiors, so it is a good idea to tour the building, making a note of where you should be and when.

△ Reinforced concrete is a rather unfriendly material, but it has a certain graphic quality that is brought out in strong, textural light. Colour shots could be subtly altered by using weak colour-correction filters.

Pentax LX, 28 mm shift, Kodak Ektachrome 64, 1/60 sec, f11

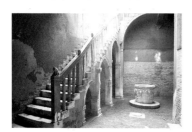

△ A corner of a courtyard in the Palazzo Fortuny in Venice encapsulates perfectly the warm and mellow atmosphere of the whole place.

Pentax LX, 28 mm shift, Kodak Ektachrome 200, 1/250 sec, f11

▷ Dappled light softens the impact of the strong geometric shapes in this picture of a convent school in Meknes, Morocco. The figure at the window brings the photograph to life.

Pentax LX, 28 mm shift, Kodak Ektachrome 64, 1/125 sec, f8

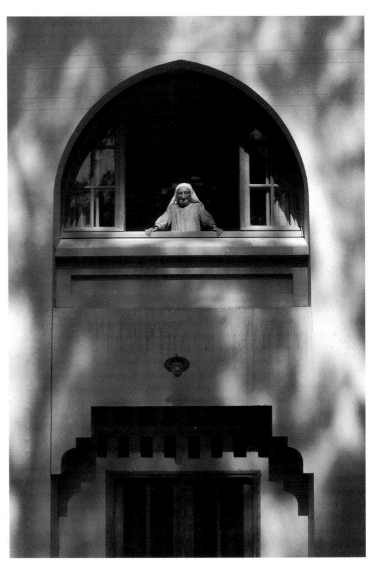

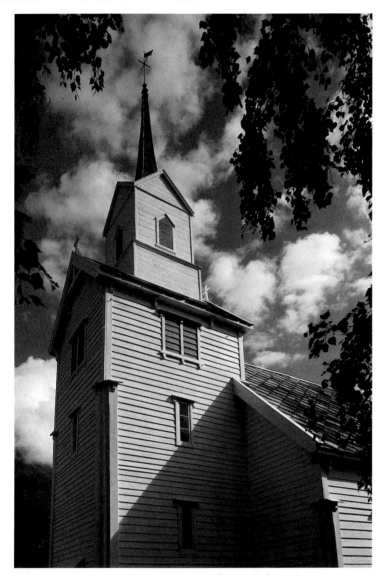

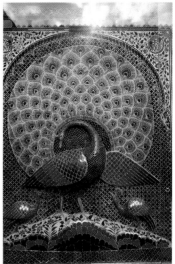

△ Islamic architecture abounds with intricate and detailed mosaic. This peacock motif had to be photographed through glass that was carefully cleaned. The lens was pressed against the surface to cut out reflections.

Pentax LX, 35 mm Kodak Ektachrome 64, 1/250 sec, f8

◁ A Norwegian timber-framed church built largely of rectangles set one upon the other. A low viewpoint was adopted to convey a feeling of power.

Pentax LX, 28 mm shift, Kodak Ektachrome 64, 1/250 sec, f8

◁ This colonnade at St Peters, Rome, is a mass of shapes that lead the eye into the picture. The lone priest is the only clue to the vast scale of the building.

Pentax LX, 28 mm shift, Kodak Ektachrome 200, 1/250 sec, f11

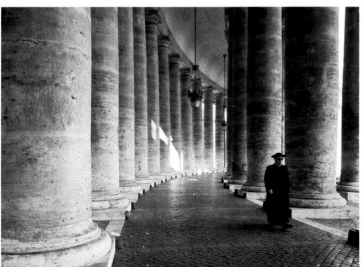

See also:
SPECIAL LENSES pp14–15
FRAMING THE SUBJECT pp20–21
FOUND STILL LIFES pp168–169

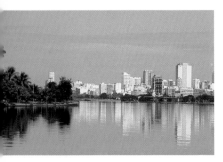

M aking pictures of distant buildings and cityscapes has many parallels with landscape photography. Instead of fields, trees, rocks, and sky, the picture elements are manmade structures such as suburban housing estates, office blocks, and bridges. But the quality of light is still of prime importance. Buildings can completely alter their appearance under changing weather conditions and this will affect the mood of the picture. Skyscrapers, especially when clustered together, as is so often the case in thriving commercial centres, may look forbidding and claustrophobic under heavy cloud and dull light, but in the bright sun of early morning they can be transformed into shimmering towers of reflective glass and steel. At such times the effect of a little sun on the building is often magical, seemingly out of proportion with what is, in fact, a common event.

△ Individual skyscrapers are not usually very beautiful. They need to be grouped for their full effect to be appreciated. These, in Brazil, are also much improved by their lakeside setting.

Pentax LX, 50 mm, Kodak Ektachrome 64, ¹/₅₀₀ sec, f8

Architects often plan their buildings with a 'front', the side which they present to the world, but buildings are also very often designed to look their best in a particular light. The most successful buildings are also sensitively placed within their surroundings, an aspect which can be best brought out by exploring the distant view.

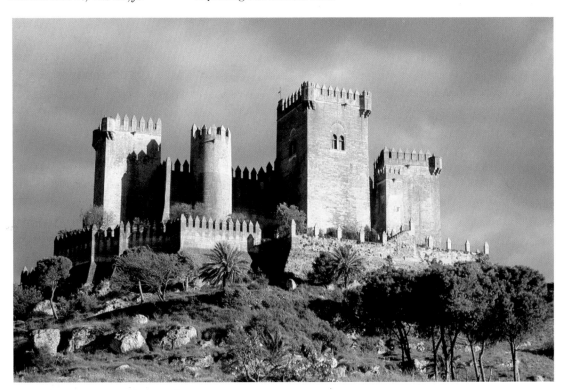

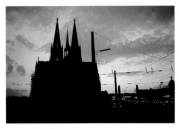

◁ Cologne's ancient cathedral is surrounded by a sea of ugly buildings which, because this picture was taken at dusk, are largely hidden.

Pentax LX, 28 mm shift, Kodak Ektachrome 64, ¹/₃₀ sec, f8

△ A shaft of evening sunlight breaks through summer storm clouds to spotlight this Spanish castle near Almería. As a result, colour, texture, and form are all enhanced in the near-perfect illumination.

Pentax LX, 135 mm, Kodak Ektachrome 64, ¹/₂₅₀ sec, f11

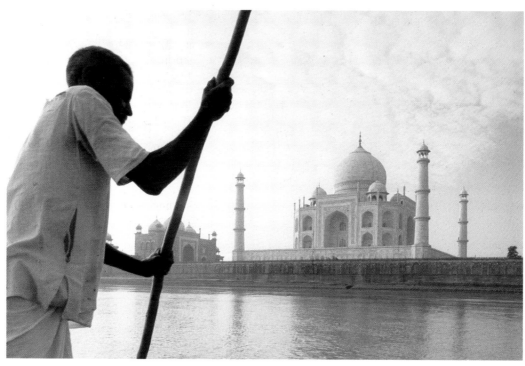

△ An unusual view of the Taj Mahal has been given a sense of scale and depth by framing it against this ferryman. A low viewpoint and the hazy lighting conditions heighten the impression of space.

Pentax LX, 28 mm, Kodak Ektachrome 64, 1/60 sec, f22

▷ The 'Rule of Thirds' is an aid to picture composition and recommends division of the picture area into thirds, creating an imaginary grid of lines with four off-centre intersections. These lines can act as a guide for dividing the picture up – note the Taj Mahal shot – and the intersections indicate balanced locations for the centres of interest within the composition.

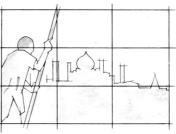

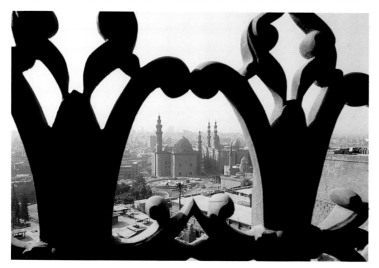

◁ Architectural features sometimes form excellent frames for distant scenes, hinting at detail in similar buildings.

Pentax LX, 28 mm, Kodak Ektachrome 64, 1/125 sec, f22

See also:
EXPLOITING TELEPHOTOS pp12–13
LANDSCAPES pp60–75
FRAMING THE SHOT pp148–149
MANMADE PATTERN pp156–157

MANMADE PATTERN

The manmade world reflects humankind's natural desire to see order in the environment and the perceptive photographer can often detect an underlying pattern, revealing it for the rest of us. Photographs of patterns alone can be intriguing, though they are rarely more than a design in themselves. However, pattern used as a compositional element is frequently a source of strength in an image. In black and white photography, patterns tend to be abstract because they usually obscure and confuse depth. Texture's role, which may appear to be similar, is in fact quite different, because it helps give the picture a sense of depth. Coloured patterns evoke an emotional response – we see bright, warm colours, for example, as being closer than dark, cool ones. In our urban environments patterns take many forms; some can be appreciated close-to, others only from a distance. They are always worth seeking out to add a further dimension to your cityscapes.

▽ There are many occasions, as with this exposed interior of a New York tenement, when a pattern is made up of organized but irregular elements. The broken plaster, open stairs, and peeling paint constitute intimate, telling detail.

Pentax LX, 135 mm, Kodak Ektachrome 200, 1/250 sec, f8

▷ The classic helicopter view of Manhattan illustrates human pattern-making on a grand scale. Flying presents useful opportunities to the photographer but you have to ask which side of the aircraft it is best to shoot from before boarding.

Pentax LX, 28 mm, Kodak Ektachrome 64, 1/500 sec, f6.3

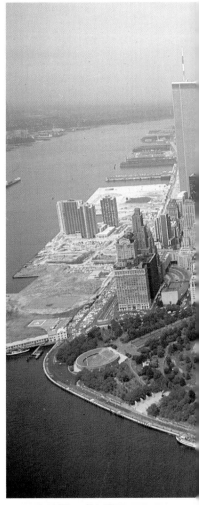

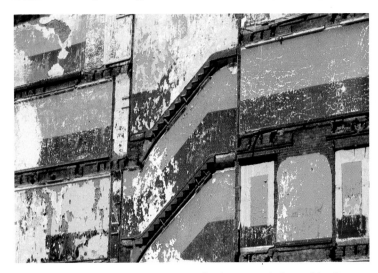

▷ A pattern is formed by the decaying spars of a pier silhouetted against a setting sun. The poignant atmosphere of this photograph derives from the slow but inevitable breakdown and collapse of a formerly ordered structure.

Pentax LX, 50 mm, Kodak Ektachrome 64, 1/125 sec, f8

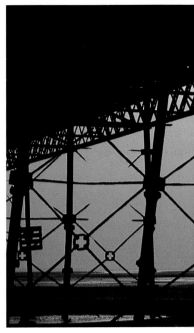

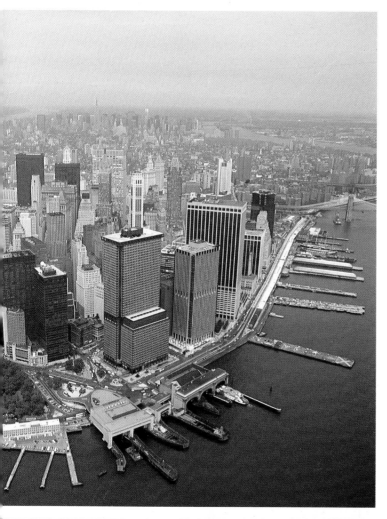

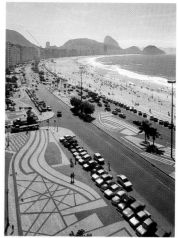

△ High viewpoints in cities frequently reveal pattern that is hard to see at ground level. These exotic pavements in Rio de Janeiro, designed by Robert Burle Marx, form part of an overall order when seen from the air.

Pentax LX, 28 mm, Kodak Ektachrome 64, ¹/₅₀₀ sec, f16

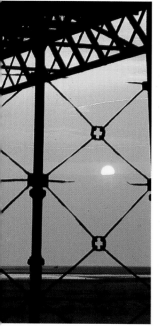

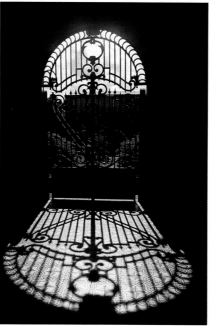

◁ Wrought iron work presents some of the most beautiful and intricate of manmade patterns. Often it is based on natural motifs. Here it is only the shadow that reveals the complete design.

Pentax LX, 28 mm, Kodak Ektachrome 64, ¹/₂₅₀ sec, f16

See also:
EXPLOITING WIDE-ANGLES pp10–11
FRAMING THE SUBJECT pp20–21
SHAPE & DETAIL pp152–153
THE DISTANT VIEW pp154–155

STUDY IN MOSAIC

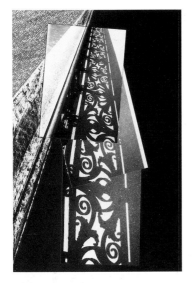

T aking interesting photographs of buildings is frequently made more difficult by the surroundings – for example, interesting buildings are often sandwiched between high-rise office blocks. It is difficult to exclude unwanted or distracting surroundings from conventional shots, but a novel approach can pay dividends and produce far more interesting pictures.

One approach is to marry up separate shots of selected areas, keeping verticals upright, so that the resulting image is a realistic view of the building. Alternatively, a more interpretative approach can be adopted, creating a mosaic that presents an impression of the building and emphasizes its impact on the senses. For this type of approach it is important to take time to walk round the building first, searching out interesting viewpoints and gaining a sense of the architect's design. The photographs may be taken from one position, or you can change viewpoint and/or lenses. Try to start out with a firm idea of the result you want, but be prepared to shoot plenty of film to ensure that you have lots of material to work from.

△ This image consists of a combination of photographs and crayon. The photographs were taken in Versailles, near Paris and show the intriguing shadows thrown by ornate railings that border a pathway.

Olympus Pen-F, Fujicolor HR 100, autoexposure (Photo: Auberon Hedgecoe)

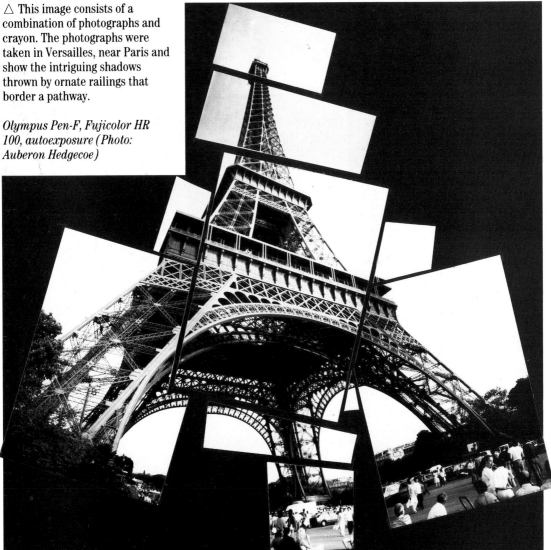

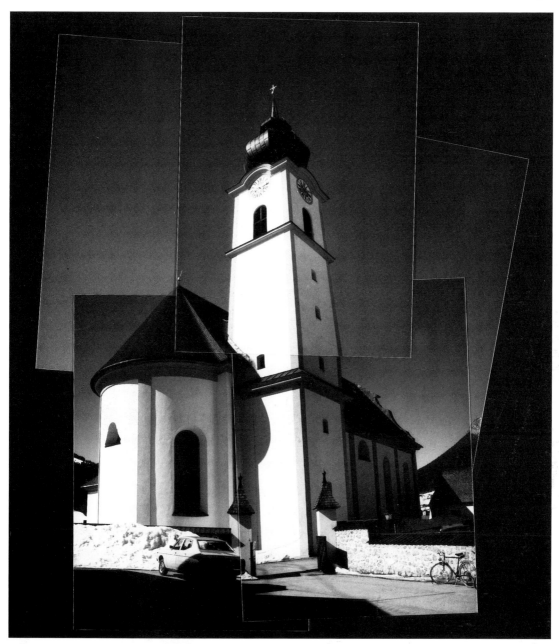

◁ This picture of the Eiffel Tower was made from over a dozen separate enprints, taken on a simple automatic camera. Despite the limitations of the equipment, the final image presents a radically different view from those taken by other visitors that day.

Olympus Pen-F, Fujicolor HR 100, autoexposure (Photo: Auberon Hedgecoe)

△ Few buildings conform to the rigid rectangular shapes of modern office blocks. Reflecting this fact, the mosaic here creates an irregular outline that furthermore refuses to conform to the rigid boundary of a single print. The varying print density enhances the effect of the mosaic.

Olympus Pen-F, Fujicolour HR 100, autoexposure (Photo: Auberon Hedgecoe)

See also:
FRAMING THE SUBJECT pp20–21
INSTANT IMAGES pp56–57*
SPLITTING IMAGES pp136–139

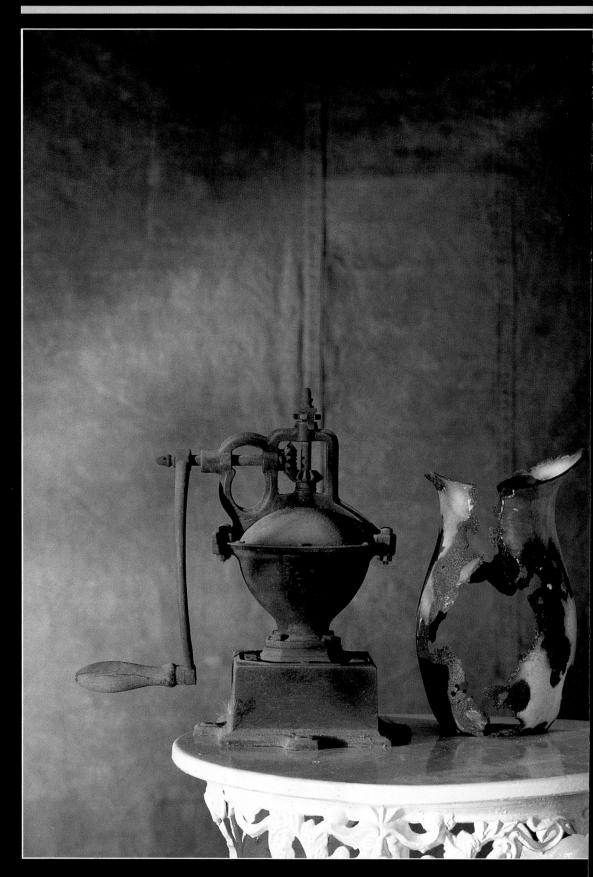

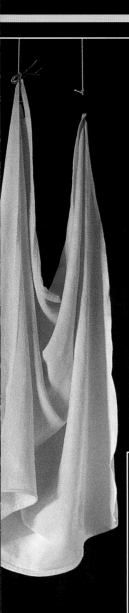

In the confines of a studio, the photographer has full control over the picture and success is born of a creative mind, careful application of photographic techniques and, above all, a clear idea of what the final image is to be, at whom it is aimed, and what it has to say. Failure is entirely the photographer's fault. This is a harsh reality, but it does benefit the photographer by highlighting his or her shortcomings. The studio is, therefore, an ideal learning environment, not only for acquiring new skills – and in the studio you have to be something of a Jack of all trades – but for exploiting creative catalysts and developing a personal photographic style that is uniquely your own.

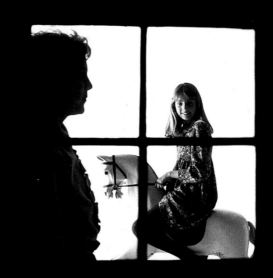

THE STILL LIFE

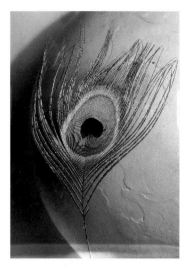

Lighting is one of the most important factors in still-life photography. Whether it is good or bad, lighting has a profound effect on the realism and mood of the picture, so it is very important to get it right. One of the commonest faults is to swamp a still life in bright light from a bank of lamps, thereby spoiling any hope of revealing form, texture and tone. Simplicity, both in arranging the composition and in deciding on the lighting required, is the key to success here.

In nature, illumination comes from one source – the sun, helped by reflected light from the surroundings. Its direction is usually from above or from one side, and only one set of shadows is cast. Imitating natural light and using one main light source is a good way to start. Having arranged your composition, decide on lighting that will be in keeping with the image. Hard, directional light from an oblique angle will reveal detail and texture, highlight smooth surfaces, and suggest energy and strength, but you must be careful that shadows do not confuse the effect. Diffused illumination from a large source is ideal for displaying form, emphasizing tone, and portraying a softer atmosphere. It is particularly suitable when you are using set-ups that contain a large number of items.

△ Only two lights were used for this picture. The white ball was placed on a white card and lit with soft, directional light from a large floodlight. A sheet of glass supported the feather above the ball and a spotlight was used to give a hard light that skimmed the surface to reveal texture and lighten tone. A large white reflector was placed over the whole set-up to provide soft fill-in light.

Pentax 6×7, 80 mm, Kodak Ektachrome 160 Tungsten, 1 sec, f45, one tungsten flood and one tungsten spot.

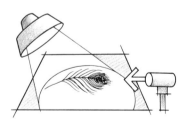

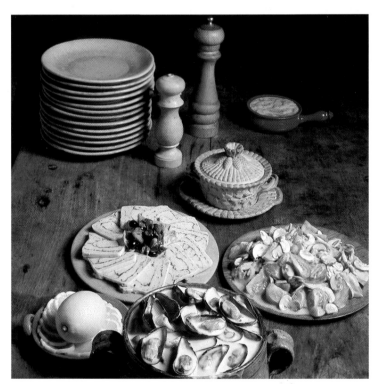

▷ Part of the brief for this shot was to evoke a rich mood. A suitable approach is to use a light soft enough to show a full range of tones, but hard enough to reveal detail and texture. A studio flash, relected off a silver umbrella, produced the diffuse light. The light was positioned close to the still life to act as a large source and shaded to give a ⅔ stop fall-off in brightness towards the back of the shot.

Hasselblad, 60 mm, Kodak Ektachrome 64, 1/250 sec, f16

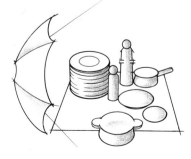

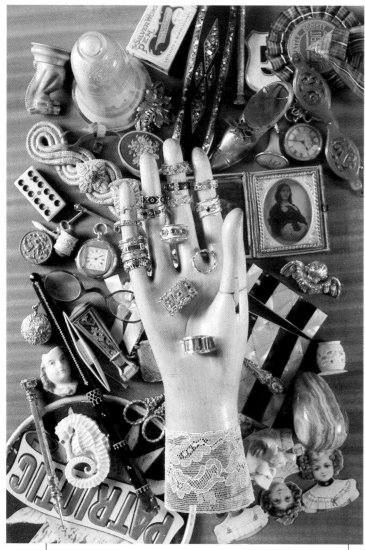

◁ Victorian rings were the main subject of this picture. The memorabilia were added to strengthen the atmosphere. The resulting complex jumble of shapes suggested an overall soft light as the best illumination. In this picture the objects were placed in front of a large north-facing window. White reflectors were placed opposite the window to lighten shadow areas. The hand is supported above the other items so that these could be recorded slightly defocused, giving additional contrast.

Linhof 6×7, 90 mm, Kodak Ektachrome 64, ½ sec, f22

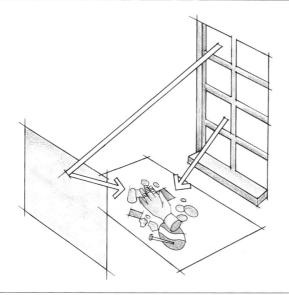

See also:
SOFT AND HARD LIGHT pp18–19
BUILDING A STILL LIFE pp164–165
FOOD, GLORIOUS FOOD pp170–171

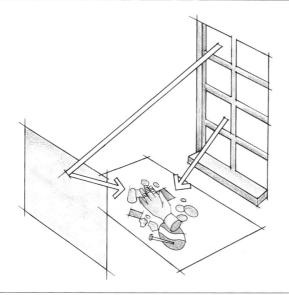

BUILDING A STILL LIFE

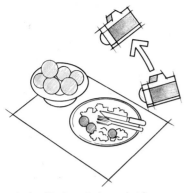

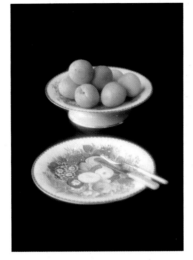

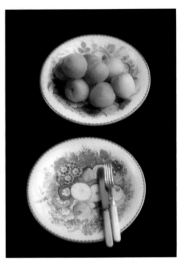

△ ▷ Choice of viewpoint is crucial to the final result. From certain angles, shape and form can be quite distorted, so care has to be taken that their appearance does not detract from the arrangement. Also, make sure that outlines are not confused and that the viewpoint selected places the emphasis correctly. The only difference between these two pictures is a change in camera position from 45° to the subject plane to nearly overhead, as illustrated in the diagram.

Pentax LX, 100 mm macro, Kodak Ektachrome 64, ¼ sec, f22

Still life is one branch of photography where the results are entirely the product of the photographer's skill. The choice of subject, lighting, viewpoint, and arrangement is solely the photographer's responsibility, so that still life is an ideal subject area in which to develop photographic expertise.

Constructing a successful still life depends on having a clear vision of the idea or theme that is to be photographed, for starting out without a clear conception of your picture is usually fruitless. A still life does not have to be complex – frequently it is a simple arrangement given a sympathetic treatment that leads to the most striking and lasting images.

The key to a good picture is to build it up slowly, step by step, checking the effect of each additional element's contribution through the viewfinder, and paying attention to lighting, texture, tone, form and mood. Sometimes, one object, carefully positioned within a straightforward setting, makes a complete picture, but try a group of old clocks or kitchen tools – anything, in fact, that is easily accessible – for pleasing results.

▷ Although this arrangement of peaches might appear to be very simple it did take some time to complete. All blemishes had to be carefully hidden, and the colour and shape of each fruit had to be balanced with the others and positioned so that the eye is lead straight into the composition.

Pentax LX, 100 mm macro, Kodak Ektachrome 64, ¹/₁₅ sec, f22

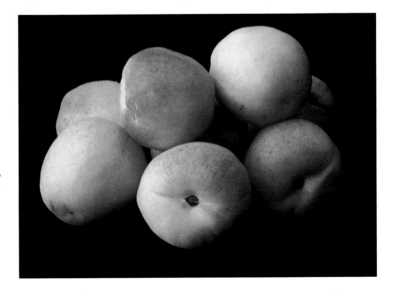

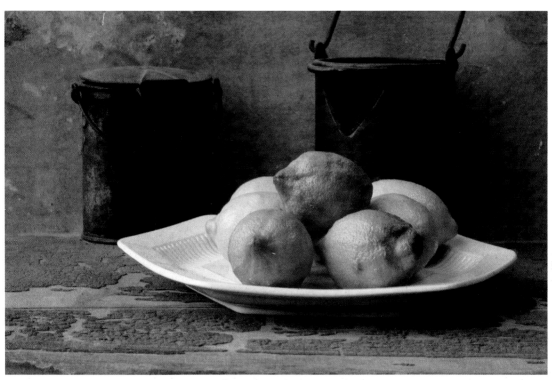

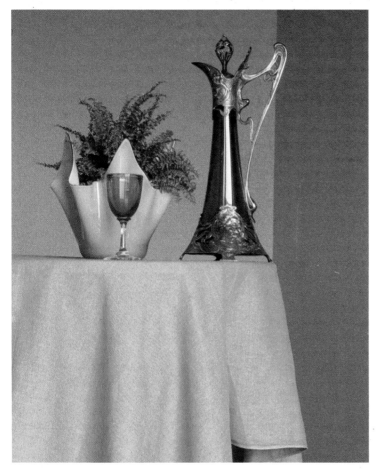

△ It is not only perfect specimens which make a successful still life. Strangely formed or blemished examples sometimes provide intriguing pictures. Under-ripe lemons with a greenish tinge were in keeping with the sombre mood created by the background. The lemons' colour also contrasts strongly with that of the plate.

Pentax LX, 100 mm macro, Kodak Ektachrome 64, ¼ sec, f22

◁ The original intention was to concentrate on the objects on the table, but it was clear that the tablecloth and the walls made an attractive, contrasting setting.

Pentax LX, 28 mm shift, Scotch (3M) 100, ⅓₀ sec, f16

See also:
SPECIAL LENSES pp14–15
NATURAL REPETITION pp112–113
THE STILL LIFE pp162–163
FOOD, GLORIOUS FOOD pp170–171

STUDIO SILHOUETTES

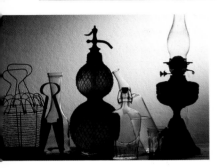

△ Straightforward still-life silhouettes can be made with no more equipment than a sheet of white paper, an Anglepoise lamp, a tripod, and a camera.

Pentax LX, 100 mm macro, Kodak Ektachrome 160 Tungsten, 1/125 sec, f8

A silhouette is an image in which a dark shape is set against a bright background. The lighting is arranged so that detail is suppressed in the main subject and the shape is emphasized. Creating a silhouette in the studio is one of the easiest of photographs to set up; the only problem is in providing a sufficiently large area of bright and evenly lit background.

The best subjects for the silhouette treatment are ones with easily recognizable shapes, such as faces and figures, tools and implements, and animals and plants. To prevent specular reflections ruining the effect, it is sometimes possible to coat shiny objects with a dulling spray or with water-soluble black poster paint. Some translucent objects – bottles are the obvious example – also make intriguing silhouettes.

Having chosen the subjects, it is a matter of arranging them so that their identity is not confused by presenting an ambiguous and cluttered outline. The background need be nothing more elaborate than an indoor windowsill or a sheet of white paper. As with any still-life, working with a tripod frees the photographer to fine-tune the set-up and check the results through the viewfinder, before committing the image to film.

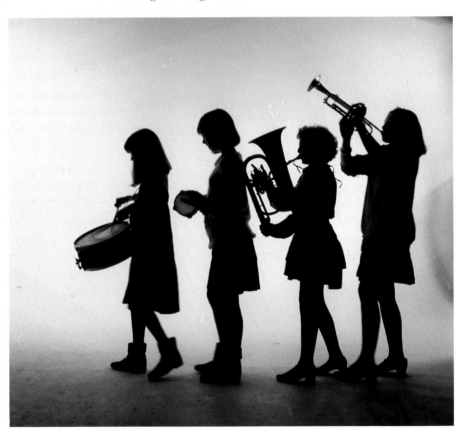

△ You need a good deal of studio space for a silhouette like this one. Outdoors, a wall or hill top are good alternatives so long as the background is at least three stops brighter than the subjects. A strong sense of movement is conveyed but the posing was exact, clearly defining the outlines.

Pentax LX, 50 mm, Kodak Ektachrome 160 Tungsten, 1/125 sec, f8

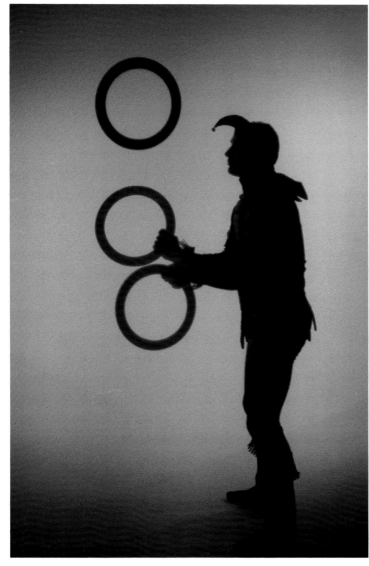

◁ It's fun to add colour to silhouettes. This shot was done by putting a ×3 red filter over the lens, but it can be done by covering the lights with colour gels or bulbs and by using coloured background paper.

Pentax LX, 50 mm, Kodak Ektachrome 160 Tungsten, 1/30 sec, f8

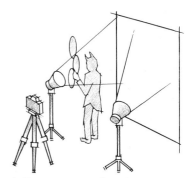

△ To create a good, even backdrop for silhouettes it is best to use plain, white background paper and light it from each side with tungsten floods or studio flash fitted with a standard or flood reflector. Place the lights about 2 m (6 ft) from the background and check for evenness of illumination with a meter – it should be 3 or 4 stops brighter than the subject.

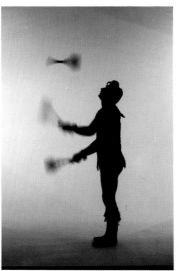

◁ An alternative approach to moving silhouettes is to use a slow shutter speed to create blur. The same lighting set-up was used here as for the children's band but with them dimmed; too bright a background might burn out the image of the clubs.

Pentax LX, 50 mm, Kodak Ektachrome 160 Tungsten, 1/30 sec, f16

See also:
CREATIVE EXPOSURE pp16–17
OUTDOOR SILHOUETTES pp86–87
A SENSE OF SPEED pp126–127

FOUND STILL LIFES

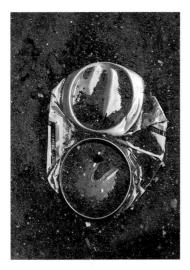

A still life is an arrangement of inanimate objects photographed as an image in their own right. Usually a still life is thought of as being constructed by the photographer who, through skilfully handling light, composition, and materials, creates a pleasing image. But this need not be the only approach, for you can photograph found objects that form an attractive arrangement themselves, without your intervention as the designer of the scene.

The skill in making fine still-life pictures from chanced-upon objects lies in selecting a small but significant area that makes a complete composition. Often, familiar everyday items are the substance of such photographs but they are seen with a fresh view that may highlight shape, design, function, spatial texture, tone, colour or relationships. Although it takes an observant eye and an imaginative mind to come up with strong pictures, the beauty of making still lifes from found objects is that it can be done with the simplest of cameras.

△ This flattened can's stark tones and sculptural qualities suggest eyes, a mask, or ominous reflective sunglasses.

Pentax LX, 50 mm, Kodak Ektachrome 64, ¹/₁₂₅ sec, f11

▽ Windows facing the street are sometimes used to display prized possessions such as this classical figure. The figure may not have merited a photograph in its own right, but the additional interest in the picture comes from the presence of the toy robot opposite it, perhaps placed on the sill by a child in imitation of his parents' pride.

Pentax LX, 50 mm, Kodak Ektachrome 64, autoexposure, f8

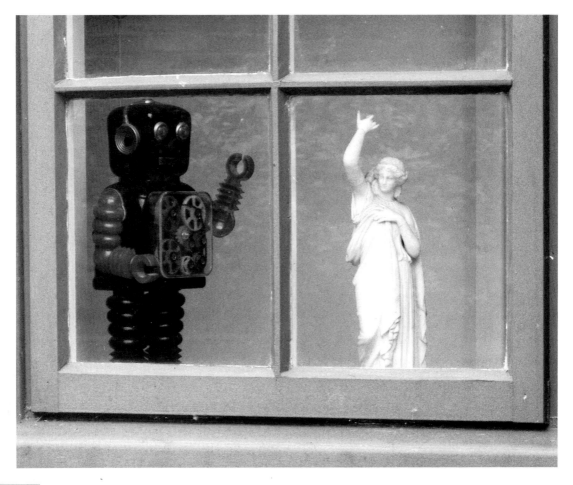

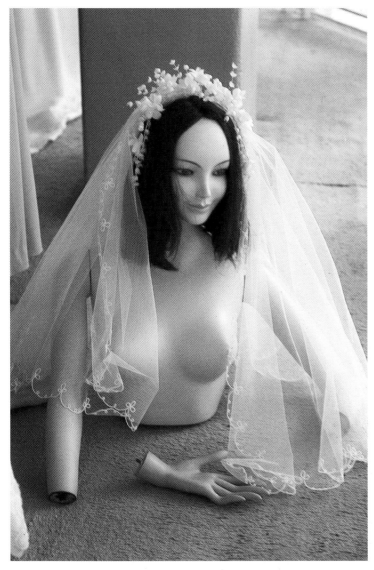

◁ The expression of this mannequin, pictured in a state of undress and dismemberment, conveys utter obliviousness of its state, which gives the picture a surrealistic quality. As the photographer has little or no control over light and arrangement in found still lifes, the successful image often depends on the ideas and associations that it gives rise to.

Pentax LX, 50 mm, Kodak Ektachrome 64, 1/125 sec, f11

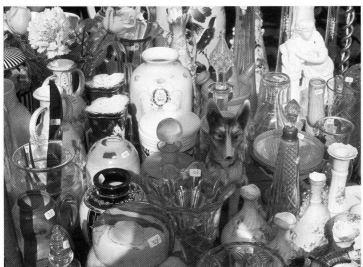

◁ Shop windows, especially those of antique shops, provide a never-ending stream of picture material. Here, an impression of a vast quantity of objects has been created by concentrating on a small part of the crowded display.

Pentax LX, 35 mm, Kodak Ektachrome 64, 1/250 sec, f8

See also:
SOFT AND HARD LIGHT pp18–19
FRAMING THE SUBJECT pp20–21
NATURAL REPETITION pp112–113

FOOD, GLORIOUS FOOD

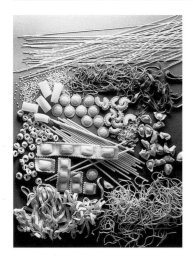

One of the basic aims of still-life photography is to make the subject appear real — so viewers of the picture are given the impression that they could reach out and touch it, feeling texture and shape. Good food photography goes one step further, producing an image that makes the viewer salivate, or even smell the aroma of the produce.

Pictures of complete meals that appear in recipe books are one of the hardest subjects to tackle in photography. In fact, the dishes are often cooked specially to look good in front of the camera — and not for their taste.

Simpler subjects to tackle are arrangements of the raw ingredients — a bowl of fruit, produce from the garden, or even dried beans from a packet. Even so, microscopic attention to detail is needed to arrange such everyday items in a way that looks attractive on film.

As you are close to the subject, and realism is essential, the smallest apertures available on your lens must usually be used.

△ Shot lying simply on a sheet of black paper, this shot of the incredible variety of pasta available from a local store becomes a collage of shape and pattern, rather than just a straight photograph of food.

▷ A simple trick used in food photography is to accessorise a shot of cooked food with the raw ingredients that were used in it. A photograph of a steaming fruit pie, for instance, will be shown next to a bowl of succulent apples. Here, the modest dish of a fried egg is made to look the more appealing because of the presence of a carefully-arranged basket of the raw ingredient.

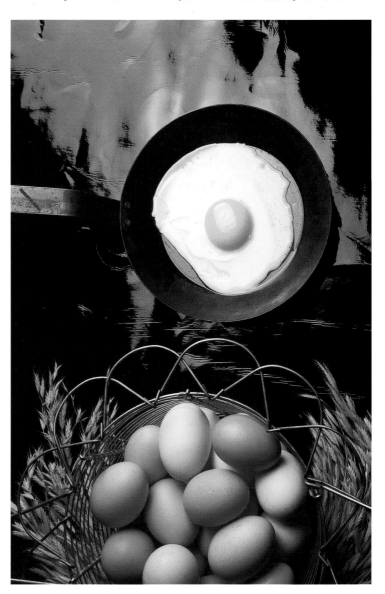

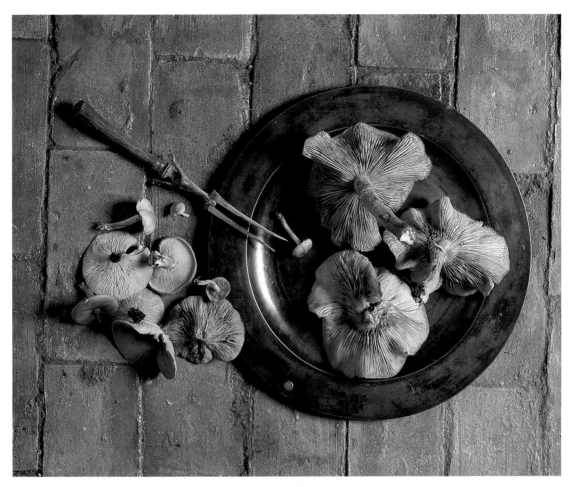

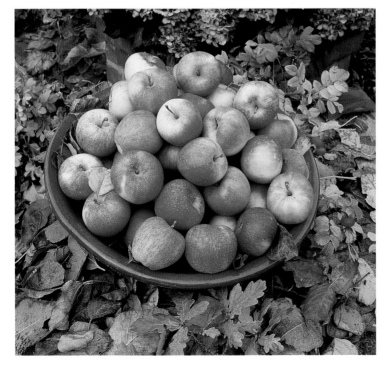

△ The intricate form of these mushrooms makes an ideal photographic subject, but it is their careful arrangement with two simple props and a sympathetically-coloured background that makes the shot.

◁ Even, diffuse lighting and a background of garden foliage have helped accentuate the colour and uniformity of this bowl of apples.

See also:
SOFT AND HARD LIGHT pp18–19
NATURAL REPETITION pp112–113
THE STILL LIFE pp162–163
BUILDING A STILL LIFE pp164–165

THE HUMAN FORM

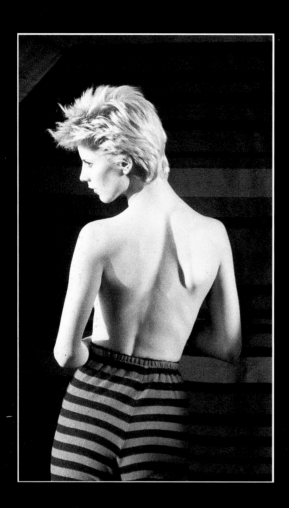

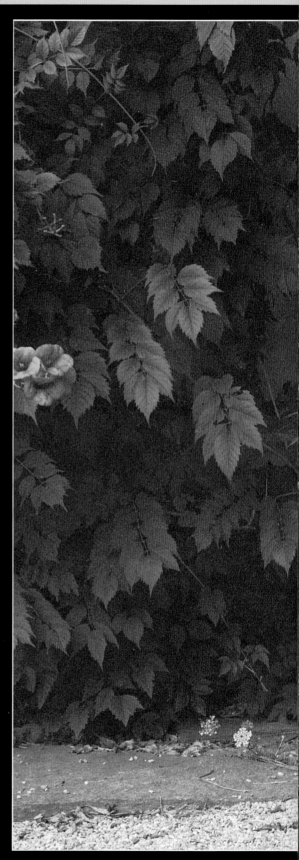

The human form is one of the most demanding subjects, but it is also one of the most satisfying. It has enough inherent interest to gain a viewer's attention, but to keep it and gain his respect requires both taste and artistic ability. There is no denying the erotic nature of a nude figure – an aspect exploited in glamour work – but the subject is much more than that, and it can be said that if you can make outstanding images of the nude then you will be able to photograph anything.

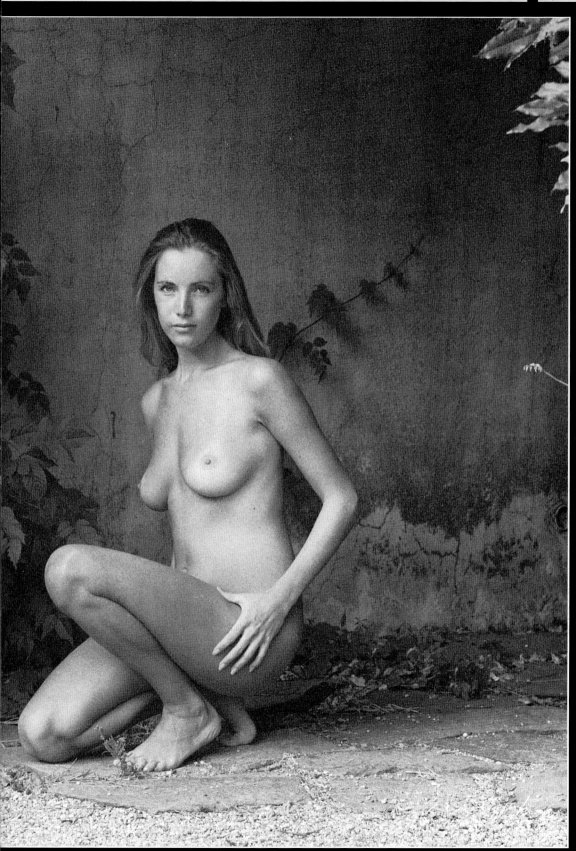

THE HUMAN FORM

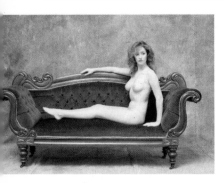

△ Fast film and soft light can highlight skin texture as well as form. The model was lit by a large, overhead window and white reflectors placed close to the camera ensured that shadow areas were well lit.

Pentax LX, 50 mm, Scotch (3M) 1000, ¹/₁₂₅ sec, f16

Photographing the nude is always a challenge, whether you are an experienced professional or a hesitant amateur, but the subject need be no more daunting than landscapes. In fact, nude photography and landscape work have many pictorial and technical aspects in common, and photographers frequently move from one to the other or combine the two, using the landscape as a setting. Geological formations can be used to echo the human form and to counterpoint skin texture.

The selection of a good model and an appropriate location will depend on the ideas that you want to present. To start with, the best approach to nude photography is to make basic images of the human form, keeping props to an essential minimum and using daylight whenever possible. Concentrate on the poses and framing alone. Soft, directional light is ideal for revealing overall shape and form. Because shadows do not have a dramatic impact on composition, the model and photographer are free to exploit the pose and viewpoints.

For your first attempts at making nude studies, choose a model you know. Failing that, it would be an advantage to use an experienced model, perhaps from an art school, who is used to adopting relaxed and natural-looking poses without the more blatant sexuality prevalent in glamour photography.

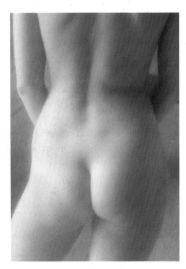

△ Often the simplest pictures are the strongest and first-time models will be more relaxed with semi-abstract shots like this.

Pentax LX, 135 mm, Kodak Ektachrome 64, ¹/₆₀ sec, f8

▷ Props that add to the context of the picture or that help the model relax are useful. Beds and couches make a natural setting.

Hasselblad, 80 mm, Kodak Ektachrome 200, ¹/₃₀ sec, f16

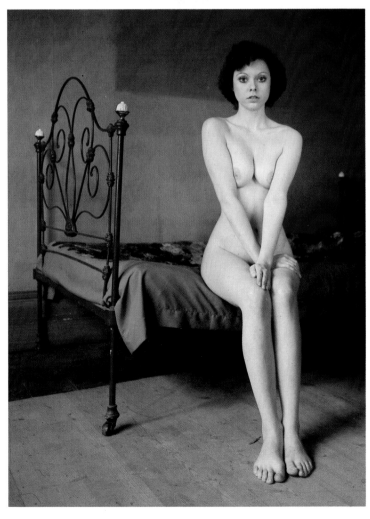

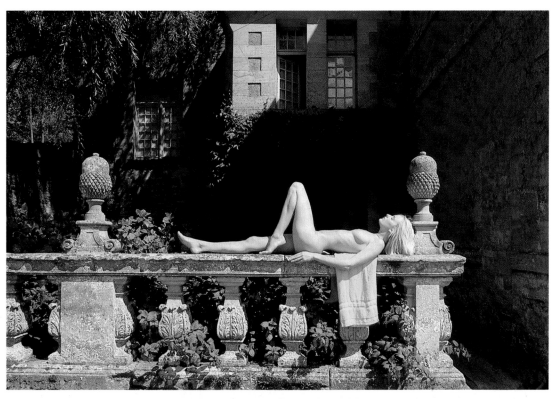

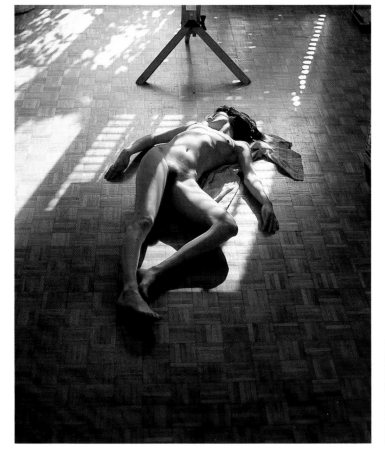

△ Outdoor locations can provide an ideal setting for nude pictures that contain a hint of innocence and sensuality. Simple settings are the most successful. Here the girl's languid form is set against a dark, contrasting background for added clarity.

Pentax LX, 50 mm, Kodak Ektachrome 64, ¹/₁₂₅ sec, f8

◁ The similarity between the colour of the wooden flooring and the model's golden skin tones make this an almost monochromatic picture where the emphasis is on light and form.

Pentax LX 28 mm, Kodak Ektachrome 64, ¹/₆₀ sec, f8

See also:
SOFT AND HARD LIGHT pp18–19
CLOSE ENCOUNTERS pp34–35
THE SIMPLE SETTING pp44–45
IN THE GARDEN pp114–115

KITCHEN GLAMOUR

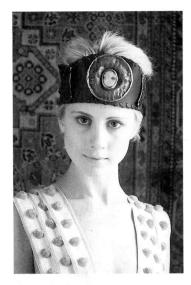

△ The ornate belt, when worn on the head, suggested an ancient Mediterranean outfit. This was provided by several feet of curtain braiding. The background is an Indian carpet and the light was from a north-facing window.

Pentax LX, 50 mm, Kodak Ektachrome 200, 1/125 sec, f8

▷ An upturned lampshade brought to mind an Egyptian priestess's headgear. To complete the outfit, all that was needed was a hastily-cut bin liner.

Pentax LX, 85 mm, Kodak Ektachrome 200, 1/30 sec, f11

See also:
SOFT AND HARD LIGHT pp18–19
CLOSE ENCOUNTERS pp34–35
BEHIND THE SCENES pp50–51

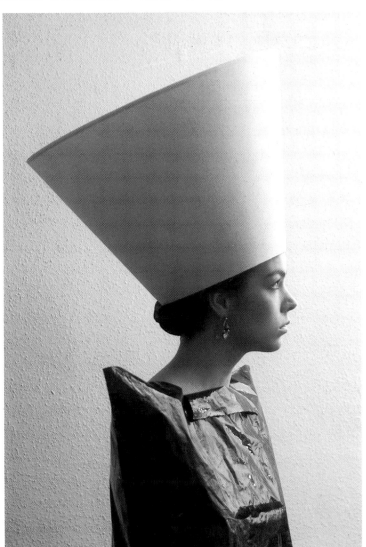

Most people enjoy dressing up, and you can exploit this to produce unusual and interesting pictures. Traditionally, costumes are created with clothing cast-offs, but more surprising, shocking, and amusing pictures can result from using readily available household objects. Apart from obvious items, like curtains, you can use unusual objects like buckets and refuse sacks. Take every opportunity to exercise your imagination and present everyday items in a new light.

Once you start a dressing-up session, you'll find everybody involved will come up with a continuous stream of new ideas. Children, in particular, enjoy these sessions. The best costumes and pictures are those that relate to an overall idea or theme. This means selecting items that relate in colour, shape or function, and arranging them to compose a balanced design in much the same way as you would when deciding what goes with what when dressing for an evening out. Often one piece of furniture or household equipment will suggest a garment, and then it's a simple matter of finding other suitable props to complete the image.

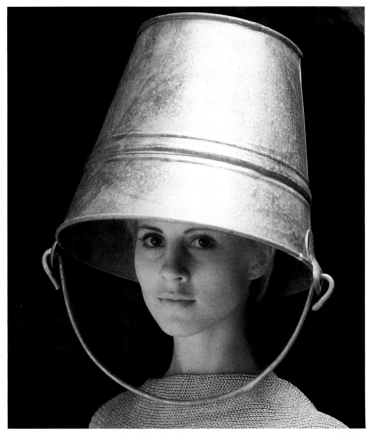

◁ The most unlikely objects can be pressed into service. A silver shawl has been draped over the model's shoulders to keep within the overall colour scheme suggested by the bucket. A reflector was used to give even lighting to the face.

Pentax LX, 85 mm, Kodak Ektachrome 200, ¹/₃₀ sec, f11

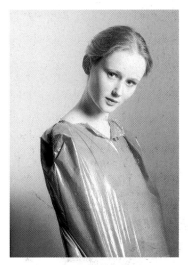

△ A plastic refuse sack as a dress. The simple composition and symmetrical shape of the sack have been enlivened by posing the model slightly diagonally and setting her head at an angle. Light from a large window provided the lighting and a silver reflector was used to fill in the shadows.

Pentax LX, 85 mm, Kodak Ektachrome 200, ¹/₆₀ sec, f11

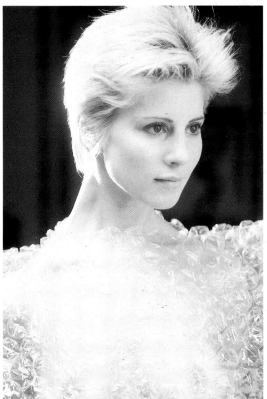

◁ The plastic bubble packing material used in this shot has a fascinating texture which reveals a new dimension as an article of clothing. The model's face was lit with sunlight – two reflectors were used to lighten shadows – and a 500 watt tungsten lamp provided the warm rimlight.

Pentax LX, 85 mm, Kodak Ektachrome 200, ¹/₁₂₅ sec, f8

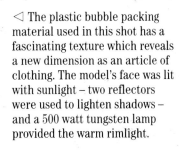

177

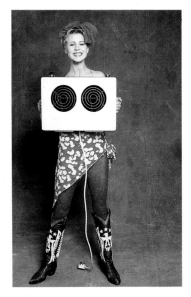

Photography tends to be about reality – its interpretation is usually purely representational – so when we see pictures that are obviously false, it can be unsettling. Optical distortions are blatant in their effect, but images that contain familiar objects presented in unusual relationships are more subtle in their effects and trigger off different emotional responses in the viewer, ranging from mild amusement to a sense of disquiet.

Perfectly commonplace items can be used to good effect and, in the most successful images, it is the very fact that everyday, mundane objects are presented in an alternative light that creates interest. Viewers are asked to re-evaluate the way they see things, perhaps seeing them in terms of shape, volume, and design rather than in terms of function or place. The idea is to give people a visual jolt, as well as some mental stimulation, which means selecting items that have strong graphic shapes and placing them out of context for symbolic or aesthetic effect. Including a human figure, particularly a beautiful female form, will make the image more disturbing. The final interpretation of the image's meaning can be left wide open.

△ Humour, rather than the notion of 'false attachment', is the key to this visual pun.

Pentax LX, 50 mm, Kodak Ektachrome 64, 1/60 sec, f11

▷ Here it is the juxtaposition of elegant shapes and role-changing that creates interest. The visual message is presented in a clear and uncomplicated composition, but ultimately the viewer is left to make his or her own interpretation of the image.

Pentax LX, 50 mm, Kodak Ektachrome 200, 1/60 sec, f8

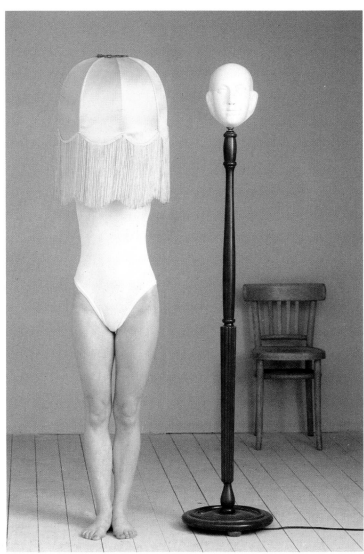

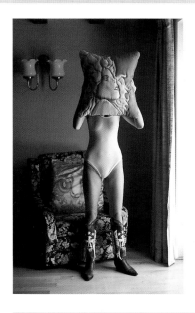

◁ The anonymous nature of beauty in modern society is the theme in this picture. The chosen form is a visual pun using the cushion as the trigger for the idea.

Pentax LX, 50 mm, Kodak Ektachrome 200, ¹/₆₀ sec, f16

▷ Another ambiguous message. But the replacement of the girl's body with a suitably shaped mirror reflecting an image of furniture perhaps suggests that the housewife is herself regarded almost as a piece of furniture.

Pentax LX, 28 mm, Kodak Ektachrome 200, ¹/₃₀ sec, f11

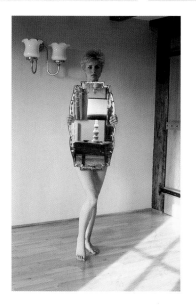

◁ This picture is built up around straight-sided geometric shapes and patterns, the model's shape acting as a counterpoint to the symmetry of the composition. There was no intention of producing an image with a message; it is simply the result of experimenting with unusual props – in this case an empty chocolate box tray.

Pentax LX, 50 mm, Kodak Ektachrome 200, ¹/₃₀ sec, f8

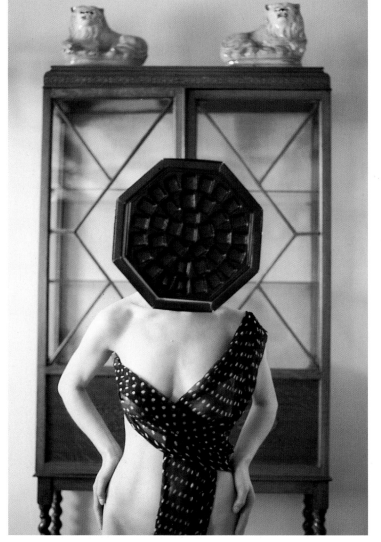

See also:
SOFT AND HARD LIGHT pp18–19
ARTIFICIAL LIGHT pp88–89
KITCHEN GLAMOUR pp176–177

FRAMING THE FIGURE

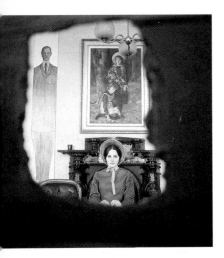

Framing is a strong compositional device that serves a distinct function in portrait pictures. It should not be confused with simply photographing a person in a setting. A setting may provide extra interest or provide more information about the subject, but a frame is used to contain a subject, add emphasis, and direct the viewer's attention.

The most important reason for using a frame is to isolate the figure and create impact, but there are other, slightly more subtle reasons for using a frame. If you use a frame in the foreground, you can increase the sense of three-dimensionality in a picture. Or visual ambiguities such as 'false attachment' may be played upon. In a complex scene, the figure may be given extra emphasis, or the frame used as a device to hide distracting or confusing elements. Whatever the function of the frame selected, remember that it must be in sympathy with the subject, and not obtrusive or distracting.

△ To direct the viewer's attention to the two sisters in the painting and the seated figure, a close foreground frame was used to hide the rest of the room. The asymmetrical shape of the frame adds interest and, because it is in shadow, its neutral tone does not detract from the main subject.

Hasselblad, 150 mm, Kodak Ektachrome 200, 1/15 sec, f11

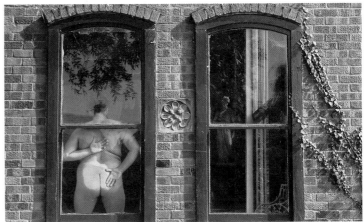

△ Warm, afternoon sun has brought out the texture of the brickwork which is punctuated by the two symmetrical windows. Two frames create a sense of ambiguity and the eye flicks from one to the other, comparing the nude in one with the sculpture glimpsed in the other.

Hasselblad, 80 mm, Kodak Ektachrome 64, 1/125 sec, f11

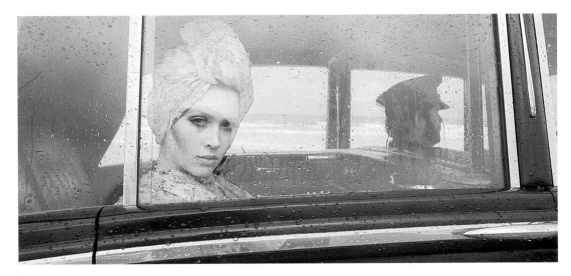

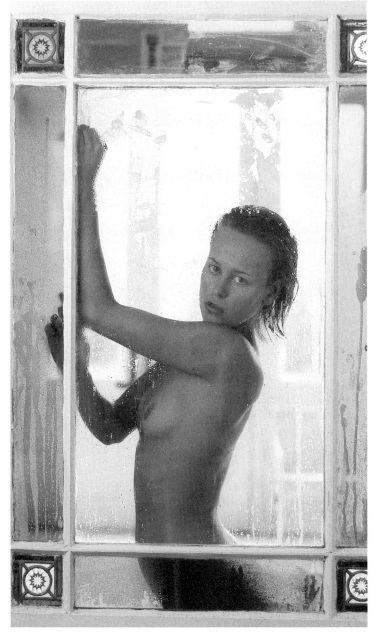

◁ A rich-toned rectangle of glass complements the paler tones of the girl's skin seen against the neutral background. Bright frames need to be used carefully, otherwise they dominate the subject, but here the girl's shapely outlines stand out in strong contrast and retain the viewer's attention. The shot was lit with a quartz-iodine lamp that was diffused through a wire scrim covered with a blue gel to give it daylight colour balance.

Hasselblad, 150 mm, Kodak Ektachrome 64, $^1/_{125}$ sec, f8

◁ This picture illustrates the use of a frame as a means of providing additional information about the subject. The girl's face is surrounded by the outlines of an expensive limousine, which suggests that she is used to living in style and comfort. The rain-splashed glass shows the protection afforded by the car and hints at the luxurious cocoon that wealth brings.

Hasselblad, 80 mm, Kodak Ektachrome 200, $^1/_{250}$ sec, f8

FANTASY FIGURES

▽ The transparency of diaphanous materials is determined by the relative brightness of the illumination on each side. If the brightest light is on the viewing side then the material is relatively opaque and its colour and texture are clear. A bright light on the far side makes it more transparent, revealing more of the scene beyond. For this shot the front lighting from a window has been carefully balanced on the far side by a reflector (see diagram) so that the nude figure can just be seen through the damp cotton sheet. Where the sheet is in contact with her body the transparency is increased.

Pentax LX, 50 mm, Kodak Ektachrome 160 Tungsten, 1/60 sec, f11

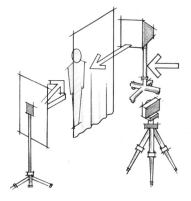

In the earliest days of photography the naked figure was often covered with soft diaphanous materials that revealed form but subdued intimate detail. The result was an idealized image of woman as a mysterious and romantic creature. The tradition has continued to this day, but with a different twist; the modern climate of overt sexuality has transformed the flowing cotton robes into the wet T-shirt look.

Harking back to the early pictorialist approach, but using modern colour materials, it is possible to produce strangely haunting images with an ethereal atmosphere. Subtle tints and colouring lend a strange kind of reality to the covered forms. Many types of material are suitable for covering your model, the best being neutral or white cotton, muslin, linings and gauze. Choose soft fabrics, as they drape naturally and cling when dampened. Lighting needs to be carefully balanced so that the covered figure is visible, and there should be sufficient light on the cloth to reveal its colour and texture.

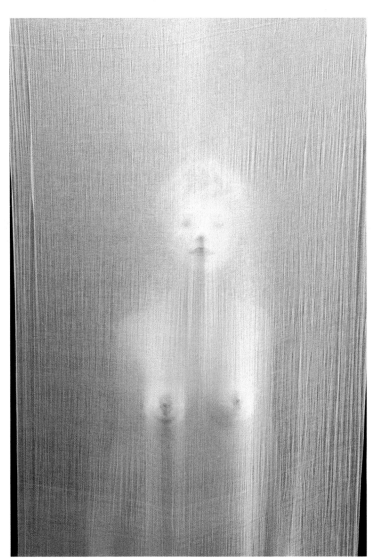

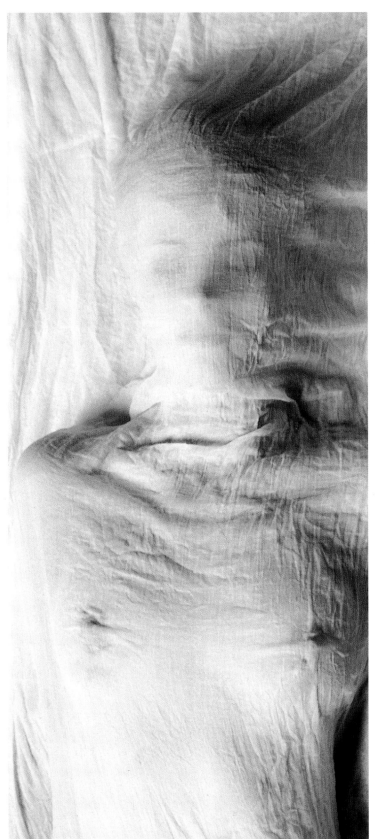

◁ To create this image of a shrouded nude the model was asked to lie down on a white board before being covered with a single layer of muslin. The cloth was dampened to make it cling to the model's body and reveal her outlines more clearly. Light came from a single window and a reflector was placed on the shadow side to lessen the contrast between bright and dark areas.

Pentax LX, 100 mm macro, Kodak Ektachrome 200, $^1/_{125}$ sec, f11

See also:
SOFT AND HARD LIGHT pp18–19
BENDING REALITY pp38–39
KITCHEN GLAMOUR pp176–177

AN EYE FOR BEAUTY

▽ Outdoor beauty pictures are ideal for shots that require a natural look. Choose a model with natural good looks and excellent skin. Settings that provide simple backgrounds in soft, delicate tones that will complement the subject are best.

Pentax LX, 100 mm macro, Kodak Ektachrome 64, 1/125 sec, f11

Pictures of beautiful women often concentrate on the face: a frontal view, close-up and made in soft, diffuse light that throws little or no shadow and reveals a minimum amount of modelling. It is, therefore, essential that the model has extremely clear skin with a fine texture that will look attractive even in enlarged images. For professional work, such as advertisements for cosmetics or jewellery, a model with symmetrical features is preferred as her prime job is to enhance the product. For the less demanding requirements of an experimental or amateur session, a symmetrical face is not necessary and a touch of 'character' often adds interest. Hair styling and make-up in studio work are normally handled by professionals and their role is crucial to the success of high-quality beauty shots. Some models are trained to apply make-up, but very few can style hair as well as a professional. Therefore, even the amateur photographer, when taking beauty shots, is advised to seek the aid of the local salon or hairdressing school, where they will often help you in exchange for some useful publicity pictures.

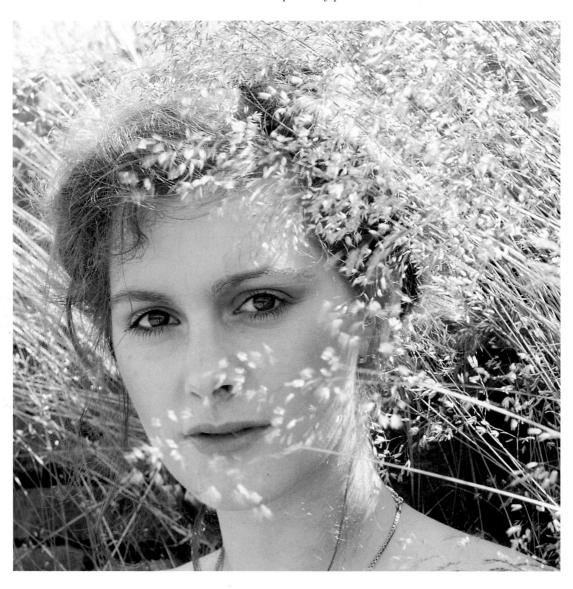

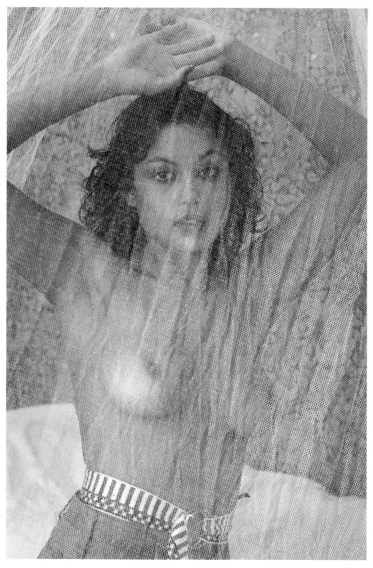

◁ On location, it is sometimes necessary to photograph in the hard light of direct sun which creates contrast that is too high to be flattering. One way to overcome this is to erect a cotton diffuser over the model, softening the light. Here, the spray of a convenient fountain was used as a soft-focus filter, diffusing the highlights and lowering the contrast.

Pentax LX, 135 mm, Kodak Ektachrome 200, ¹/₁₂₅ sec, f8

◁ A common practice for evoking a romantic atmosphere in beauty portraits is to shoot through a screen to diffuse the image. This photograph was made using a sheet of butter muslin as a diffuser, but other suitable materials include light netting, transparent plastic, and thin cotton. Emphasis should be on the model, not the screen, so make sure that there is ample light on her face.

Pentax LX, 50 mm, Kodak Ektachrome 200, ¹/₃₀ sec, f8

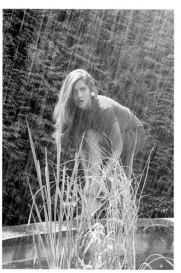

See also:
SOFT AND HARD LIGHT pp18–19
CLOSE ENCOUNTERS pp34–35
THE HUMAN FORM pp174–175

THE CLASSIC NUDE

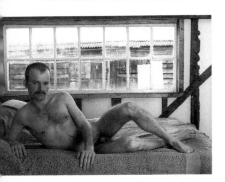

△ Sometimes it is possible to photograph models in their own homes where they are most likely to feel at ease. If you are lucky, as with this man's house, the rooms will be large enough to allow the use of a standard lens or a short telephoto for most shots.

Hasselblad, 80 mm, Kodak Tri-X (400), ¹/₁₂₅ sec, f16

The studio is not always the best place to photograph a model. He or she may find the atmosphere too sterile, or even intimidating, and would prefer to be photographed in a more natural setting. The setting may be indoors or out, but the main aim of abandoning the studio is to create a more relaxed atmosphere, particularly if your model is to be nude. Photographing nudes on location also has the benefit of solving the problem of what props to use, and how to obtain them.

Overall, soft directional light is best for photographing the nude, because it both reveals the form of the model and illuminates the setting without making it too dramatic or imposing. Outdoors, a sky with thin cloud gives the right kind of soft, directional light. Such light has a beautiful quality that reveals form and texture. If you wish to get the same kind of lighting in direct sun you can place a large screen of thin white cotton or gauze between the model and the sun to soften its direct rays, using reflectors to soften shadows and reveal details.

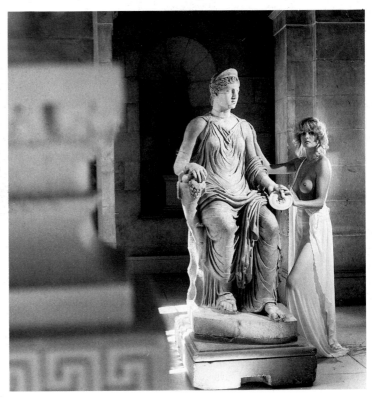

△ The best locations provide their own props and have an atmosphere that is creatively stimulating to both model and photographer. This picture was taken in an English stately home that revealed new and exciting settings at almost every turn. Here it was the classical figure with her flowing robes that inspired the dress and pose of the model. Lighting was carefully arranged so that the tonal values of the stone figure and the model's body matched each other.

Hasselblad, 80 mm, Kodak Tri-X (400), ¹/₁₂₅ sec, f16

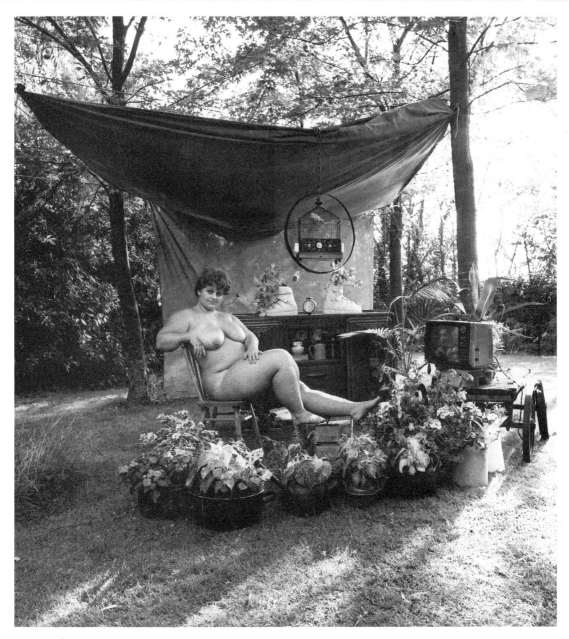

△ Naturist camps are not always
as back-to-nature and spartan as
their public image sometimes
suggests. In true British tradition,
all the trappings of civilized, even
luxurious, life have been
transported and set up as an
exotic outdoor sitting room next
to a caravan. The woman's naked
form is ample in its proportions
and in the Rubenesque tradition.

*Hasselblad, 60 mm, yellow filter,
Kodak Tri-X (400), ¹/₃₀ sec, f16*

See also:
SOFT AND HARD LIGHT pp18–19
BLACK AND WHITE pp22–23
THE SIMPLE SETTING pp44–45
BEHIND THE SCENES pp50–51

MIRRORED IMAGES

▽ Mirrors make excellent frames for simple pictures, as well as contributing to the atmosphere of the image. The model was lit with a single spot lamp.

Pentax LX, 100 mm macro, Kodak Ektachrome 160 Tungsten, 1/60 sec, f8

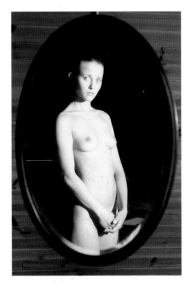

▷ In this picture an aging 17th century Venetian mirror with a mottled surface has been used as a background to complement the young model. Soft, directional daylight from two opposing windows highlights the girl's form and a reflector, placed near the camera, lightens the shadows.

Pentax LX, 85 mm, Kodak Ektachrome 200, 1/30 sec, f22

The conventional fixed viewpoint of a camera lens can be, in some circumstances, severely limiting. One of the most important things about a mirror image is that it is laterally reversed – right is left, and left is right. We are so used to seeing ourselves in a mirror that we are often surprised when we see ourselves in a photograph the right way round and as we appear to others.

The mirror's reversing effect has played on man's imagination for centuries, and has featured in legends, poems, plays and stories right up to the present day. So, too, has the way that, when a mirror is broken, the fragments each reflect a complete image, not part of it. In ancient times mystical properties were conferred on mirrors, and even today's mirrors' unusual properties make them an intriguing subject.

A single mirror can be used as a frame, reflecting one image; a pair of mirrors opposite each other will reflect a huge number of images, disappearing into infinity. Mirrors can be used to create bizarre double images, reflect a new foreground, or cover an obtrusive background and, used in conjunction with painted backdrops, they can create successful illusions.

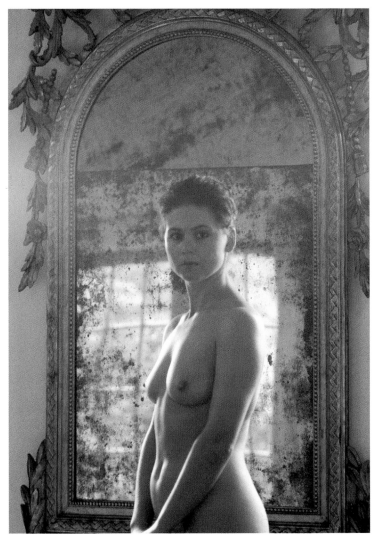

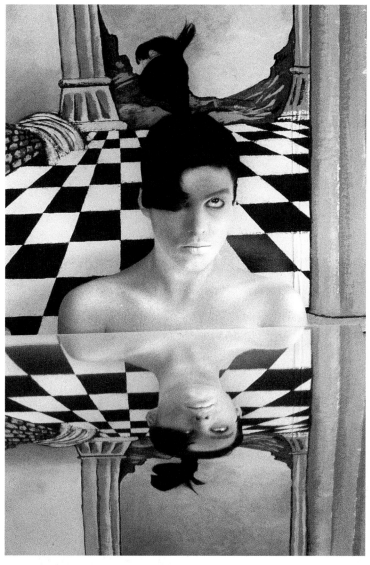

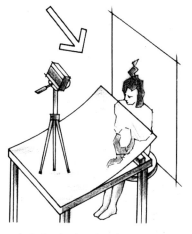

◁ △ Intriguing double images can be made when the background provides interesting shapes and illusions of perspective. The model was made up with theatrical paints and sat just in front of the mural, legs outstretched beneath a low table. A small, wooden block was placed on the table and a plastic mirror laid on top with an edge against the model's shoulders. The block bowed the mirror's surface, distorting the reflection.

Pentax LX, 85 mm, Kodak Ektachrome 200, ¹/₆₀ sec, f16

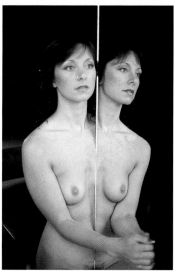

◁ An almost endless variety of views and shapes can be created by altering the relationship between the mirror and the subject. One of the most effective ways of using a mirror is in a double portrait like this one. If the edge of the mirror was blacked it would disappear, strengthening the image of a two-headed nude.

Pentax LX, 28 mm, Kodak Ektachrome 200, ¹/₆₀ sec, f16

See also:
BENDING REALITY pp38–39
LIGHT ON WATER pp70–71
FRAMING THE SHOT pp148–149
FRAMING THE FIGURE pp180–181

INDEX

A

action shots 12, 48-9, 120-31, *140-1*
age, portraying 34, *35*
angles of view 10-11, *12*, 14;
  unusual 144-5;
  see also viewpoints
animals *117*, 118-19, *118-19*, 144
aperture *13*, 14, 16, *28*, 84, *85*;
  depth of field *11*, 38, *108*, *112*
architecture 10, 14, 98-9,
  145, 150-9

B

background 28, 40, 50, 58, *58*,
  103, *138-9*
beauty portraits 184-5
birds 118-19, *118-19*
black/white shots 22-5, 64, 74,
  74-5, *75*, 156
blur 28, *108*, *117*, 118, *119*;
  accidental 12, *117*;
  action shots *49*, 126, *127*, *167*
bracketing 16

C

candid shots 12, 42, 48, *95*, 97
candlelight 88, *88*
children *37*, 40, 42-3, 48-9, *48-9*,
  93;
  babies *34*
cityscapes 18, 98-9, *145*, 155,
  156, *156-7*
cloning *29*, 31
close-ups 12, 14, *70*, *108*, 110, 116;
  portraits 10, 34-5, *35*
clothing *40*, *51*, *93*, 176-7;
  using different 58, *58-9* ,
  104-5
clouds 18, 19, *62*, *64-7*, 65, *72*,
  82, *82*;
  filters 74, *74*;
  scudding 68, *68*, 69
colour 16, 18, 19, 20, 22, *24-5*,
  58, 70;
  for blur 126; c.
  altering *27*, 28, *29*;
  and filters *64*, 72-3, *74*;
  pale 65, *67*, 78, *79*;
  of sky *66-7*
composition *71*, 84, 96, *96*,
  132-49, *155*
contrast *16*, *17*, 22, *59*, 64, 74
cropping *13*, 20, 56, 142, *143*,
  149;
  on computer 28

D

dawn *66*, *67*, 68, *112*, *122*
depth, emphasizing/minimizing
  18, *19*
depth of field 10, *11*, 12, *15*,
28, 38, 48, 122;
  close-ups 34,116;
  wildlife 118
design 58-9
diagonals *20*, 134-5, *134-5*, *177*
digital techniques; imaging 26-7;
  manipulation 28-31;
  montage *28-9*
distant shots 10, 154-5
distortion 12, 14, *15*, 80;
  deliberate 28, 46, *137*, *145*;
  with mirror 38
documentary 90-105
double image *57*, *80*, *189*
drapery 182-3

E

echoing elements 40, 149, *149*,
  168, *170*; in portraits 50, *50*,
  186
e-mail 26
essay, photographic 100-5
evening *19*, 52, 54, *54*, *66*, *67*,
  78-9
exposure 16-17, 48, 56, *63*, 70;
  for artificial light 54, 88;
  for flare 84, *85*;
  multiple 138-9
expressions, facial 34, *34*,
  130-1, *130-1*, 140, *140*, *149*
eyes in portraits 34, 118, *119*, 130

F

farm 100-1, 118, *118*
film 16, 26;
  format 20, *20*, *35*, *47*;
  f. speed *22-3*, 78, *92*, *95*,128;
  infrared 74, *75*;
  tungsten *47*, *54*, 84, *146*;
  warming *56*
filters *24*, 46, *56*, 72-3, *108*,
  110, *152*;
  black/white shots 64, 74;
  digital effects 28;
  fog *24*;
  graduated 72, *72*, *73*;
  neutral density 64;
  polarizing 64, 72, *72*;
  radial zoom *73*;
  skylight *73*;
  square *73*;
  ultraviolet 72, *73*
firelight 88
fixed focal length lens *see*
  lenses: prime
flare *11*, *71*, 78, *78*, 84-5
flash *28*, 54, *84*, *92*, *96*, 104,
  123, *135*;
  studio 40, *44*, *47*, 48, *55*,
  162, *167*
floodlight *81*, *162*, *167*
flowers *24*, *52-3*, *80*, 108-11
focal length 10, 12, 14, 86,
116, *127*
foliage *52-3*, 74, 86, *171*
food 170-1
foreground *69*, *72*, *73*, 78, *82*, *86*;
  wide-angle lens 10, *104*, 146
fragmenting images 136-9
framing shots 20-1, *20-1*, 65,
  142, 148-9;
  buildings 152, *155*;
  human form *43*, 180-1
freezing movement 124-5, 124-7

G

gardens 52-3, 108-11, 114-15
gels 46, *181*
glass, reducing reflection in
  72, *153*
glass sheet *57*, *162*
graininess 22, *22-3*, 54, *75*
grid lines *21*, *155*

H

hands and feet 34, *47*, 104
haze *73*, *75*, *79*, *108*, *155*
headlamps 54
helicopter, shots from *156*
highlights *15*, *17*, *72*, 80, *82*, 89;
  unwanted 72
historical record 98-9
horizon 10, *11*, *69*, 128;
  rule of thirds 20, *20*, *21*, *71*
human form 172-89

I

image manipulation 22, 26, 56,
  57, *72*, 136-9
insects *116*
instant pictures 56-7
internet 26

L

lamplight 54-5, 88, *89*, *166*, *181*
landscape 20, 61-75, 78, 114, *147*;
  l. format 20, *147*
lenses 10-15;
  fisheye 14, *15*;
  macro 12, *12*, 14, *14*, 110,
    116-17;
  mirror 14, *15*;
  prime 12, 14, *14*;
  shift 14, *15*;
  special 14-15; *see also*
    telephoto lens; wide-angle
    lens; zoom lens
light 14;
  artificial 88-9, 104;
  back l. 86;
  dappled *152*;
  diffused 18, *18*, 19, *19*, 48;
  direction of *17*, 18;
  fleeting 68-9, 82-3;
  hard/soft 18-19;
  low-angle *78*, *109*, *144*;

ACKNOWLEDGEMENTS

The Author and Publishers would like to thank the following people for their assistance in the production of this book:

Chris George for his help on the text; Charlotte Darling and Suzanne Metcalfe-Megginson for their design and DTP work; Jennifer Macintosh for administrative support; Simon Ward-Hastelow for his assistance with the pages on computer imaging.